The Women Writing Science Project

In collaboration with the National Science Foundation, The Feminist Press announces *Women Writing Science*, a series of books that bring to life the story of women in science, engineering, technology, and mathematics. From biographies and novels to research-based nonfiction, *Women Writing Science* will celebrate the achievements of women scientists, explore their conflicts, address gender bias barriers, encourage women and men of all ages to become more scientifically literate, and embolden young women to choose careers in science.

base ten

A novel by
Maryann Lesert

Afterword by
Florence Howe & Sue V. Rosser

The Feminist Press
at the City University of New York
New York

Published in 2009 by The Feminist Press at The City University
of New York, The Graduate Center, 365 Fifth Avenue, Suite
5406, New York, NY 10016

Library of Congress Cataloging-in-Publication Data

Lesert, Maryann.
Base Ten : a novel / by Maryann Lesert.—1st ed.
p. cm.
ISBN-13: 978-1-55861-581-6 (pbk. : alk. paper)
ISBN-13: 978-1-55861-593-9 (library : alk. paper)
1. Astrophysicists--Fiction. 2. Women scientists—Fiction. 3. Self-
actualization (Psychology)—Fiction. I. Title.
PS3612.E75B37 2009
813'.6—dc22
2009009275

Cover design by Black Kat Design
Text design by Teresa Bonner

Publication of this volume is made possible, in part, by funds
from the National Science Foundation and
from Sara Lee Schupf.

13 12 11 10 09   5 4 3 2 1

For Greg, Max, and Rory,
who have been there through
the best and the worst of this
writing journey. To them,
I dedicate this story of wonder,
frustration, and love.

CONTENTS

1. Day One—Settling In   1

2. The Great Rift   13

3. Time   22

4. Day Two—Sully's Depot   27

5. Day Two—Sunset   35

6. A Long Smokies Day   39

7. Peia Again   49

8. Day Three—Inland   51

9. Couples   61

10. Open Drawers   67

11. Day Four—South Manitou   72

Life on the Main Sequence   87

12. The Call   90

13. To the Roof   101

14. Something and Nothing to Prove   112

15. Day Five—The Old Man   119

16. Bad Mornings   131

17. Day Six—The Lighthouse   142

White Dwarf   151

18. Any Woman   153

19. On the Star Deck   159

20. Evelyn Young   170

21. Pictures   193

22. Time in Heaven   204

23. More Pictures   214

24. In Tens   222

25. Day Seven—His Body   227

Red Giant   231

26. Namesake   233

27. Day Seven—A Theory of Dreams   240

Binary Systems   249

28. Day Eight—The Waters of Hamlin   251

29. Day Eight—Telescope of Trees   255

30. Day Nine—Late Night Radio Call   265

31. Day Ten—Back to South Manitou   275

32. Day Ten—What Mishe-Mokwa Knows   283

33. Day Eleven—Call Home   286

Glossary   299

Acknowledgments   304

Afterword: Balancing Lives for
Women (and Men) in Science
by Florence Howe and Sue V. Rosser   306

Works Cited   322

1

Day One—Settling In

AFTER THE BLEACHING SUN AND asphalt of the expressway, Jillian's turn onto Forest Trail was a turn into a world of color. Yellows, greens, browns, blacks, heightened against a turquoise sky. Turquoise! The water, the big lake, must be feeding the sky.

She had driven the busiest route on purpose—taking 23 north from Ann Arbor, 96 around Lansing, through Grand Rapids and on to Muskegon—to remind her, as she headed further and further north along Lake Michigan's shoreline, why she needed ten days alone. More than days. Through days filled with hiking to near exhaustion and nights standing at the water's edge, open to the stars, open to everything the stars had always meant to her, she would listen. She would listen so intently that only the cold water lapping over her toes would remind her she was of Earth, but still part of a great infinite stir.

She passed a huge, brown sign with yellow-gold letters stamped into its painted wood, *You are now entering the Manistee National Forest*, and she slowed to take it all in: the bright yellow patches of poplar and birch leaves among the darker greens of oaks and pines, and the forest floor covered with ferns, deep greens tinged with rust. It had been an especially hot summer. Even the air flowing through her windows felt saturated with hot and cold and color, and she breathed deeply, smelling the overly sweet scents of wildflowers in the sun, the tang of pine in the shade.

For ten or twelve miles the road cut straight into the woods, and she couldn't help thinking of her usual drive home: from the highway to the land of strip malls and research buildings on Victor's Way; past apartment complexes and condominiums and houses too big for their small lots; to her taupe, two-story house with a dormer, built on a mild hill. Before the neighboring fields were developed, before street lights, they had been able to see some stars.

The road began to bend and as she steered back and forth past the campground loops, the Violet, the Oak, the Orchid, and the Hemlock, she could smell the lake. Occasionally, she spotted dark shapes deep in the woods. Black rounds looked like bears or figures staring back from behind the trees, and they made her think of Jack and Manny and Peia. Motherhood brought so much anxiety and fear. She had become so strong and so responsible for them, but so worn down from her self, and those shadows—tree stumps, she knew—felt like warnings.

Ten Days in the woods was not going to be easy.

But it was going to be.

When Forest Trail ended in the only parking lot for miles, Jillian opened her door, feeling the lake's power gust in the wind. She jogged a pathway of recycled planks, tunneling through trees that rose from dirt as soft as ashes. The dark powder seemed to brew from the bulging roots that wove themselves across the ground. Yes, this was a time to rejoice. A time to reconnect with her joy. The path opened onto a broad deck and she stood, overlooking the dip and swell of the dunes and beyond that, nothing but water and sky.

A sky sometimes frustratingly clouded with moisture, but a sky she and Kera had listened to for years, a beautiful, long-afternoon turquoise sky.

She closed her eyes and felt the sand and water and light wrap around her, billions of tiny photons and water and air molecules colliding with her skin from all angles.

Day One, One, One. And I made it.

To her left the Dune Ridge trail began where timbers had been laid into the dirt to prevent erosion. It would be dark soon, under those trees. She had to hurry.

Back at the car she checked her gear one more time. Her roll pack was stuffed with water, pouches of tuna, cheese, protein bars, and trail mix, one aluminum pan, and a tiny coffee percolator. She was roughing it, yes, but she couldn't *be* without coffee. Her clothes were all set: wring-dry nylon outfits, three bras, three pairs of underwear, tank tops, and a bathing suit. She had packed an assortment of necessities: one hundred feet of corded rope, a flashlight with extra batteries, a simple first aid kit (salve, bandages, liquid sutures), and treated kindling sticks.

She took out her topographical maps—two large sheets taped together—and smoothed them out across the car hood. She could have planned the trip using GPS on the computer, but the quadrangles, each representing seven-point-five minutes of earthly rotation in painstaking detail, reminded her of earlier days when she and her father, and later, she and Kera, headed off into the night with telescopes and a pocket logbook. The act of smoothing out the pale green and white sheets and locating the best observation points had always been the required sufferance before the adventure. And now, her first truly solo adventure would take place in the heart of this undeveloped tract of dunes and forest fourteen miles wide by twenty-four miles long, an expanse of solid greens and blues bound only by the white of Ludington to the south and Manistee to the north. The spot she had marked—44 degrees, 5.4 minutes North, 86 degrees, 28.5 minutes West—was a four-mile hike away.

At five o'clock, she settled her pack across the back of her hips, clasped the belt, and unbuckled her watch. Here she would live by the sun and the moon and the stars, the water and the wind and the sky. She threw her watch into the trunk and locked the car. Pausing on the observation deck, she said a quiet goodbye to the few people she could see in the water below, their splashes cut by the wind in her ears. As she turned to face the trail, she was acutely aware of the one-after-another density of the trees.

Earlier in the day as she drove across the state, she had pulled into rest areas and paced, reciting her Manistee Mantra:

Ten Years of marriage.

Ten Months of planning.

Ten Days to make it.

And between each, she had whispered, "Day One. One. One."

Already, the act of driving away had weakened the stranglehold of home. Freedom made other things important: the kids' faces, Jack's hands on her shoulders as she packed his lunch (he should have known something was wrong). The deceit of her smiles, though she had made sure to say to the kids *See you soon,* not *See you tonight.* A day-trip wasn't going to bring about change. She needed space, that precious feeling of endlessness, to figure out what came next. At one point, she had taken out her base ten triangle. To think that a triangle, a diagram, could reset a life! But then, realizing she had taken more of Jack with her than she intended—she didn't need a list to tell her how she felt—she threw the drawing in a garbage can and hadn't stopped again.

Those tens had been important. Ten Years of staying close to home because she couldn't bear to miss their nightly "Tell About Your Day." She couldn't miss the chance to boost Manny back up when he'd sat on the bench for losing the basketball three times. His body was growing and everything about him was loose and sloppy. He'd get that tightness back. Because music was for Manny what the stars were for her. She understood. Why didn't they? Because Jack didn't notice those vague pauses between Peia's words, those shifts in her gaze and the crooked grins that said she was having trouble with friends. Some new grouping of girls was shutting her out, and because it hurt too much to blame her friends, she was trying to figure out what she'd done wrong. Ten Years of developing software for other researchers because she could, because working at Burton's wasn't a bad job. Ten Years because she could still hear, clearly, Manny's cries the one time she did leave: *Let me come with you! I can help.*

Her boots clumped across the deck until her heels hit dirt. This was what she had to do: put one foot in front of the other and walk. Stepping over the timbers with her ankles flexed hard, she entered the path of trees.

She let the kids' faces pester her, remnants of long glances from the night before flooding her mind. She'd take the kids with her, but not Jack. No. She had never shared this place with Jack; she wasn't about to pack him in with her now. Standing over Manny and Peia as they slept, she had worried that her anxiety might leak into their dreams. She had lain parallel to Manny on his bedroom floor, knowing the slightest pressure on his mattress might wake him. Peia was either on or off, moving or asleep. Jillian had been able to touch her face. It helped to think of their faces now—Peia's darkly golden and Manny's so fair and blonde—when her back, the back of her legs, the back of her pack even, burned to turn around. To turn around and check, not for someone or something really, but to capture, visually, confirmation that the world behind her was being sealed off by the trees, that she was being folded into the forest.

The trail narrowed and grew darker, but turned often—thank the universe!—toward the water, and Jillian stopped at several overlooks to take in the endless expanse of blue, turning lavender now on the surface. Up and down root-grown and sandy slopes she bounced, with the green forest rustling around her and the sandy-aqua shallows rolling silently far below.

She estimated, using the sun's position, that it was seven o'clock when she climbed to the absolute crest of her dune. Four miles in two hours, perfect. Sweating profusely, she dropped her roll pack in the sand and sat, breathing in for three, out for three, in for three, out for three, feeling wonderfully exhausted and small.

A breeze blowing all the way from Wisconsin, over ninety miles of water to the west, ruffled her clothes. Behind her, to the east, the woods were fourteen miles deep. From her spot two-hundred and twenty-seven feet above the big lake, everything before her was deep and blue and green. Several strands of hair clung, dark and limp and stringy with sweat, to the sides of her face. Her hair stylist had said that her intense face needed some framing, so she'd allowed him to cut a few jagged bangs. Now, gathering the sweaty strands and preparing to set up camp, she regretted the cut.

She found a swell of sand that rose between two lines of trees. The first, poplars and birches, were clean moist trees. They'd provide good shade. The pines behind them would keep the bugs away and their needles made great kindling. With her folding shovel she leveled the sand, remembering the days when she and Kera used to lie on the slope of the dunes, their telescopes set up on the ridge or down close to shore. If they slept on uneven ground, or worse, with heads lower than feet, she would wake disoriented.

She ran rope through the tent's corner rings and bow-tied the loops around two young birches, then stood back with a smile. The climber's knot worked. Her tent puffed with the breeze, but only the flap flew into the wind. She'd set the tent parallel to the lake with her door facing north so that the wind, typically out of the southwest, could blow in through her windows and out through the flap. It was working. It was all working.

By the time she finished rolling out her bed, sealing all noncanned food in plastic containers, and rigging her hook-n-cable between two trees—where she hung her food fifteen feet above the ground to prevent any curious black bears from getting into it or coming close to her—the sky was streaked with reds and oranges.

She laughed at herself as she ducked into her tent to sweep the floor with her hands. She never would have made it to the Depot before dark. What was she thinking? She must remember the back country rule: never overestimate your speed. Two miles per hour, that was the most she could count on.

Tomorrow, she would hike to the Depot. Tomorrow would come soon enough.

She gathered twigs and dried needles, used one kindling stick and two bursts off her lighter, and sat beside a fire. Strands of clouds—way off to the west and heading north, she wasn't worried—were undercoated in fuchsia. Reds and purples fanned into lavender overhead, and within minutes, she watched the reds reach out and draw back. Now, all she had to do was wait, enjoy her fire and wait. But waiting, without the stars, left her vulnerable to the catch in her chest when she followed the colors of the sky southward and thought of them all, two hundred and fifty miles to the southeast, over the trees, at home.

Jack would have read her note several times. *Ten Days*, he would have read and reread, not quite understanding the duration, *maybe more. Who knows? I've never done this before.* The *this* in her note had been carefully dropped in to suggest the act of putting herself first. Restarting a life continually put on hold. Taking time that should have been hers all along, time that she was taking, now, to figure out how to salvage her science. She had planned to pack the note in his lunch so that he'd find out she was gone after the fact, but then she'd decided that was wrong. Her note announced nothing new, certainly nothing she had to hide. So she asked him to stay until the kids left for school, which created a stir. Jack was always the first one out the door. She handed his lunch to him and said, simply, "I'm leaving."

"So am I," he'd said, bending toward her to give her a quick kiss, as if she meant *I'm leaving for work*.

"No," she said, and he stopped, perplexed, as she handed him the note.

His pale blue eyes were so relaxed, so unlike hers. She felt embarrassed, remembering how he'd followed her to the car, looking back and forth from the note to her, saying "What am I supposed to tell the kids?" He had stood there in that loose-backed posture, nervous she figured.

Before she could call her plan silly and decide not to drive away, she'd put the car in reverse and called out as she backed down the driveway, "Tell them I had to leave. Something to do with the Planet Finder project."

The kids had heard her talk about the conference, watched her, night after night, poring over old drawings and images of her and

Kera's last spectral studies at Lick. They knew she had exhumed something important, very important, and her time to present was drawing near.

Jillian pictured all of them in the big bed, Jack pulling Manny and Peia close. That's how Jack expressed his love, he pulled everything to him.

The crackles of her tiny fire echoed into the woods and she turned, several times, knowing there was nothing behind her. But the hairs on her neck rose when she didn't look. A dune chair—she would dig a dune chair with an arch for her neck, just as Kera had taught her that first time Jillian had spent a few nights at the Depot on her way back home from school. Her parents had been so surprised when she didn't come home immediately that June. But they weren't hurt. Jillian had found someone like herself, a girl who drew with math and loved the stars.

Just a few feet down from her tent, into the slope of the dune, she dug her own shape into the sand. Over and over she sat and pressed her body into the slope; finding creases that needed smoothing, she scooped and smoothed again. The sand cooled and the horizon warmed with an intense, cerulean glow, an oceanic fullness of color her mother had always loved. The brighter stars: Altair, Vega, Lyra, began to appear. To the south—she couldn't help it, she kept looking south toward the Depot, toward home too she supposed, though home was far to the east and over the trees—Scorpius was visible with his orange-red heart, Antares. She squinted, reducing her view to lights and darks, searching for clusters and nebulae beyond Sagittarius's cocked arrow. If the skies remained clear for the new moon, she might see the central bulge of the galaxy, where millions of hot, white stars orbited in a chaos of heat.

To the north, Cassiopeia cleared the trees. Soon, the queen of the night sky would drag Andromeda, Perseus, Aries along with her. What an incredible black backdrop for Capella, Algol, Aldebaran, the orange eye of the bull.

And finally, the Pleiades would emerge, zenith blue.

Movement below drew her eyes to a dark form on the beach—a man?—walking near the water. In the water? The only way she could tell where the sand ended and the water began was by concentrating, locating the sound. It was probably a shadow from her own memory, a walking representation of her wife mother-leaving-anxiety. Or was it a hiker, struggling to focus in the half-black, half-gray of early night. She remembered that spooky pre-black time, filled with shadows and noise, with bugs and flying squirrels and foraging raccoons. The sky and the air would cool to true black and grow quiet. In the Porcupines and the Smokies, she and Kera were often separated by hundreds of meters, but they always knew the other was near. They had their radios and they'd chat.

She found the Corona and used one of its brighter stars to draw an imaginary beam from her, to the star, to Kera, down in Houston. Kera, too, was on the water.

It was a man; she was certain by his gait. And now, seeing her in the light of her fire, he knew she was alone. As he passed below, she imagined his profile straightening with his upward gaze. She bent her arm at a ninety-degree angle and waved, only slightly, a mannish gesture. This was one of the real dangers in being alone: being discovered alone. But no. From two hundred feet below, he wouldn't know she was a woman. She stayed with his slight form, losing it and finding it several times before it faded completely.

The water's movement, the wind, the pauses between gusts that wiped out all sound, she knew, played many tricks. But now he was gone, and she felt truly alone. Soon, the direct hard light of the stars would burn away the gray and the obscurity. She doused the fire and went to get her binoculars.

Jack would be feeling alone too. He would spend hours, perhaps, each night, trying to figure out how to maintain his morning labs, get a lecture prepared for evening, and still manage the kids' busy days. But—was he being tested as she was? Lying in bed with the kids pulled around him like pillows?

She set her binoculars on Albireo, sighing at the beauty of its pairing: pale yellow and bright blue, such a successful binary couple. She fuzzied the focus and the two stars blended into one, twinkling green. Ah, but even her favorite couple would be in trouble if they added a third or a fourth body. Gravitational suicide.

She panned for other stars, trying to ignore her immediate surroundings. But the snaps and rustles behind her—entirely too regular—had her constantly bolting and twisting, searching the trees. Pesky squirrels! Raccoons would be much noisier, much easier to identify.

Or, it's that man. He's doubled back.

Now, that was it! Yes, there were miles and miles of woods behind her, with no one she knew or trusted nearby. That's exactly why she had come. She could either scare herself all night, listening to the moans of the trees and imagining the forest vapor as breath, or find a way to settle in.

She decided to go halfway down the dune, rationalizing the move. If anything was going to come at her—some strange nocturnal hiking monster, a pack of coyotes, her passing shadow-man—she'd have plenty of time to hear and feel the disturbance. She grabbed her knife (for a man), her driftwood club for an animal. She'd light the club on fire and jab it at a bear or a coyote. She'd jab it at anything that got close.

Jillian dug another sand chair, closer to the water and more upright, but when the sudden romp of a whitecap rumbled on shore, lying back at the slightest angle made her feel vulnerable. She sat up, trying to ignore the chill rising from the sand. She was here for the stars! All the physical work, this location, it was all designed to bring her back to the stars. And the night sky required patience. Patience.

She relaxed her eyes and followed the Milky Way to the southern horizon, where Sagittarius was sinking into a band of purple. She tried to lie back; tried to breathe in for three, out for three; but an increasing number of black flies, flying silently in the bowl of the dune, began to bite at her ankles.

Another fire, close and constant—that's what she needed. She trudged up the dune, club in hand, to fill her arms with kindling, and in her trudges up and down, Jillian designated her chairs high and low dune chairs. Two star viewing choices, every night. And later, when she was feeling brave, she would sit at the water's edge, float maybe.

She carved a sand table close to her low dune chair, chopping in and smoothing the sand away with the side of her hand, again trying to ignore the chill. She arranged the largest twigs into a teepee, lighting the kindling at the base of her new, tiny fire, and though she had planned a sleepless night, the tiny puffs of heat warmed her and she dozed. She imagined herself afloat on the silvery-black water, lulled by the waves, starlight streaming through her. Jack stood above her, his palm under her back, supporting her. She had never been able to float. He twirled her slowly around, his head cocked to the side, his mouth open barely. When he smiled, the blue in his eyes deepened with tiredness, and Jillian knew she was being foolish. She had vowed not to associate Jack's smile, or his hands, or his eyes with comfort.

Peia came to her next, fast and hard, her dark-rimmed eyes lit up with obstinance, stomping her foot in her black go-go boots. Peia's strength lay in her commitment to her emotions. She was going to stomp and stomp anyway, so Jillian took her long, narrow foot—Peia was so tall already, at eight—and stomped it ten times. Ten times for ten days without Peia's glare.

When Jillian was young, like Peia, she had asked her father, *Do you think the stars watch us like we watch them?* They both knew the answer, of course, but her father, always teasing, had said, *Wow. How many eyes would a big guy like Betelgeuse have?*

Through Manny's eyes—because Manny was always watching her and she watching him—Jillian saw herself curled into that world of sand, water lapping from below, the forest pressing from above. She felt the sky overtaken with Manny's colors: his eyes a dark mixture of blue and gray, like hers, but flecked with gold. Perhaps she was seeing the first of the Perseids. She had timed her stay to coincide with the meteor shower. No, it was Manny, insistent: How could she love this world more than them? Jillian wanted to explain. It wasn't that she loved the stars, or the lake, or her research more than them, but she needed to understand, once and for all, how to deal with the longing. How could she tell tender, young, idealistic Manny—almost thirteen years old and just beginning his own quest for self—that sometimes you simply couldn't get what you lived for?

From deep in the forest, perhaps from her own unconscious, came the cool vapor of an even deeper question: How could she ever, ever, tell Peia that having a second baby had marked the beginning of the end of her very own quest?

Finally, the Pleiades appeared. She had learned, after years of observations, to track the movement of the stars through uncooperative eyelids, waking herself when her target drew near. With her binoculars pressed to her cheekbones, Jillian studied the brightest stars in the cluster, seven beautiful young stars whose light was incredibly purple through the specialized coatings on her lenses. And then, feeling as if she had accomplished a great goal—her best night of seeing in such a long time had not gone to waste—bitten by the flies and nearly out of twigs, she retreated to her tent.

She lay inside with the mesh windows fully unzipped and tried to keep watch for the movement of the stars. But the image of the man kept popping into her mind. Sometimes, as her eyelids met, he appeared between the trees or under her food cable, rattling her plastics to wake her. Other times, she woke just as he was about to stick his head in the tent flap. Exhausted, she grabbed her club and her flashlight and with her sleeping bag wrapped around her, she walked down to her high dune chair and backed her way into it. Trying to find comfort in the muffled waves and the glittery trail of the Milky Way, she looked up at the Pleiades, clouded with moisture but still present as a ring of light, and sighed—a sigh so frustrated and pained that she might have cried if she were not so intent on listening to the air around her.

But then, sick of crying, she called out, over the lake, "What do you want from me?"

The sound, the sheer noise of it felt good. She looked up at the stars, all of them now, accusing her of not longing, not fighting enough for them, and she repeated in a whisper, "What do you want from me?"

But then her question, sent out over the lake and into the universe, sounded as misdirected as a question could. And it brought back a sickening memory.

Peia was a tiny baby, maybe six or eight weeks old. She was hungry, always hungry, but not like Manny. Peia was a gorger. She would breast feed furiously then turn her head and spew out Jillian's milk. Hungry again, she would scream for more.

One night, Jillian was walking around and around the house with Peia screaming in her arms; screaming, with another hour to go before there could possibly be enough milk to feed her again, and with sleep so far away, Jillian had snapped. Her arms shaking, she lifted Peia above her, not way above, but above. She held the screaming baby over her face and whisper-screamed, "What do you want from me?"

She hadn't truly shaken Peia. As soon as she hoisted her and let the question go, she watched Peia's head barely rock, side to side, maybe a centimeter forward and back, but she hadn't shaken her. Jillian's hands supported her baby's neck, her mother-hands cradled the back and sides of Peia's baby-head. The shaking had come from her own, tired arms. Still, her baby's face bobbed and took notice. Peia, hoisted in the air, stopped crying.

Filled with an awful, aching guilt, Jillian had held Peia close, settled Peia's tensed stomach across her forearm and gently bounced her from kitchen to living room and back while Peia screamed and Jillian cried. She had been alone with both kids, day and night it seemed, with Jack teaching and setting up a new lab, and she had snapped. She had snapped. She hadn't truly shaken Peia, of course she hadn't. But what if she had softened the bobble of Peia's head in her own memory?

Astronauts, some of the women Kera met in training, said they all went through it. Some kind of internal breakdown was necessary before they could settle into the isolation. Even on the ground, in simulator tests, if they were left alone on one of the space station pods, they felt it.

With black flies bombarding her face—they were after the moisture in her tears— Jillian lit the end of her driftwood club and planted it next to her in the sand. She would get through this night and nine others. She would, whether she slept or not.

She looked up at the Pleiades, now slightly west. Wisps of moisture were gathering above, blowing in off the lake. Individual stars within the cluster were no longer crisp, but their combined light, with the boldness of aqua and the resonance of periwinkle, shone through.

From the universe, she should ask for patience. There was some flaw in her, at work against her. She apologized to the Pleiades. She had never told anyone—not Jack, not Kera, not even her mother— about that night. She looked up at Cassiopeia and gave voice to her fear.

"I'm sorry."

Jillian always feared she had caused some defect in Peia that made her behave in hard, fast, emotional ways. She had sheared Peia's tiny spinal cord or ruffled her growing nerves. Strangely enough, as Jillian faced the Cassiopeia in the sky, the Peia in the sky seemed to smile.

"I'm sorry," Jillian said again.

2

The Great Rift

KERA WAS ON BIG SABLE'S spiral staircase, ahead of Jillian a rung or two, holding the flashlight as they stepped deliberately to Kera's cues.

"God, this is an odd sensation," Jillian said. The leafy pattern of the wrought iron steps cast shadows on the outer wall of the lighthouse as they climbed. "It feels like we're going around in a huge circle, doesn't it? Around and around and around."

"Keep your hand on the wall," Kera cautioned.

"I am." Jillian was hyper-aware of the iron spiral that held the steps together.

"How many windows have we passed?" Kera patted each stair with her front foot, testing.

"I'm having enough trouble watching my feet, now you want me to watch windows? Are you crazy?" Jillian was engrossed in her own system: one, two, shove it toward the spire; three, four, shove it toward the spire. They were climbing the downed lighthouse (its historic light taken down for repairs) in the dark. That had to be some kind of record for hardship endured for a good night's viewing. She tapped Kera on the back, "We're crazy," and Kera stuttered forward.

"Jilli!" The flashlight wobbled, spraying the walls with dancing leaves, but Kera held onto it, thankfully. "Whoa."

"Big whoa." Jillian patted for Kera in the dark. "Sorry."

"You feel that? I've got to sit a minute."

The spinning sensation was powerful. Jillian looked down, trying to gauge how far they'd come—not even halfway, from the looks of it. "It's the competing spins, the physical force through the stairway and all these shadows swirling around." She set her feet—one crammed into the central spire, the other heel against the outer guard—and looked up. Through the rectangle of the open trap door above, she saw the stars: huge and tiny and medium points of luminescence, all incredibly distinct. "Hey." She found Kera's shoulder. "Look at the stars."

"It's the Milky Way." Kera sat, holding her head. "I don't know what's up. My sinuses, I guess. I've climbed this light a million times."

Yes, Kera had said that the Milky Way, from the vantage point of lying on the lighthouse walkway, surrounded by miles and miles of darkness, would leave Jillian speechless. What Jillian saw now wasn't an expanse but a crop, a cropped image that seemed to lend more definition to each star within the tiny rectangle of sky.

"Shine the stairs for me." Climbing a twist above Kera, Jillian stopped and sat. She tilted her head back, cheek pressed firmly against the center pole, and whispered, afraid to break the moment. "Turn it off now."

"Don't move then," Kera whispered back. "Stay put."

Jillian had no desire to move. She was transfixed by the stars.

She and Kera were two weeks into their four-week retreat at the Depot, time they'd set aside to outline their PhD proposal for the Space Consortium. Arnie, their advisor at Michigan Tech (Dr. Arnold Schmidt as he was known in academic circles) had told them not to bother coming back unless they brought him an outline he could take to the doctoral committee. Arnie was kidding, somewhat, but their time was running out. He was counting on their proposal, hoping their project would be one of the first joint ventures between MTU, the University of Michigan, and a growing number of universities interested in sharing equipment, faculty, and new research. A PhD in Astronomy from the University of Michigan, without having to commit to three years in Ann Arbor where the stars were drowned out by the lights of Detroit, was a great opportunity. And no one was counting on a successful proposal more than Jillian and Kera. After splitting up for the previous summer's research projects, they knew what it was like to be the only woman on a team.

Jillian had participated in a Syracuse study, using computers to create simulations of the heat and pressure mechanics within stars. Her graphics were linked to images retrieved from the observatory, stars in all stages of the stellar life cycle, images Jillian had selected herself. She'd fared better than Kera mostly because she'd kept to herself. She created the graphics and the guys assembled the show.

"Kera. Look up, through the trap door."

The stars, framed by the doorway, were so dense that when Jillian let her eyes relax, she felt she was seeing what the ancients saw, the Greek's band of milk.

Kera's two-toned voice split, rising low and husky. "They're perfect."

Jillian wanted to tease—*Save the Lauren Bacall for some guy*—but she felt the tingle of a new idea and she didn't want to lose it. "More than perfect. Look near the edges."

Kera cleared her throat and that vibratory mix of low and high returned. "Sharp, aren't they. Much sharper than usual."

Yes. Ultra-sharp, as if the stars that butted up against the open doorway were throwing less light, less glare. "Explain interferometry to me."

"Why? You know what it is."

"I know. I know. But just let me hear it, step by step."

Kera's study of detectable radio wave emissions from objects in space had bored her senseless. She had gone to the desert, imagining sitting high above a mountain canyon, wearing headphones and listening to sounds bouncing off asteroid, and found herself instead the only woman at a small, three-dish radio array in Arizona assigned to daytime frequency observations, watching a single amplifier needle for an occasional, nonregulated bounce. She'd been bored, yes, but she'd learned a lot about the process of combining signals from several telescopes.

"Well, interferometry, literally, means to interfere and to measure. As light moves toward us, it waves up and down in crests and troughs. So, if you know the exact distance from one wave to another, which is wavelength, you can combine the light from two or more telescopes so the peaks of the waves match up. To get the brightest, highest resolution picture possible."

"Okay. Now." Jillian looked down, purposefully trying to connect with Kera, though all she could see was the puff of Kera's thick hair. "Supposedly, you can do the same in reverse, right? Instead of intensifying the light, you can nullify it, by combining several telescopes."

Now she could see Kera's upturned face. "In theory, yes. Once you have a working interferometer, you can interfere constructively or destructively with the lightwaves, but it's complicated. The idea is to delay one set of waves by exactly half a wavelength so the peaks of one wave combine with the troughs of another and they cancel each other out, and then you have to repeat the process over and over to suppress the light to any noticeable degree."

"What if we didn't have to? What if we could mask the brightness away?" Jillian scooted down the stairs. "Can you climb again? Here, let me take the light. We'll keep it along the center pole, then these damn leaf shapes won't keep spinning around us."

A twist or so below the trap door they sat side by side, looking up through the rectangular window, and Jillian tried to explain the odd set of images and ideas that were converging in her mind. "There's this thing we do at the print shop, called spreads and chokes." For years, Jillian had spent her summers doing camera work, pre-press, at the shop.

Kera sounded doubtful. "Okay."

"We use these really bright cameras to shoot type, in the plate-making process. It's hard to explain, but basically, the light from the camera is so bright that it bounces off the surface of the plate and back into the photographic film, and the glare causes the type to get all fuzzy."

Jillian continued, knowing Kera would understand, eventually.

"You can't get rid of the source of the glare, the big camera, so what we do is create these masks that mask out all the extra, unwant-ed light."

Kera nodded and shook her head, a sign that she was with Jillian but didn't know where they were going. "What are you saying? That we could mask out the star?"

"Well. Kind of. The type is actually created when light passes through the type shapes in the film. When you're working with com-plicated type or a really big image, it's hard to keep it crisp, with all the glare. So what you do is enlarge the type, blow it up a percentage or two. That's the spread. Then you combine the spread with anoth-er shot, a percentage or two smaller. That's the choke. As light passes through the spread and then through the choke, you end up masking away the glare, which leaves only the straight throughput of the let-ters. The light you want to pass through to create clean, high-contrast type."

"Jilli. I don't mean to be mean here, but the whole analogy thing has never been your strong point."

Oh, how true! She had such trouble, sometimes, communicating ideas she could see. "Hang on a minute." She shook off her backpack and dug for her graph pad and a pen. "I'm thinking we could use the same process, with the opposite goal. Instead of trying to increase the throughput of starlight, we'd mask it away."

Kera raised an eyebrow and left it there.

"Here, shine the paper for me. Think of this really bright camera as the star, and the plate as the back end of the telescope. The end point where we're focusing the light into a final image."

"Okay."

"Between the camera and the end plate is this film. The film that has all the type shapes on it." Here, Jillian drew a simple square with a few letters of type on it.

"Okay. I guess."

"Why couldn't we do the same with starlight? Mask the light away before we make the final image?"

"And you're getting all of this from up there." They both looked up.

"Yeah. And the shapes too."

Jillian raised her hands above her, shaping her fingers in a tiny rectangle. "If we could block even part of the bright starlight coming toward us, what would be left–"

"I got it—is anything that was reflecting light. I got it! What would be left is anything around the star that wasn't producing its own light."

"Exactly. What would be left would be any light caught on the surface of something else."

"Like a planet."

"Like a planet."

"But what would we end up with?"

As if on cue, they both reached skyward, putting their hands together and making different shaped crops. Jillian made a tiny rectangle and positioned it in several locations over a particularly bright star. "I don't know, but we could certainly do some calculations and figure it out."

Kera leaned into Jillian, stretching her arms above, cropping a wide, then a smaller rectangle, then a square. "It's the edge then." She looped her fingers into a circle and placed them above Jillian's tilted face, as if to demonstrate. "It's the edge that's going to make the difference."

In a way, the trap door was acting like the opening of a telescope, except it was small and rectangular, not round like the body of the lighthouse. "It can't be that simple," Jillian said.

But it was. They climbed to the deck and tried out all sorts of instantaneous lens creations. They put two sextants together in the shape of a diamond; they isolated a tiny slice of space with one clipboard above and one below. They worked their hands and fingers into different sizes and shapes, augmented with rulers, pens, opened and closed bookspines, and reasoned their way through the potential results. Why not? They'd be crazy if they tried to explain the idea anyway. Why not try a cat's eye? Kera placed her hands, cupped with a cat eye opening, in front of Jillian's face.

Square, oblong, a slice of a trapezoid—they drew and discussed all kinds of masks.

"You know," Kera stretched the edge of her pinky fingernail over the center of a star while zooming her other hand, flattened, toward the blocked image. "We might want to try a simple occulting device first, like they use to study the sun's corona. Occlude the body of the star, then work to reduce the halo around it."

"Maybe," Jillian agreed, dipping down and watching as Kera's fingernail blocked the main light of the star. Her other hand acted like a visor, which, as she thought about it, was a good analogy: a visor blocks the sun's rays from reaching your eyes, but the sun still shines on the road. "Kera. Maybe this seems too simple because it is."

"Oh no you don't. I was just beginning to believe."

"Really?"

"Totally. Even if we did end up combining images, way down the line, we'd still have to come up with some masks. I don't know about visible light though, Jilli. Radiowaves are so much longer, so much easier to work with."

Of course radio was easier. The radio dishes Kera had worked with were all banged up and made out of crude mesh. But their mirrors would have to be nearly perfect to catch and combine the tiny, higher-frequency waves of visible light.

"That's where Arnie comes in," Jillian said, well before she understood what she was saying. Arnie could pull together a few lab physicists and engineers. And Kera probably knew more than she realized about combining waves and troughs—troughs, yes, the dark valleys between the peaks. If they could mask away some of the light, first, then cancel out the bright peaks of what was left, they might actually get a look into the area immediately around a star. Other planets must be orbiting other suns, but because the area around a star was so impossibly bright to observe, no one had ever actually *seen* such a planet.

"You know what?" She turned to Kera, feeling her own grin spread wide. "We're going to build our own."

"Our own what?"

"Our own light-blocking, mask-testing observatory."

"What!"

Jillian held her clipboard open as she drew. First, the barrel of a telescope, and then she inserted masks: over the end or somehow positioned out front; in between the primary and the secondary mirror, where the light was first focused; and finally, at the back end of the telescope, at the pupil plane, where all of the light from the telescope was refocused and captured as one tiny final image. She put the clipboard in Kera's hands and tapped a drawing of a mask with several slats, light spreading out in distinct areas, creating dark bands in between. "Eventually, we'd probably have to combine images, to get a really high degree of contrast between dark and light. But for now, you're right, we need to find the right mask."

Kera scratched at Jillian's drawing. "We'll keep it simple at first, try different shapes and see what we get." She drew a cat-eye opening, with light beams radiating out at certain points. "You know what? This could work. This could work." Light fanned out above and below Kera's cat-eye mask, but off to the sides there were vast triangles of darkness.

Above them, in just one spiral arm of the Milky Way, were hundreds of millions of stars. How many solar systems, planets, moons, were drowned out by that light? Modern telescopes weren't all that different from the ones Brahe or Newton used. And the more scientists studied light, how it illuminated the interactions between atoms and particles and matter, the more they were amazed how little science knew about the other 70 to 90 percent of the universe: that portion of the observable universe called dark because we could not see it. We couldn't even imagine it. Astronomers were peering farther and farther into space, using light's beam to define astronomical distances, its hue to label stars heavy in this element or that, but no one knew what exactly it was that moved with or between light. It was astrophysics' inside-out version of geophysics' outside-in shortcoming: geologists scoured the earth, the moon, meteors for elements of life, but they still didn't know what was 4,000 miles below, at the center of our very own planet.

"We'll be mistresses of the dark," Kera said. "Like Vera Rubin. Course, we'll be as ridiculed as Vera, too. You really think a simple mask would chop away the light like that?"

"If it doesn't, it won't take us long to find out." But if it did, they could move to different locations, try variations on masking, work toward combining images.

"Kera. Think linked, masked mirrors."

"Let's not forget, Jilli, Vera's dark matter doesn't seem so far out now, but the poor woman nearly left science for good."

"No, she didn't nearly leave. She was nearly left out. There's a difference." Jillian motioned for Kera to move closer. "But who's laughing now? We can do this. I know we can."

"We might want to look close to home."

Meaning: start small. Study some sun-like stars with the potential for Earth-like planets. Oh, to discover a planet or a nearby solar system! To actually *see* one.

"That's right. But for now, we're going to sit here all night and test shapes. I hope it stays clear."

The Great Rift in the Summer Milky Way, a dark expanse that stretched from Deneb, the eastern star of the Summer Triangle, all the way to Scorpius in the South was clearly visible above, where the black of night spread down from the dome and subtle blues condensed to a line of purple that would remain on the horizon until dawn. They had the best of nights.

"We're not going down that staircase until dawn, anyway," Kera laughed. "It didn't bug your head?"

"A little, I guess. How many telescopes do you think we could handle, if we were mobile?"

"I don't know. Two? Four? How mobile?"

They had come in search of clusters and nebulae and the brightest splay of stars either of them had ever seen south of Houghton, and they'd discovered, perhaps, a research project that could keep them together.

"Arnie," Kera said. "Arnie will love it."

Jillian wasn't sure. Just before they'd left Houghton for their month-long hiatus, Arnie had talked, excitedly, about how wide-open computer modeling was. She could apply her models to problems as huge as supernovae and the age of the universe or as weird as time warps, worm tunnels, black holes. People like her, Arnie had said, who knew their way around imaging software could model, on a small scale, a universe that was too large to see. Still. No one, not even Arnie, knew how important it was for Jillian and Kera to stick together.

"Kera. Do you realize we can go anywhere?"

Kera spread her arms out wide: over the lighthouse rail, over the faraway silver-black of the water, into the purple-black sky. "Anywhere."

All they had to do was prove the *potential* for searching the area immediately surrounding a star; the *potential* for finding another planet, and NASA or any number of funding sources would, as Kera liked to say, "go ga-ga over it."

"Exactly," Jillian said. "Now draw."

3

Time

SHE HAD PURCHASED THE CLOCK for two reasons: it was chrome, which would match the cherry of their renovated kitchen; and its numbers were huge and stark and black, perfect for teaching Manny how to tell time. She would pull the huge clock off its perch above the kitchen table and lay it in Manny's lap. They would take turns arranging the minute and hour hands in different positions, quizzing each other. If Manny forgot that 2-3-4 was equal to ten-fifteen-twenty he could count the bold individual hash marks, one for each minute.

The three of them were bellying their way across the living room floor: Peia in a diaper, dark and gooey with baby-fat rolls (Jillian had to take great care to wash into those creases during bath-time) and Manny, long and skinny-white in shorts. At five, his face was beginning to look more boney and defined. Jillian had been feeling uneasy about teaching Manny how to tell time, but she had to, didn't she?

And then Peia found the clock. Jillian saw her eyes enlarge and then she lunged for the television stand, Manny and Jillian beating her to it, pushing videos out of her reach.

"You like the clock, huh baby?" Manny cooed. "You like the clock?"

Peia yanked with her strong arms and lay on the clock. Her wild dark hair hung over the clock's huge plastic face, shaking as she shook with excited throbs from her legs. But then she quieted, studying the clock's hands as they moved with an audible hitch. *Tick* with a hesitant backstroke, then *tock* pushed the second hand forward.

Manny pulled the clock to him, turning the buttons in the back. "Look at that, baby. I can make the hands move." Peia smiled and slapped at the clock, squealing as she scooted toward it. Manny loomed over the clock with her, and, discovering his reflection distorted and elongated in the clock's chrome rim, he moved his head closer and farther, making long stretched-out noises. "Big Manny," he said, whoo-ing away, "Little Manny," while Peia throbbed.

And Jillian saw, so clearly, what marriage had in mind.

She tried to explain it to Jack, how it hurt in an odd, self-inflicted way, to be managing bids and supervising other scientists-turned-computer-specialists, instead of digging into projects like Syracuse's "Supernova in a Can," those hot new computer-generated simulations that would normally, naturally, be hers.

She'd kept her word, hadn't she? She had taken three full months off, except for occasional phone calls and emails needed to oversee a bid. She would talk Nikki through the specifics of time and people needed to develop a networkable imaging system for sharing data between observatories, or a computer modeling program to take in the mass, chemical composition, and luminosity of recently discovered brown dwarfs and simulate their birth and development. Were they failed stars? And then Jim, the company founder, would step in to write the proposal, sending it to Jillian for final tucks and revisions, because, as bright as Nikki was, she was an electrical engineer, used to dealing with hard-wired realities. Jim knew how these projects could grow. He knew enough to take the time it *should* take them and multiply that by three. Jillian was trying to enjoy this time, supposedly a summer respite for her and Manny and Peia, but there were relationships between the numbers. Jack was working six and seven days a week while she was only now working up to three. She tried to explain, but Jack wouldn't have it. He would hug her or jostle her elbow and tell her, "You'll get back to it." As if it were all about *her*.

She loved thinking of Jack in a jacket and jeans, that clump of dark hair hanging over his forehead, the pale blue of his eyes heating up as he paced back and forth in front of his students, excited about genetic mutations and chromosomal splicing. But that was enough. She didn't want him hanging around after class for all those doorway conversations, hours of abstract, supposedly scientific talk-talk-talk that really wasn't work at all. He was eyeing the new Lab Director position. She knew that pressure: not wanting to miss a single opportunity to show your commitment. But that didn't mean she didn't want him home. Home shouldn't be her and the kids, always her and the kids. She wanted him home.

Peia slapped the clock so hard that the minute hands bounced in and out of action. Her hair shook as she stretched out her baby legs. She was adoring the clock, smiling at its hands, its button nose, its huge black numbers as if the clock were the face of someone she loved, as if the clock face were as worthy of adoration as her brother. But it wasn't a face. It was a clock. And just as Jillian had been teaching Manny, one day she would teach Peia. One day, in an instant, Peia would come to realize that those long black hands dictated when she could let her thoughts go, when it was time to get dressed, eat, go to school, dream of a better world. And in that instant, just as Jillian had witnessed the flash and then the quiet hurt on Manny's face the night before, Peia would feel robbed, cheated of her magic.

Why was she doing this? Teaching such limits?

Bed-time, school-time, listen-time. To do this at that time, think about that at another time, when your heart begged to do an entirely different, potentially disorderly activity was overtly mechanical. It was numbing, dumbing, wasteful.

Jillian scooped Peia up and away, with Manny looking on, confused. He thought it was the noise, the noise of all that banging, and he pulled back on Peia's feet. "She won't hurt it. She won't hurt it, Mom."

Jillian had always had moments of duality, sitting in classrooms copying diagrams from an overhead while images from home—the fields and the farms and the sound of her hiking boots clumping over dried stalks in the dark—ran somewhere felt but not seen. But everyday, now, she was living as two selves: the self who longed to take big, clumping steps anywhere, anywhere around the neighborhood, along a trail, from one complete thought to another; and the mother-self, who shuffled from polyurethaned wood to short shag all day. Mother washed bottles at night, alone, while Father fell asleep on Manny's floor. He was working much more than they had planned. She could tell the stories and Jack would wash bottles, if that was what she wanted. But she enjoyed hearing, from such a sweet, close distance, Manny's giggles and Jack's awful French accent, "But I am Pierre and those are my meatballs!" And bath times when Jack would call her away from the sink to watch Manny's rendition of Cocker's "You Are So Beautiful," Jack singing "You are so beautiful," and Manny's arms reaching toward her, his high voice belting out, "To me! Can't you see! Ee-ee-ee-ee!"

But Jack got away, always. Jack got away.

She gazed into Peia's huge dark pupils, certain there was some innate spirit about to be destroyed.

More and more now, Jack embraced university-time: lab-time, lecture-time, building tenure-time. And the more he removed himself from the conflicts of home-time, the more his clocks tightened a web of responsibility over hers. Someone had to be present. Was that what marriage had accomplished? Forced her and Jack into a continuous struggle, both of them believing they needed and deserved their own time and space? And the marriage clock was strong—*tick* for one child; *tock* for another. Its beat forced her to pass on that oldest of impositions in the most subtle, insidious way. Who, after all, was teaching, living, modeling limits? *Mother.*

Peia squirmed in Jillian's arms, twisting toward Manny.

"Mom. Let her play."

Sometimes, Jillian wondered if Manny told Jack about these moments.

"Mom. Let her play."

It was their first night in the Smokies—their first night of getting used to a whole new set of variables called location—and the mist rising around them seemed to be both stifling and heightening their excitement. Standing on either side of the huge boulder that marked the very summit of Mount LeConte, Kera and Jillian watched a cool gray mist rise from the deep crevices below. Moisture: an astronomer's worst nightmare.

Kera pointed skyward, irritated. "Since when does mist rise like this? It's creepy, isn't it?"

Jillian tried to stay positive as she opened the aluminum case marked R-SS for her masks, the Rectangular and the Super-Slat. The foam lining glowed like a liquid paste in the dark as she reached in to grab one of the sleeved masks. "It'll fade. It has to."

Kera's was marked CC for Cat-eye and Concave. They were going to test that curve in both directions, throw light up and out and side to side.

"It better." Kera helped Jillian lift the ten-inch telescope onto its base, carefully seating the delicate but strong metal tubing that cradled the mirror in a criss-cross of supports. They tightened the side screws so the barrel remained in a straight-up position. All they had to do was let the telescopes acclimate. That was all.

She slipped on a pair of photography gloves before handling the mask she and Kera had created, the first one, an opaque disk with a tiny rectangular opening, laser-cut for accuracy. Cutting the masks had taken much longer than expected. One of the techs in the laser lab could have cut the masks for them, but they wanted to build every piece. She surveyed the mask with her red light, making sure it was perfectly seated between two gelatin pads that would allow it to adjust to temperature and humidity. For tonight, they'd leave the masks out front, at the pupil plane. Later, they'd move them to the mask-box with a CCD camera they'd designed to add on to the backend. Throughout, they'd compare masked results to images produced with a simple occulting disk at the focal point. Their masks needed to show at least some improvement in light-nulling capability if they were going to commit to further study.

"Hey, check this out." Kera's voice, coming from an unexpected position, startled Jillian. She'd thought Kera was still standing behind her, huffing about the sky and waiting for her turn to use the one eyepiece they'd had time to put together. She checked up, an automatic reaction. The dome, straight above, was beautifully clear, but the mountain, all around them, was being engulfed in a thick, climbing mist.

She found Kera standing near the edge of the settler's wall that bordered the lodge. They traded "Wows," watching their tiny researcher's cabin disappear in a puff of mist, and the two of them stood with their arms outstretched, waiting for the mist to reach them. Gauzy streams of fog overtook the summit and blew over them with a strong breeze, and they climbed to the top of the boulder to watch.

Darkness on LeConte was exactly as Ranger Brad had described. Once the fog swept over the mountain, fingering everything in its path as if taking assessment of what belonged and what did not belong, the cool gray moisture balled itself back down into the valleys below and the dome was completely clear, cobalt, and seething with light.

"Above us only sky," Kera whispered.

And then, as if time did not matter, even as she felt herself waking, again, to turn off a sore shoulder and hip, Jillian heard in the vacuum-like chill of LeConte's receding mist a familiar metallic rumble followed by a low, steady whir. Rumble-hum, and the dome of a giant telescope opened to reveal a widening band of stars and black sky.

Rumble-hum, and the sky opened wide.

4

Day Two—Sully's Depot

THE DEPOT LOOKED LONELY. The long, two-story house where Kera had grown up stood in its yard of sand as if it were guarding the forested dunes behind it. Standing across the street, staring at the old railroad depot Kera's parents—Kate and Mitchell Sullivan—had converted into a bed and breakfast for summer researchers, Jillian could only think *the Depot looks lonely*.

Morning light had come slowly, over the course of several miles. She left camp well before sunrise, walking in and out of scalloped edges of water with the sky just beginning to purple, climbing to dryer sand, at times, to hear the squeak. She tried to remember why the white sand of Lake Michigan made such a noticeable noise. Was it limestone? The presence of glass? She couldn't answer. She walked with voices and emotions of the night before still in her mind, thinking again of bottle washing: standing over the sink feeling like a failure when Manny was a baby, scrubbing and wondering why he was so skinny and when she would feel strong enough to return to the observatory. Years later, with Peia, she'd stood over hot lemony suds understanding what it was to feel glad for night's precious moments alone.

Rounding the three-humped dune that marked the end of the national forest and the beginning of Ludington State Park, she had stopped walking to take in daylight and to clear her mind. Turning to face the western sky, she'd felt that old sense of relief (a long night over) mixed with sadness; out on the horizon, cobalt paled to a minty blue that drowned out the stars. By the time she jumped rocks at the lighthouse and, two miles further down shore, walked waist-deep through a watery field of petrified pillars at the old beach house pier, the sun was yellow-white and hot.

Now, standing across the park entrance road, gazing at one of her favorite places in the universe, Jillian sank to her knees. In all her summers with Kera, she couldn't remember the wind off the lake being so hot—Iowa hot—and humid. She squirted water over her head, but that brought thoughts of Peia and her teammates squirting themselves after a soccer game, so she shook the image and the water from her eyes. Solitude, it seemed, was going to take its own sweet time.

She managed a smile for the Depot's sloped front porch, remembering how the painted boards with their sand-filled gaps felt under bare feet. And Kate's rockers—she remembered sitting in the high-backed rockers Kera's mother made from planed driftwood and stringy lake weeds that she dried and greased all summer. The porch, lined with Kate's rockers, was empty. She had missed the morning commotion.

Hours earlier the porch would have been crowded with naturalists, botanists, biologists, all types of scientists and academics who rented rooms at Sully's Depot. Guests would have sipped strong, organic coffee with Kate and Mitchell—naturalists who had written their share of books and guides—while organizing their thoughts and packing for the day. Many of the Depot's guests, realizing they had spent too much of June and July observing the birds, lake levels, the zebra mussels, would have spoken in quick quips, not bothering to sit or chat. The end of August was near. Time for the scientists of summer to wrap up and head home.

A man, too young and too tall to be Kera's father, opened the screen door. He waved and Jillian's face grew hot with embarrassment. She was kneeling at the side of the park entrance road, way too close to the pavement. Kneeling and staring as if she had dropped down, overtaken by a sudden need to worship. She crawled to higher sand. Sitting on top of the drift, away from the road, she would look like a hiker taking a rest instead of some desperate seeker.

The man sat and looked out over his laptop screen, staring toward the water, then began to type. And there sat Jillian, a thirty-nine-year-old woman with a doctorate in Astrophysics, longing for something magic and irreversible to happen. What did she expect the Depot to do? Send an electromagnetic wave of healing? Open some strand of her previous existence? Restore her tired, sweaty body and the hope draining from her soul?

Two old wooden train cars—a passenger car and a caboose—sat cockeyed, beached in the sand as if a giant toddler had been playing with toys and left them hitched but badly angled, next to the house. They seemed more orange than Jillian remembered. Years ago, when she and Kera spent summer nights lying on the roof of the passenger car, the cars were creamier in color, painted a thick, glossy tan. Now, aged and oxidizing, rust colored the wheels (oblong from years of heat and immobility) and the back of the caboose had sunken into the sand.

Jillian laughed, remembering the train yard she'd first imagined when Kera described her home. "You have railroad cars in your yard?" Jillian had pictured brown, numbered railway cars, metal ones with no windows.

"Not like that," Kera said. "You're thinking freight cars. These are old, really old, from a passenger train that got buried during a sand storm. The whole place was under a few feet of sand."

They had just met, at Michigan Tech, and everything about Kera seemed instantly certain. "No one calls you Jilli?"

"Not really. People usually call me Jill."

"Well, I'm going to call you Jilli."

It was 1979, turning toward the eighties, yet she and her new roommate were the only two women in physics. Physics with honors, what had she done?

Driving through Wisconsin, Jillian and her parents had stopped at every rocky overlook along the Lake Superior coast. In the Porcupine Mountains—Michigan had mountains?—the three of them stood on the Lake Superior trail, trying out Scottish accents, her father sighing, *Aye, we could be in Scotland.* There were so many cliffs and such impressive thundering waves, and they woefully underestimated the time it took to drive across Michigan's Upper Peninsula. Jillian had arrived at Michigan Technological University one hour after her freshman orientation group had departed for the campus tour without her.

Her mother, from the start, let the tears flow. "Oh, baby, I'm so sorry. We were going to have such a relaxing morning, weren't we?" Her father's sunburned face paled and he hugged Jillian for so long that her lungs literally ached when he released her. She stood, waiting for him to rib her about all the men or blowing up the lab, but the ribbing never came. Her father was going to cry.

So she packed her parents into the station wagon—"The coast of Scotland, after all, does beckon!"—and watched them drive away, her mother zig-zagging the wagon each time she turned to look back. "See you soon, baby! See you soon!" The last Jillian saw or heard of her parents was her father's "Gayle, watch it. Gayle!" And then she stood in the center of her dormitory room, alone—until Kera came bursting in: tall, red-haired, and springy.

She threw her long arms around Jillian. "I am so glad to see another girl! Man! Did they tell you we're the only ones? Everything's been warped back to the fifties up here!"

Later, Kera showed her those awful drawings, some scratched in ink and thicker ones drawn in marker. They were unpacking. Kera parted the hangers to make room for Jillian's clothes, and there they were: breasts hanging, breasts with eyes, breasts being mouthed, squeezed, and—pinched? Crudely drawn breasts covered the heating duct that ran up the back wall, dividing their closet in two. "Yeah," Kera said. "You gotta love the stick figures with breasts section."

Jillian had stepped back, feeling at risk. Kera was practically flat, but Jillian, she was a lot more out there. She'd hung out with lots of guys in high school and sure, she'd gotten looks at track meets. She'd done her fair share of looking back. But none of the guys she knew, not a one of them—had they?—had ever treated her like that.

"Don't worry. We'll get our own set of markers." Kera grabbed some hangers and waved Jillian's eyes away from the top, where the drawings were most crude. "Hey, cool jeans." But the drawing of a woman on her back, legs up in the air, with a caption reading "Hail, Hail the new College of Education!" had already made its impression. Why hadn't anyone tried to cover it up?

She and Kera went everywhere together after that: up and down the elevator; to check out the basement laundry room; introducing themselves to two other girls they found on their floor. (Science Education majors, Jillian was instantly afraid for them.) They filled out a maintenance request to paint their own closet, and later, after an orientation dinner of miner's food—the Dean explained that the half-moon of pie crust filled with beef and carrots and potatoes was a pasty—the only two women in physics went outside.

They walked the path to Houghton's infamous blue bridge and crossed over cold purple-blue water with the lights of both towns, Houghton on one side and Hancock on the other, flickering up the hills. It was August, and it was already cold.

When Tech's admissions packet arrived, Jillian had stroked the glossy aerial photo of campus, loving the colors: red buildings strung along a river so blue and so deep they called it a lake, Portage Lake. (Rivers in Iowa were brown, never blue.) And the land itself, the Keweenaw Peninsula, curled like a knobby finger into the deepest, darkest, meanest of the Great Lakes, Lake Superior. She knew the college was going to be male and technical and remote, but when she'd read in the Physics department's brochure, *A well-trained physicist can do anything*, she was certain. She had no intention of ending up in some particle lab, slamming protons and electrons together or apart, but to get anywhere in astronomy, she needed a good base in physics and math. What better place than the desolate shores of Lake Superior, one of the darkest areas in the world?

"Does it snow in Iowa?" Kera asked.

"Oh yeah. Sometimes, when the wind blows down from the plains, the snow freezes like lace over the roads."

"Well, forget the pretty lace. Here, they get lake effect snow, which means it comes and it stays."

High above the "School of the Mines" an historical marker described how the chairlift at the very top of the school's ski hill had been converted from an old mining tower. Lying in the damp grass, Jillian watched as the aura of the Milky Way came alive with light, more and more stars popping through its gassy image minute by minute.

"Wow. Now we know why we're here."

She was cold but it no longer mattered. Neither did the pink-tipped stakes, taller than the station wagon, that rimmed the roads around campus. "Snow stakes," Kera had slapped her leg. "Snow stakes for the plows."

Looking down on square campus buildings huddled along cold dark water in two long rows, she thought about their future. Dorm life would be a challenge, but outside, with the brightness and the density of the stars, they'd make it. She wondered if her parents had reached Minneapolis yet, whether her Mom had stopped crying and whether her Dad had ever started, and she admitted as much to Kera. She was homesick already, and a little scared.

"The boobs?" Kera's voice softened. "Yeah. They got to me too."

Kera lifted a hand to the sky, her palm open and flat and moving with her gaze, as if she were touching the stars. Jillian was tempted to tell Kera about her mother, Gayle; how the two of them, on the darkest nights, convinced each other they could see colors in the spaces between the stars. But that was a little too far out. Gaseous clouds, sure, with the naked eye.

"What's your favorite?" she asked instead.

And Kera had answered without hesitation, "That'd have to be the Pleiades. Man, it's dark up here, isn't it? I love their color. Zenith blue."

"Zenith blue." Jillian had repeated. "That's so cool. Like the peak of the universe."

The man on the Depot deck was gone. The zenith, directly above, was blue-white and hot, and Jillian's head was still pounding. She opened another bottle of water and guzzled. The Depot couldn't restore possibility to her life. No. And Kera—Jillian was not going to go that route and feel jealous. Kera had gone through her own kinds of sacrifices to get where she was. The last time Kera had visited, she and Peia had spent hours applying ridiculous amounts of make-up, eye shadow and three-toned blush they'd walked to the dollar store to buy. They'd come home wearing matching flip-flops and made fun of Jillian when she cautioned them about cheap make-up and skin sensitivity. And later, when Kera and Peia sat in the grass playing hand-clap games, dandelions stuck in their hair, Jillian had felt so proud and so sad. Not for Kera, as she and Peia lifted each other to their feet and performed some secret hand-shake, some hand wobble that went skyward and then a spin and a clap behind their backs. Not for herself as she stood watching Kera and Peia, both so tall and lean, dancing in the front yard. But for both of them, for herself and for Kera, because from the beginning Kera had not let anyone or anything get in her way; because Jillian had let everything stand in hers.

The wind lifted her hair and moved on, uninterested, lingering in patches of dune grass in the Depot yard. Kate and Mitchell wouldn't dream of planting a non-native ground cover. Jillian stood, smiling at Sully's Depot, feeling a fresh wave of longing for Kera's parents and all those airy, wallpapered bedrooms. But what would she say? *I've picked out a great cliff. You know, Nordhouse Dunes, that tract of sand and trees and ferns that no one ventures into.* No one except the serious back country camper or a runaway Mom.

Through waves of heat, she pictured herself and Kera—twenty, fifteen, even ten years ago—lying on the top of that rusting passenger car, talking under the stars.

Always, one of them would point up and say, "Someday."

And the other would echo, "Someday."

Of course the dreams she and Kera voiced in the dark, only to each other, were big. Huge! To take their masked telescope and later their first crude coronagraph and use it to prove that masking away the blinding glare of a star's light was possible. To apply to NASA and keep applying until they both made it, whether they were employed at one of the research centers or down in Houston or out on the cape. If they were right, and they could eventually apply the masking concept to the biggest of visible light telescopes, someday—someday— they might actually *see* another planet.

Wasn't that what dreams were? Nearly unattainable goals? Like her father had always said, "Goals you can catch. Dreams you have to keep pushing for."

She turned back toward the water, shimmers of white lapping along the tops of its silvery, midday surface, now knowing what Day Two was. Exhaustion Day. And she was going to push. Push her hips and her knees and the soles of her feet. Push her sunburned face and her stinging shoulders, where the straps of her daypack were digging in. She would push beyond the beach house, beyond a nap at the breakwater, push on for another four miles past that lowest point of flat hot sand and scruffy pine brush. She and Kera had accomplished so much: their very own Suitcase Observatory and their initial attempts to prove that masking could work, and then their early, terribly early light-nulling research in California. Together, they had earned time on one of the most powerful telescopes in the country. Together, they had seen stars pooled in the bowl of that incredibly shallow ten-foot mirror.

Now separated, their lives were different: Kera, out of astronaut school, waited for a spot on any mission; Jillian worked at Burton's because Jim's central office was half an hour from home, because Peia had good friends, and because Manny had his music. Because they were all happy, and Jack was so rooted he'd never seriously considered anything but staying put. She had had to leave them, then, to continue her research. She'd had to. And somehow, she'd prepared for the discomfort of long-term separation. But—she'd had no idea what she was getting into: the slow forgetting of exactly what Manny's new teeth looked like or how his voice sounded. How the skin on his hands felt so soft when he used to lay his hands over hers and they would stroke the satin edge of his bear blankie together. Manny liked, always, to be in contact, much like Jack, and that knowledge was with her for every subsequent decision.

Day Two. Was the second day in space the hardest? After you'd rocketed through Earth's atmosphere, floated beyond Earth's colors, and realized you were truly, completely surrounded by nothing but cold, black space?

"Someday," she said to the hot blanched sky. Someday Kera would have to come back to her with the answer.

5

Day Two—Sunset

HER HEAD HAD FALLEN, TIRED. Thank the universe, she was going to sleep tonight, and she hadn't missed the sunset, not the best part. The sky was just beginning to swell with pinks. She sat up, wrapping her fleece tightly around her, breathing the beginnings of night. It was the scent of darkness that had taken her back to LeConte, the moisture climbing the dunes reminiscent of the mist that had engulfed her and Kera the first night they'd tested their telescopes and so many nights after; the smell of darkness and moisture and the hope for good stars.

Arnie had loved the masking idea from the beginning. "When something this simple comes up, it's either ludicrous, or, and I think you might have something here, it's so simple that ten teams will jump on it." They didn't want anyone else jumping on it, of course, so they tested the first prototype on an engineering bench, directing beams of light through crudely cut two-inch masks, and they were able to show, with a blank card stuck in the light path, that light passing through certain masks was redirected in fairly predictable patterns. But what they really needed to know was how the telescope and masks would perform together, how they would handle the normal diffusion and any additional diffusion the masks themselves might create. So, not quite a year after she and Kera had formed finger-masks on the lighthouse walkway, they were driving to Gatlinburg, Tennessee, *Gateway to the Smokies*. They'd secured a researcher's cabin in exchange for teaching some star gazing classes and helping out, as needed, at the lodge. She could still remember Gatlinburg's awful light: the reds and oranges and blinding greens of pole-barn tourist attractions that lined the strip. And when they'd driven as far as they could, they checked into a pink motel with a heart-shaped bathtub. Yet for all of Gatlinburg's garishness, she had loved the Smokies: the yellow-green leaves tinkling like faint bells, the llamas that carried supplies up the mountain because there were no roads, the neon orange of the sunrise. Jillian would take the Smokies sun with her forever, its brilliant orange, like the soil; the way it clung to the peaks and burned neon for ten minutes before muting to yellow.

But even then, she was beginning to feel the first inklings of illness back home.

That very first night, as she and Kera had lain head-to-head on the boulder that marked the summit of Mount LeConte, she'd expressed her uneasiness over her father's cough. They had driven to the Depot and to the farm before driving off to Tennessee, and Jillian had noticed, right away, the way her mother kept watch.

"I saw my Mom looking at him, like it hurt when he coughed. And Gayle's not exactly the doting type."

Both Manford and Gayle had insisted the cough was allergy related. He'd been helping out on the neighbor's farm as he had every summer for years. "It's the damned dust," her father had motioned her off. "Dry season."

And Kera had pretty much agreed. Cupping her hands under her head, watching the sky above them, she'd tossed it off too. "Ah, by now he's back in the classroom, terrorizing freshman with big math. But man! What a rush that would be, wouldn't it? Driving a combine!"

So many things had collided back then: Jack, their telescopes, her father's illness. Perhaps that was the pain of love and family, that feeling of fusing, of being overwhelmed by the energies and the needs of others and no longer being able to separate or extricate yourself. The stars knew that: life was born of heat and pressure.

But their goals were much simpler then: to capture the slightest suggestion of something, anything, orbiting a sun-like star and to avoid serious entanglements with men.

We go in with a good pair of binoculars and a hefty roll pack, but no man.
A man is too damned heavy to pack!

Leaning back to watch the subtle recoloring of new darkness spread eastward overhead, Jillian knew what needed to be said. There was no sun*set*, after all, only a slow turning away.

If she could talk to Jack and Manny and Peia, she would tell them light does not fade, light seeps; seeps away and slips under the horizon in stages from bold to brilliant to pale.

Of course, they would all look at her blankly and walk away, and she understood, to some extent, their inability to listen to her waxing poetic about light rays and colors and the elements of life sprinkled throughout the universe by a million dead and dying stars. Still, if they knew the stars as she did, if they could bear to listen, she would tell them it was all in the staying.

First, there is the spread of bold light—a surprise of power as if the sun has revealed its inner furnace—and the sky burns liquid white, searing an oblong of white into the west.

White yellows and the orb of the sun, expanding, turns a brilliant yellow-orange. An orange still hot with white and it highlights every cloud wisp, every curl of water, backlights the curve of the earth, every tree. Oranges and pinks burn from within the shapes in the sky, puffing up clouds and heightening waves.

And then white, pushed back, climbs into the blue. Turquoise and jade spread upward like a cooling gel behind billowing pinks and reds, creating a contrast so intense that the clouds begin to live and breathe with color.

The brilliance, the life, tunnels into everything in its path and swells there—in your heart, almost unbearably—as a catch, a surge, an inability to comprehend. What could be greater?

And then as if to answer, the sky flattens in relief. Colors reach their peak, overpowering everything on Earth. Trees, water, even clouds appear as patches of flat gray—dark, unimportant shapes in light's way. For this is light's turning point, the point when most people pack up their lawn chairs and look away.

Light—fractured but left the lone witness to its many shards—reaches out into the sky and puts itself back together.

Purple chases after thinning light, staining light's edges and pulling its colors back. Reds and pinks reassemble in the west, shrinking into rich violets, bloodied pinks, and finally a pale, pale rose.

In the beginning, the fracturing of light looks like life: bold, brilliant, unhampered. In the end, colors smolder with sadness, retreat. But in truth, the progression from bold to brilliant to pale is more about fracturing and reuniting. Colors separated yearn for wholeness.

Colors of light, gasses in the atmosphere, shards of yourself, yearn for wholeness.

Watching, waiting, it's the fracturing that's unbearable. Because day after day light reminds us that wholeness is possible.

Wholeness. *Right.*

The lakewind surged and Jillian sat up to meet it, filling her eyes with the last of day's color. It was one thing to have survived the first night. It was quite another to go into the second night, knowing.

6

A Long Smokies Day

IT WAS THE MORNING OF their second Night Sky class, and Kera wanted to run down the mountain. She leaned back and gave her boot laces a severe tug. "I say let's go for it. We've got, what, ten hours before we need to head out to Cliff Top?"

Employees of the lodge, Kera and Jillian included, used short but steep Alum Cave trail to get back and forth to work. Every year, new records were set for fastest descent, ascent, and variations on the theme: Round Trip. The "world" record included leaving the lodge; descending the trail; driving to Gatlinburg to purchase junk food and beer (neither were allowed to take up space on the llama train); and the return ascent—all of which a pair of young men supposedly accomplished in three hours and forty-five minutes.

Jillian could run eight-minute miles on flat land, half that pace would be pushing it on LeConte. And Kera, with all her lanky flailing, was way too inefficient. "Less than four hours? It's hard to believe that record hasn't been stretched a bit." She grabbed her short hikers with the non-slip soles and started lacing.

At nine o'clock exactly Ros gathered the crew to give them a ten second countdown, and they were off, lodge guests calling out "Good luck!" and "See you on the upside!" as they crested the summit and dropped down to the rock ledges below.

The rest was a blur of passing landmarks. At the neck of the cliff, instead of testing for dampness by flattening their boots, they hung onto the cables and ran across the chiseled rock. In the Smokies, there was always the roar and the trickle of water. Slowly, urgently at times, it brought down rocks, boulders, mountains. There was the brief clearing where they saw Gatlinburg sitting thousands of feet below, looking like nothing more than a swipe of misplaced gray. Finally, they maneuvered the heath bald, pushing their way through thick tangled vines, hopping over the small scratchy version of rhododendrons.

At the car, Kera dropped the keys twice, and twice said emphatically, "Shit!" which made hikers gathering at the trail head look at them even more suspiciously than they had when the two women came running across the wooden bridge and jumped three stairs per stride as they raced away from the river.

Jillian both regretted and consoled herself on her decision not to drive. Kera aimed the Jeep in and out of curves, and as the tires squealed through the last tunnel, she accelerated into the Gatlinburg strip. After a month on LeConte, the pole buildings with their shingled facades and brightly lit signs advertising *Carnival*, *Go Carts*, and *Hill Billy Golf* seemed more than wasteful—the town seemed sinister, blinking with excessive light. They both sighed sometimes, sitting on their Cliff Top ledge, thinking that in another twenty or thirty years, the lights of Knoxville and Gatlinburg might drown out the stars. She looked over at Kera, slapping the meat of her palms on the steering wheel and begging the light to change, and thought, *Here we are, in the Great Smoky Mountains, with a dream of a research job, and the clearest sky yet on the eve of the new moon, and we're racing for junk food and beer. How far we've come.* "This is too much fun!"

Kera, who passed every car they came upon, was first off at the light. "No! Not too much, just fun!"

They strategized: Jillian would head for the beer, Kera would dash for tortilla chips and salsa and Jiffy Pop popcorn, which could be popped over an open fire. They'd discovered that pleasure when a guest shared her popcorn with the two of them and everyone else who was drawn to the luscious, buttery aroma. Meals at the lodge were hearty but there were no frills, no sweets, no popcorn.

At the Kroger, they talked over the aisles and left the cashier a three dollar tip, opting to run while she fingered the change. Kera drove in wide, banked circles, and Jillian tore paper grocery bags, wrapping beer bottles before packing them in their sacks. They gulped from cold (cold!) bottles of pop and stuffed potato chips and chocolate bars into their mouths.

"Now this is disgusting!" Jillian's voice shrieked with the tires through the first tunnel. In the cement gleam, headlights strobed and Kera's hair blew back in thick, blinking shards.

"Think about it!" Kera yelled. "Have you ever gone an entire month without chocolate? And men?"

As they pulled into the parking lot, Jillian prepared to hop out as soon as Kera parked, but her timing was off. She hopped as the Jeep rocked backward, and she fell out. The bottles she had wrapped hit the ground, and though they didn't break, they rolled out of their wrappings and away.

"Get back here!" Jillian crouched after them, but Kera didn't seem to understand, she was looking up and away. "The beer! The beer!"

Jillian followed Kera's gaze and saw two men walking toward them. She stood, straightening her baseball cap, watching them chase down her roll-away beers.

Kera's low voice sounded beside her. "The universe is listening."

Jillian had noticed the blonde's bare torso, red-brown and muscular, but her gaze was drawn to the tall one with dark hair. He wore a sleeveless shirt, ripped at the collar, and she noticed his shoulders, how straight he stood.

Kera whispered. "Record. Men. Record. Men."

"We can still make it." Jillian readied her backpack. "I say, let's go for it."

"Hey," he called out, raising a beer, and she noticed his eyes: intensely white-blue.

The blonde looked in Kera's direction. Did men discuss such choices or follow a simple first-glance, first-dibs rule? "The guy at the park office gave us a newsletter and we recognized your pictures. You're teaching a class tonight, right?"

Brad had put their pictures in the park newsletter?

"That's us." Kera touched Jillian's arm. "Now what?"

"Well." Jillian accepted the bottle Jack handed her as he introduced himself and his friend, thinking, he must feel the stares, all the time, people drawn to his eyes. On Earth blue was cold, but out in space blue was hot. Short-wave, ultraviolet hot. "Thanks. I say we take a minute to wrap them up tight and we beat it up the mountain. We could still come in under four hours."

Kera raised one eyebrow.

"All we can do is try."

"That must be some important beer," Jack said.

Jillian blushed. She hated how easily she blushed. "Yeah. We're looking like serious researchers about now, aren't we?"

"We have to make it back," Kera said, "in less than an hour and a half."

"Up to the lodge?" Jack asked.

His milky irises were rimmed with a darker, brighter blue. They were stunning, and Jillian was staring. "Sorry. We have to run, literally."

Kera took the last bottle from the blonde.

"What about yours?" His hand lingered near hers. "Your name?"

"Kera," she called out as they back pedaled toward the trailhead.

Jack smiled as Jillian stumbled backwards, and she lifted a beer. "It's hard to explain how important this is." His head dropped back and he let out a loud, easy laugh.

They walked a few steps before turning to wave.

"Real men," Kera sighed. "We're leaving two good-looking— you saw the chest on that one—men behind."

Bounding back up the trail, they wondered: were they coming up for the class? They stopped to look and listen, but when they found themselves alone on the trail, Jillian took the lead. "All right, that's enough. Let's dig in."

Up top, Kera pleaded with Ros to let them add their journey to the list. They'd missed the record by only eighteen minutes. "Come on! You have to know how excruciating it was to turn away from two young, good-looking men. Look around, Ros. Imagine the commitment."

Jillian pictured Chris's tanned chest and the curl of dark hair that hung near Jack's eyes. "They were stunning."

In the end Ros awarded them second place, and Jillian wrote a summary next to their names: *Second place, round trip, including: descent to Alum Cave parking lot; drive to Gatlinburg for chips, salsa, popcorn, and twelve bottled beers; lively discussion with two men; and the return ascent—total time: four hours, three minutes.*

"Second place." They consoled each other as they shuffled toward the tiny cabin they'd grown to love. Sometimes, late at night, it appeared to be teetering on the edge of the mountain world, held up only by fog.

The next time Jillian saw Jack, or rather, sensed him, she was standing on the smooth-rounded peak of Cliff Top, waiting for Kera's cue. Kera was demonstrating the Zenith and how to measure degrees with an arm extended up from the horizon: flat at zero, straight up at ninety, and forty-five in between. Jillian had already done their "Red light at night, keeps the stars in sight" talk, introducing their audience to the idea of a new (dark) moon. Now, she stood thinking: they had such a good audience, these were hikers, they'd love to know that short-lived events such as solar flares caused waves of gases to pelt Earth's atmosphere and set it aglow, that the northern lights were literally the touch of the sun. And with just a few more words, she could explain the colors as they star-hopped, how different stars with different chemical compositions radiate light at different temperatures, creating Betelgeuse's red, Antares' orange, Rigel's bold blue. How visible light, in fact, was only a portion of the total light spectrum, that portion matched exactly (due to evolution) to the light our eyes were accustomed to receiving from our very own sun. Jillian listened to Kera, trying to figure out how to work it all in.

"We're at Zenith, right? Now keep adding. Ninety plus another shift half-way down to one-thirty-five, all the way down to one-eighty. Horizon to horizon, zero to one-eighty."

Kera had made Jillian promise not to wander all over the universe as she had in their first class. But that was just Kera. She thought people were too concerned with their day-to-day lives to notice the ground, let alone the stars. People would get too confused and ask too many questions, but Jillian was sure their audience would love to know that the sun rang like a bell and had a solar wind. She was listening for Kera when she was distracted by movement at the back of the crowd. Chris and Jack. She knew it! He hadn't forgotten about her.

Chris sat near the back, but Jack continued to feel his way through the crowd, stooping toward the front. For a second she was afraid he was going to walk right over Cliff Top's rounded edge, but he sat, easing toward her, and she blushed. At three-hundred-sixty degrees, she was supposed to jump in with Earth's location in the galaxy. She had missed Kera's cue.

Kera bumped her and Jillian blushed again.

"Okay. Jillian's going to take you through a little star hop. While she explains the location of each star or constellation, I'm going to shine my little red light." She paused, as she had during their first session, with the red light under her chin and her mouth making that ridiculous, bloody-toothed grin. The crowd laughed. One little voice cried out.

"We goof around sometimes," Jillian forced a chuckle, hoping Kera would let the face-making go. Last time she'd panned the crowd with her llama lips. Jillian sensed the concentration of the crowd, and she wanted to appear intelligent, at ease, in front of Jack.

"But it isn't really that dark out here, is it? Years ago people used to navigate by the stars. And our eyes were probably accustomed to seeing in less light. Think of your eyes as light-gathering tools. That's what telescopes do." She could feel Jack's faced turned up and following hers and a thought struck her; his eyes would look pure white in the dark. "We use telescopes to gather light and the stars tell us their stories. Stars are born, they go through life stages, and they live on for generations, passing on their elemental structures like we do." Not with genes, but with elements. "The stars make heavier and heavier elements with every generation. That's why we say light has a history. Everything we know about the universe, we've learned from light."

"That's right." Kera jumped in, looking at her with the *What gives?* face. "I'll shine my arm with the light and make the movements Jillian describes. If you can't find the target, don't be afraid to speak up. We want everyone to go home knowing how to locate objects in the night sky." Kera must have noticed Jack. She turned and mouthed "Oh!" with her eyebrows raised for emphasis, and Jillian watched Kera scan for Chris.

"Let's start with Polaris, the North Star. On a clear night, in the northern hemisphere, you can locate Polaris by first finding the big dipper. Can someone find the big dipper and give us the direction and degrees?" A child's voice called out and Kera moved to it. Kera asked the girl—Jillian thought the voice sounded like a young girl's— to point for the crowd. The little arm shone red and Jillian heard Kera's and the girl's voices chase each other through a few rolling giggles.

From the ladle of the Big Dipper, which was actually part of the constellation Ursa Major, the Great Bear, Jillian called out, "Follow the arc to Arcturus." From there, she guided them to Boötes, the Herdsman. Always the hunter and the hunted in the Greek's sky. "Some people call it the kite, but when I was young, I liked to call it the ice cream cone." She asked Kera to encircle the Corona Borealis, a not-quite-complete circle of stars. Jillian told the audience to think of the Corona as a scoop of ice cream falling from Boötes' cone. She much preferred to think of the figures in the sky as wise and playful, rather than scorned and locked in some ancient feud.

They journeyed south to the red giant Antares and Jillian pointed out the large, snake-like "S" of Scorpius. Jack turned his whole body toward it. That wasn't a good sign, identifying so strongly with a crawling serpent. Perhaps the boldness of Antares, the star most likely to supernova in the next million years, had captured him.

"Okay. We're going to wrap up with Sagittarius. Would someone like to point that out for us?"

A man's voice called out. "Isn't that the teapot?" Kera made her way over to Chris. In the red light, Chris's smile was a pink triangle and Kera's wide grin fell open. Chris feigned incompetence and Kera positioned his arm.

Jack was smiling, mouth open like Kera, watching Kera and Chris. He caught Jillian's eyes, raising his eyebrows, and she turned away. The class was turning into a chorus of eyebrows.

Jillian faced the sky as the audience saw it. "Yes. Sagittarius is often called the teapot. If you look close to the horizon, up about fifteen degrees—remember, if forty-five is half-way up, then fifteen is only a third of that distance—you'll be gazing just over the tree line." The ridge across the valley was a black curve that could have been cut from construction paper. She loved the way the night played with depth, deleting it from the ground in favor of fleshing out the vast areas around the stars above.

The crowd located Sagittarius, voicing their affirmations, and Jillian returned Jack's smile. In the dark, he probably thought his repeated attempts to get her attention were much more subtle than they were.

"If you look above the spout of the teapot, you'll see steam rising and trailing across the sky. That's the Milky Way." The crowd sighed, arching their heads back to follow the trail. "Hundreds of thousands of stars in just one portion of our own Milky Way galaxy."

She wanted to address the name: Milky Way for Hera's milk, the mother of the gods. But that was another story, a story Kera's eyes, now directed on her, were telling her they did not have time to tell.

But the bulge, as long as they were looking, wouldn't be too much. "On a clear night, in late summer and early fall, if you gaze directly past the spout of the tea pot, you might notice a vague, yellow-white glow. If you find it, you'll be looking into the central bulge of our galaxy, a ball of hot, swirling young stars."

Leave them with a *Wow*, Arnie always said. Quite a few people stayed, gathering around Jillian and Kera in small packs, asking great questions. What did they mean by the spiral arm of the Milky Way? And why could we see it sometimes and not others? Jillian decided she should add an explanation of Earth's summer versus winter tilt. As the last of them said goodbye, she switched on her red light. In the glow, Jack extended his hand.

His palm was meatier than she had expected. "Great class. I never thought, before, about what you said about light. How we've learned everything from light."

Kera approached, lighting a mock silent scream, teasing Jillian for mentioning, one night, that Kera's red-lit face reminded her of Munch's expressionist paintings of a distorted face, screaming from a sky of reds. "Hey, I'm sure she'd love to tell you all about it."

Jillian made a face that said *Stop it!*

Jack extended his arm to Kera. "That'd be great to have at Halloween."

"Someone who appreciates my humor." Kera glanced toward Chris and then back to Jack's eyes. Kera noticed, too, how Jack's eyes picked up the red. "Hey, it's our teapot guy."

For a moment, as the four of them stood in a circle, Jillian lifted one of her hands, resting it in the air above her hip to see if she could feel whatever it was—heat? magnetism, literally?—coming off Jack's body. People gave off auras, some people even claimed to be able to see them, halos of energy and color surrounding our bodies. But no. Quietly, she lowered her hand. Jack was a good-looking man on a beautiful mountain, that was all.

Really! Wasn't that enough?

Kera and Chris and Jack were all talking, slicing the air between them in quick chops and loops. Jack and Chris were in medical school at the University of Michigan. Chris held up his hand and pointed to the middle of his thumb pad—making the Michigan mitten—but Kera slapped it away. They'd just finished a year at U of M, taking classes for their PhD's. They knew Michigan. And now, there they all were, meeting hundreds of miles away. What a place, this universe! Jack and Chris were staying in Wear Valley. Did they know where that was? The school had about a hundred students from medicine, geology, anthropology, all lodged in some lover's valley.

"Did you guys ever make it out to the Bunion?" The only time Kera was any good at small talk was in the company of a good-looking man.

"No." Chris slugged Jack in the arm. "Bonehead here wanted to make sure our samples didn't get too warm."

Jack rubbed his arm, but he didn't strike Chris back. "They would have."

Chris's face seemed soft, too young to belong to someone in medical school, except for the stubble that glinted on his chin.

Jillian could feel Jack watching her as she drew imaginary lines and circles with the toe of her boot. Just like down at the trailhead, the pair-off had already begun. She would have gone for Jack, anyway. Chris was too physical. But what she really wanted, right then, was for everything to go back to her and Kera and the job ahead of them. "It was nice to talk, finally, without some timer running."

"Me too." Jack's response didn't match what she'd said. "I mean, I think so, too. Hey, would you mind if we tagged along? I'd love to see what you're doing out there."

Jillian stammered something about how small their rock ledge was (which it wasn't—it was huge and sturdy, or they wouldn't be out there); how they had to stick to a really strict system, one of them loading, the other adjusting, and Kera came to her rescue. The thought of tag-alongs pulled Kera away from all that head tilting with Chris.

"You guys should come up during the day. At night, we've gotta bust ass, basically."

"Oh. Right. That's okay," Jack looked embarrassed. "We'd get in the way, wouldn't we. I know how that is."

Chris looked over the edge. "You stay out here, all night?"

Jack didn't wait for their response. "Maybe we can all do something together sometime, when you're not so busy. I really would like to see your telescope."

Jillian almost laughed. My telescope! Kera was giggling. "Sure."

Jillian grabbed Kera's arm and they backed down the eastern slope, where they would work for most of the night. "We're hard to get a'hold of though."

"I'll leave our phone number. But, hang on. I don't know where to leave it."

Kera stopped. "Where are you guys staying, anyway?"

"In the office." Chris punched Jack again. "Jack bartered us some sleeping bags from the cook. We stirred a ton of dough."

In the morning, after observing ten targets—the most they'd captured in any night yet—Jillian and Kera lugged their suitcases along the stone path that led to their cabin. It had been a spectacular night. They'd recorded Rectangular, Super-Slat, Cat-Eye, and Concave masked images of the brighter stars: Deneb and Altair and Lyra, and then they had moved on to smaller, sun-like stars such as epsilon Pegasi and tau Aurigae tracking east to west until the first reds of dawn bled in. They didn't expect to find anything, of course. They simply wanted to record any distinct patterns of light and dark they were able to create with each mask. She'd thought about Jack's col-larbones a few times, for some reason, the way his bone structure was so apparent, but standing there tired and entirely happy about the night's imaging, it was his meaty palms she remembered as she read the note tacked to their door.

In handwriting quite large and loopy, the top portion read: *For a good time call Chris and Jack.* Below the phone number, a second hand had written: *Seriously—give us a call, we can all go into Gatlinburg or do some hiking.*

7

Peia Again

IN THE MIDDLE OF THE night, Jillian woke under her sheeny green tent ceiling. At first, she wished she had her watch, but then she admonished herself immediately: *No.* She would *feel* what was enough and not enough—sleep, truth, all of it.

Why were her thoughts of Peia so fearful?

There was a series of hills on the school grounds near their home, where they sledded in the winter. One warm spring day, they'd all ridden their bikes down the steepest slope—which seemed incredibly foolish now—but they'd made it. Adjusting their helmets for each ride and gripping their handlebars tightly, they'd pointed their bikes down every hill on the grounds, looking for the most thrilling ride. Even Peia. Jillian had figured her small bike was so close to the ground she wasn't in much danger, though she wondered, later, why she hadn't seen it—the potential for flipping end over end. Jillian's bike, on the other hand, her sit-up-straight ten-speed, pounded down the hill, her screaming with it. Laughing and out of breath, they agreed the first hill was the best and then they split up to do what they'd originally come to do. Jillian and Manny and Jack had come to run up and down the hill—Manny was getting ready for some sport—and Peia had come to rollerblade in the adjacent parking lot where they could all keep an eye on her. It was perfect for rollerblading: a huge empty lot with a slight slope from one end to the other and only one central row of light poles.

Jillian and Manny were running zig-zags down the hill, and Jack was watching from the top when they all turned toward an awful sound. Jack had breathed out "Oh no" just before, and Jillian turned to look. Peia had climbed up to the tennis courts and was in a racer's crouch, rollerblading down the paved access path that led from the tennis courts above to the parking lot below. The path was quite steep and curved and they watched as Peia made it all the way down, tucked tightly forward. Then, when Peia started to pull up and Jillian

49

thought she'd made it; when Jillian felt herself breathe again and was thinking, *That little shit! How can she do that!* one of Peia's wheels must have caught on a stone. There was an awful screech, and her body flew first upwards, her arms stretched forward and her head yanked high. And then, she hit the pavement. Jillian saw Peia's arms hit the ground and they all heard a long, loud skid. She was sure Peia's hands were being skinned. When the scraping stopped, Peia's head bobbed up and then thunked to the ground.

Manny had fallen off his first bike after taking too sharp a turn in the neighbor's driveway, and Jack had carried him into the house, looking more frightened than Manny. Manny moaned about the skin on his nose, holding a folded hand over it, and when Jillian calmly pried his fingers away from his face, she found he was right, most of the skin had been scraped away.

But this skid and the long, slow approach toward Peia seemed more frightening.

"Peia!" she'd hollered, as she and Manny broke into a run. "Hang on! We're coming!"

Peia let out a moan, which must have been more of a growl for Jillian to hear it so clearly as all three of them ran toward her, Jack's footsteps stomping through the hill as he ran. And then Peia hopped up, arms raised as if to stop them, and she hollered back: "I'm okay. I'm okay!"

The wrist guards were worn down to the metal and her helmet was cracked. Her palms were hot with tiny, gravel stones, but her skin, for the most part, was intact.

8

Day Three—Inland

JILLIAN WAS FIFTY FEET OUT, sitting on the sandbar with her back to shore, moving one foot at a time through slow, wide circles, soaking her beach ankles. Her aching legs were partly to blame for all the waking during the night: vague appearances of the cloaked hiking man and the jarring images of daredevil Peia. Still, with just a few hours of sleep, it had turned into Day Three. Already, she had made her first restocking trip.

That was her plan, to restock every three days, so she had stuffed her pack full, hoping to make it to Day Seven. Under the weight her legs felt like boards hammering down upon her ankles. Day Two's sixteen miles along the lakeshore, sloped down to the right all the way to the Depot, sloped down to the left all the way back, had left the tendons and muscles above her ankles stiff with overuse. Winding her foot around and around with the wind and the water drowning out the crunching sounds—though she could feel the grinding and popping, as if the bones in her ankles had shifted and were trying to scramble back into place—she felt victorious: over night, over fear, over sheer physical exhaustion.

In the middle hours of the night, she had discovered the beacons of the lighthouses. Manistee's first, then Ludington's, shadowed by the long bend of the dunes. She'd come out of the tent to sit in her high dune chair and to think about darkness. What was it, exactly, that she feared? She had followed the pulsing lights, Manistee's beam projecting far into the west, so far over the water she thought it was lightning, and then, following the tail of its flash southward, she found comfort in Big Sable's dim echo. Her fear had nothing to do with light or with darkness. It had nothing to do with nature. Her fear—not of being alone, exactly, but of being discovered alone—was man-made. Literally, created and sustained by men. A coyote, a bear, even a rabid raccoon would scare her. But she wasn't their natural prey. Men, human men, could be predatory. That's what women had to live with.

Watching Manistee's light race north-to-southwest, waiting on Big Sable's muffled response, she forced herself to sit still. With bright and dim blinks chasing each other in the sky, she pressed her head back into the sand and reasoned. This fear of being alone, this fear that made her suspicious of the dark, would only limit her. So she vowed to act. Each time the hairs on her neck rose, each time a sudden slap of water made her jump, she would hold onto Earth, place herself close to nature, and throw off the fear.

Later, in her tent, she had actually fallen asleep with her lantern behind her. She left it on low beam, with her nylon vest draped over it. It was senseless, lighting her tent like a glow worm. When she woke, the mesh windows were covered with bugs. But she had slept, on her own, at the crest of her two hundred and twenty-seven foot dune.

She turned slowly toward a sound—she would not whip her neck around—and saw a ranger-led group, people in various stages of hiking readiness, stream past on shore. Tuesdays and Thursdays, she remembered the sign-up sheet on the board, rangers led day-hikes. Her mind imbued the young man dressed in national park greens—shirt, shorts, mid-calf boots—with Ranger Brad's tense posture. Fast Brad had never slowed, that was true, but any time she and Kera saw him—on a mission to relocate a bear snooping around the lodge or to repair a trail damaged by wild boars—he was always eager to show them another part of his Smokies world. Jillian would never forget the time he had taken them to Gregory Bald, on the far west side of the park, a trek he made on his own each season to witness changes in the stars. Kera would never forget Brad's calves, she always said, the man had cantaloupes for calves.

This ranger walked with a relaxed stride, on the soft, level sand above the hard-packed slope. Obviously, he'd experienced beach ankles and learned his lesson. He waved and Jillian waved back. She waved to a woman in a sundress and straw hat; a young couple, both in jeans, the girl wearing what looked like flip-flops and her boyfriend walking in cowboy boots. They bumped along with their arms around each other, each holding onto the other by a belt loop. Jillian knew where they were headed. A mile down the beach, the ranger would lead them up the Dune Ridge Trail. They'd meander up and down wood-steeped hills, eventually descending to the lake where pine-brush, all that could grow in the intense heat, lined scorched lumps of sand. She hoped they had had the sense to carry water. She smiled and waved at three middle-aged hikers with day packs and safari hats. If the teen couple didn't have water, these more experienced hikers would.

A family moved back and forth in a swirling clump. Two adults, one with a day pack, the other with a baby in a backpack carrier, walked on the slope while a child stomped in and out of the waves, running loops around his parents. He'll never make it, Jillian thought. He might make two, maybe three miles, but at that pace, he'll never make it.

Another figure dressed in sage and pine-green, blonde hair bobbing from her hat, jogged up behind the family. She wore a pack belt with water bottles shoved against her back: extra water for the unprepared. The pony-tailed ranger hollered something that got pushed back in the wind.

"Lots of sun today!" Jillian called. "Have a great hike!"

Watching the group make their way down the beach, she thought about following them from a distance. She was getting tired of her thinking voice. Thoughts cycled through her head, popping up as she looked out over the water, up at the sky, even down at her own feet. Sometimes not saying anything more than: *Mm. Blue sky*, or *Bug spray*. Other times, she heard entire conversations, Jack yelling at her: *Kids change everyone's lives!* with his eyes hot-blue and his fingers webbed out hard in front of him, though she hadn't actually seen him the night they'd had that awful fight. She'd gone up on the roof to get away from everything he was saying and the tension both of them were feeding into. Tension and anger so volatile the kids had gotten scared. Manny and Peia had huddled on Peia's bed, Manny's hands cupped over her ears, and even though Jillian had only glanced their way before she yanked out the window screens and escaped to the roof, she knew Peia would have been chanting: *Make them stop. Make them stop*. Peia had heard so many arguments, witnessed so much more fighting than Manny had when he was young.

The child down the beach continued to agitate his family picture. That kind of contact, the bombardment, the grabbing and winding and slicing was what Jillian found so hard to appreciate. Did any parent? Not having a choice, not being able to remove herself when

Manny and Peia and Jack brought everything to her—whatever they had to tell her, or show her, or ask her to do for them, while she stood, trying to hold her own.

She stood in the water, looking after the hikers. How clearly she had read the group's identities. She had felt the life in them, and now, watching them leave, she felt comforted knowing that they'd pass by again early in the evening.

She walked out of the shallows and into the sand, her wet feet grinding into the sand and she narrated with the squeak: *Day Three. Three. Three.* Quartz, it must be, the glass in quartz. How was she going to reach any personal epiphanies if she stood thinking all day? Her mind was being inefficient, showing her all her failures, seizing up with the past.

But not today. No. She had to remember: fear and involvement, two dangers to avoid. She turned to face the wind off the lake, letting it ease the heat that had overtaken her. She should go inland. Get away from the water and the sky and the people who occasionally walked the beach. Pamper her tired ankles with some moist, level ground. But she'd stick close to camp. She wanted to be there when that line of hikers, angling up the dune far off to the south, returned.

She ate a quick lunch: raisins, hard roll, bag of tuna; and packed two of her topo maps, figuring she might make it as far as King's Corners, the quadrangle directly south of Manistee. Descending the interior, heavily wooded side of the dunes, she followed a steep, root-tangled trail that had her sweating profusely in a matter of minutes. On the dunes, she had smelled only heat and water. Here, she smiled with each breath of cedar and pine.

How quickly the forest changed once she put a mile between her and the last dune. In the dunes towering oaks dominated, with pines and cedars forming tiny groves or standing together like walls of a fortress. Inland, the soft forest floor was covered with ferns, some as high as her hips, and the oaks gave way to maples and beeches, poplars and white birches. The forest floor, the trees, the air changed from wind-blown brown to a lull of peaceful green.

She admired, for a second, these essential natural differences. Oaks, with their tall, upright trunks and their deep, vertical roots, could anchor themselves even in the dunes. The shallow roots of maples and poplars could spread out, enabling the trees to stabilize themselves on the surface of moist, low ground. But they were easily uprooted.

The Beech Grove trail took a sudden turn to the east. But forking off to the south—southwest, her compass said, which would wind her back to the lakeshore—she saw the faint pattern of a two-track. Clumps of grass grew over a layer of packed stones. Big stones, the kind laid for traction on ungroomed dirt. She'd driven many such rutty, chunked-rock roads in the upper peninsula.

Carefully, she folded her Kings Corners map halfway out, spreading the southeast section on the ground without disturbing the wildflowers and ivy that edged the trail. Just south of the main trail she saw the dashed boundary of a cedar marsh and a solid creek line with dots on each side, signifying a natural drain system. But there was no indication of a road. She followed the stones a bit, hoping to pick up a sense of where the road headed. Snaps and cracks sounded around her, but she refused to be afraid. The shadows moving in the cedar marsh were deer, she knew that, does and fawns eating from blackberry vines, constantly moving to keep their distance from her as she walked into their woods.

She noticed a bright spot ahead, a clearing, and a few moments later walked into a circle of trees. The ground was flat, worn down to dirt around a sloppily dug firepit, a hole with charred tree roots sticking through its sandy walls. She knelt down to touch a burnt log and her finger went right through its ashy crevasses. It was old, months old. A local party pit maybe? Why would teenagers bother to hike all the way from Forest Trail? Probably a deer camp. At least there were no beer bottles or heaps of cans left around. There was something about the trees, though.

She walked over to one and saw initials, hundreds of them, carved from two feet up all the way to the first few branches. Every one of the smooth-barked trees, even the paper birches, was covered in scars. Scrapes and gouges lined the circle-side of each tree, where it faced the others, as if the carvers had purposefully given the trees eyes to look upon each other's wounds. She eased the palm of her hand over the face of a poplar. Deep in the letters V and S she could see moist, yellow-green marrow. Someone had been there, recently.

Staring back at each tree, turning to look into its letter-eyes, she tried her best not to focus on human cruelty. *What would a group of hunters do with her if they found her out here alone?* She tried instead to

focus on the quiet persistence of the trees. She backed into the center
of the circle and stretched out in the dirt, close to nature. She lay flat
on her back watching the treetops move over patches of yellow and
blue. Moving her legs and arms slightly, palms down in the dirt, she
made an angel in the earth.

The feel of the dirt under her flattened hands reminded her of the
Winter Carnival and slushing. Wearing those huge mitts and forming
truckloads of snow and ice into tall blocks that would eventually be
carved into ice sculptures. Every department in the school and busi-
nesses all over Houghton, hundreds of people slushing day and night.

What was his name? Garret? Garner? Talk about involvement, she
had almost slept with him and she didn't know his name. They had
slushed together, spent long hours loading snow and ice and rubbing
it over the physics department's ice-version of a standing bass. Graduate students froze fiberoptic filaments into strands of ice. Strands that
would vibrate with pulses of light and those pulses would trigger
sound. It worked for a night, then the light melted the ice that held
the filaments together.

He played hockey and he was fast, but his skates didn't scrape like
a hockey player's. He glided in long, side-to-side strokes, feeling the
ice, as if he refused to fall through its shiny top layer. His arms, relaxed
and aloft, cut a path through the air but apologized, soothing all the
same. She could barely move on ice skates, especially the worn-out
skates she had picked out at the warming house. He laughed and
yanked her up when she slapped down. She remembered the way he
fixed his blade sideways against the point of hers, so she wouldn't
slide too far and fall again. After she cracked her elbow hard on the
ice, they took cups of hot chocolate up the ski hill and huddled close.
From up high they saw the ice sculptures, spot-lit and gleaming.
Thousands of tiny blue and white lights sparkled along the banks of
Portage Lake.

He tried to carve their initials into the twisted, rope-like bark of a
giant cedar, but he was clumsy with a knife.

"Let me," she told him. She worked with tiny, razor sharp blades
in the lab, snipping, peeling, shaving back wires and their sheathing.

"Strip some of the bark away," he said. "It'll be easier."

She broke through the cold, red bark, angling his knife to bevel
under deep grooves. The bark whined and snapped as she peeled it

back, exposing white, gummy fibers. She gouged with all her strength, almost ripping through one of her gloves, until the knife sunk in and she was able to make letters, their letters, one stab and stroke at a time. Whitish-green paste foamed up each time she tried to make the turn of her J, so she squared it off, his G too. From the ground, in the rising hues of the Winter Carnival, the round of bark she had stripped looked like a cold, blue face.

Kera often questioned her. "Something must have happened. Come on, he was a Greek Adonis."

Jillian made all sorts of excuses. He was blonde. He was in mechanical engineering, too structured. It was the chill in the air and all the twinkling lights, but it wasn't. Her feelings had changed from the moment she looked up at that bare, shining spot where she had skinned an artificial face in the tree. Where she kept skinning and stabbing, even after it bubbled and bled on her J. With the tree's frozen white blood trying to coagulate and seal up each scratch, she kept going. She kept going until she had finished his G.

And then, they were through. She didn't like herself anymore, with him.

Lying still, smelling the ashy dust as it settled around her, she heard loud snaps off to her left. She felt vulnerable with her face and her chest and her legs open, so she rolled onto her stomach and lifted her head, slowly. She didn't want to alarm a bear. Not at this close range.

A doe poked her head into the circle, sniffing. She stared at Jillian, curious but unafraid, and Jillian stared back. But once the doe noticed Jillian's gaze shift to her fawn—shuffling out from the trees, tugging at a berry vine—the mother deer darted into the ferns and her fawn followed. The crackling of dry twigs receded with them as the whites of their tails bounded out of sight.

Jillian picked up her pack, snugged it over her hips, and looped her way through the circle of trees, touching every white peely birch, every smooth beige beech, the gray poplars, the north-mossed maples. She looked over hundreds of carved initials, acknowledging the heat as her face flushed with guilt. She was young, under the spell of his physical grace. Still, no man was worth such a change in her principles, not even Jack.

Walking away from the clearing, she had two thoughts. If the trees had eyes, at least they must be getting a kick out of the dirt on her backside. And she remembered another something blue about that night. She had gone to his apartment and they had come close to having sex, but the spell was over. For her it was. He had paced the room, accusing her of leaving him with "blue balls."

Surrounded by the yellow-green of the Beech Grove trail she felt her face grow purple with embarrassment, for him. For him! How could he have made such a statement and actually expected her to, what? Relieve him?

Sitting in her high dune chair, cooled by the early evening breeze, Jillian watched the hiking group amble by. She'd been eyeing them since they appeared as dots sliding down the dune, over a mile away. Now, as they plodded far below, she didn't want to break their trance or hers by calling out with a human voice.

The three hikers in safari hats dragged their walking sticks instead of cleanly setting them in the sand. The young couple, still arm in arm, carried their shoes. The family, of course, struggled: Dad carrying the day pack on his chest and the older child on his back, Mom carrying their sleeping baby in her arms. Even from two hundred feet above, Jillian recognized the mother's weariness, the way she focused on the ground ahead, the tilt of her head.

Perhaps she was watching her husband's back, noticing the deep imprints of his boots pushing forward, wishing he would turn around and smile. Remember her. Take her hand so she could dig her fingers into those soft spaces between his fingers, because she *was* tired. Was that so awful to admit? That it would feel buoyant, like water, if he placed her hand in his and seemed to be towing her along?

Jillian used to feel saddened by the look of the four of them. Why did Jack's bond, father with sleeping son, make him look so much more beautiful while hers, mother and baby, made her look so tired? And she recognized, so clearly, what the tiny, tired mother below must also know: that by pulling, each on their own end, they were creating a string of tension so taut that there was nothing they could do but snap, eventually. She had seen so much of Jack's back—too much—and there was nothing more frustrating.

A quarter of a mile or so to the south, straggling behind, was an older man Jillian hadn't noticed before. His hair caught the light and it glowed so unnaturally white that for a second, she assumed her mind had created him, a peaceful—even slightly sad—older man walking in and out of the water, stopping to gaze at the lake and scoop water over his arms. Perhaps he was her visage of what Jack might become if she could wait, his bright hair a play on Jack's darkness.

But no, this man was real. He kept watch, maintaining a certain distance from the group, a hesitant distance that made him look like someone who wanted to be alone but didn't know how. She might have done the same, though she would never have followed that family. That would have been too much like life!

Jack, left alone, would pace and tap and make lists, asking himself what he could have done to keep her. To keep her, yes, because as much as Jillian wanted it not to be true, Jack would only turn back if he thought he had lost her.

She pressed her head back into her high dune chair and gazed into the sky, bluing boldly to the east, over the trees. She thought of Mr. Blue Balls and the blue face she had carved for him, and she allowed herself a few seconds to think of Jack. With his hairline receding slightly, he had let his hair grow longer again in the front. Sometimes, when he turned to her suddenly, the contrast between that dark sweep of hair and the blue-white of his eyes still surprised her.

If the woman with the baby collapsed, if she were to fall to her knees in the sand while her husband strode on—for how long? How long would it be before her husband felt the difference?—the old man would be there. Walking in and out of the water directly below, he seemed to move with half a soul, strung ahead not by his own will but by some yearning, some secret he was seeking from the others, and Jillian felt drawn to him. For a second she thought she could use him, replace that dark cloaked image that still occasionally popped into her head with his bright, bright hair. Redirect herself when she saw Peia falling. But taking anything from the old man seemed opportunistic and cruel. He looked so lonely.

Oh, boy! With sunset approaching, she had better redirect her thoughts. Another sunset like Day Two's and she might find herself turning into one of those new age evangelists of light. Convince herself that the universe had sent her the old man with glowing hair. Hail light! Hail mass! No, don't hail mass. No gravity either. Hail to the particles that pass through us all! Hail to the physicist who woke up one day, heard the beams of light passing through his blinds as music, and became convinced that light carried a message.

What if there were some kind of drag line the group had left behind, something she was supposed to follow?

No. Being around others was too physical. She needed the water, the light, the trees. Waiting was not what the universe wanted from her. This was her time to lead. How much more waiting was she supposed to be able to take?

She prepared a tiny fire knowing she would use the low beam again. And so what? So what if it meant she might sleep? She gathered her topo maps, unfolding Kings Corners and Manistee and maps of quadrants even further north. She needed to move, not follow. She needed to move.

When she woke, clear-headed, she would know where she was going.

9

Couples

JILLIAN WATCHED JACK GRILL THE burgers she had shaped into perfect circles—one, she had sculpted into a star at his request—and everything, the wooden chaise she was sitting in, the tiny cabin in the middle of some lovers' valley, everything was suddenly uncomfortable, leading to one place, to only one place.

They had been flirting for a month with the idea of touching, playing a painful game of tag. Jack resting his hands on her shoulders or cupping the back of her arms until she pulled away. Her hand on his thigh, watching the blue in his eyes grow more intense. Finally, alone on the Rainbow Falls trail—why were there no families streaming by to prevent such moments?—they had ended up in some kind of embrace. Both of them wrapped around each other. Game over.

Was it her fault? What did her eyes say when Jack's took on that got-to-have look? She had ripped off her poncho, screaming, "To hell with the rain, I'm suffocating!" Being covered in plastic was suffocating, her skin couldn't breathe. She had rolled the wet poncho into a ball while Jack stared at her chest as if he had, at that moment, discovered her breasts. And she had simply stared back. Probably to hide his face—maybe to get closer to her chest, who knows?—Jack had pulled off his poncho and wrapped his arms around her.

They had walked the rocky trail, crossed log bridges, stroked rhododendron leaves, holding hands. Holding hands, making burgers, drinking beer together on this long, wooden deck in this tiny valley filled with couples' cabins, and her insides were turning to soup. Why did he seem so calm?

Jack set a plate in her lap. "Your star, well done."

She stared at its burned edges. Laughing inside, afraid to speak out loud—the tension in her throat was unbearable—she thought: *Supernova.*

Jack knelt next to her and tipped his face to the sky. "Should be a good star night, huh?" He took a swig of her beer. His wide lips molded around her bottle and she wanted to slap him, slap him and say "This is ridiculous! You're leaving in two days!" But his lips broadened into that thin, crooked smile. And his eyes. When the dome of the sky turned turquoise and the air ambered, his eyes became more blue. And now, with the line under his cheekbone so close and his hand over hers, she was being drawn in. She imagined her fingers on his lips.

She jumped up and went inside, claiming she needed ketchup, mustard, all kinds of things, and left Jack sitting on the chaise, sipping from her beer.

She returned with her arms full of protection: chips, salsa, condiments, paper plates. There were lots of things she could go back for. "You have no idea what a luxury tortilla chips are. And salsa. Salsa! No such extras on LeConte."

He stepped toward her and reflexively, she stepped back. They stood, for too long, staring at each other. Wouldn't anything come out of her mouth? He took the plates and then the chips from the crook of her arm. So much touch.

"You're uncomfortable about being here, aren't you?"

Uncomfortable was a pebble in your shoe. This was torture! She was beginning to crave being near him: his eyes, his prominent cheekbones, his hands—she had watched the wide bones of his wrists and the skinny muscles in his forearms as he twisted off beer bottle caps. She took a deep breath and fingered the soft hairs on his forearm. "It feels so couple-ish."

He moved to the deck railing. "There were other students here, earlier in the summer. One night, there was a bear wandering around between the cabins."

Now, she dared look. "Did you see it?"

She and Kera often suspected there were bears following the llama train, smelling the food. Occasionally, when the lodge was short-staffed, they had led the llamas up and down the mountain. Once, they saw a pair of tiny dark eyes. One of the cooks told them about a mother bear and two cubs he had come upon as he ran the Alum Cave trail, late for work. The mother bear stood in front of the rock arch and blocked his way. Every time he tried to move, she shifted her body one way and then the other, stomping her heavy paws into the dirt.

Jack was still talking about his encounter with a bear. "Some idiot even tossed out a steak."

"Oh, no. That's the worst thing to do."

"The sun will be down soon." He motioned to the table where a few of her star charts and drawings lay spread out. "You have to show me your drawings."

Chris and Jack had accompanied them on a few observation nights. Chris asked a lot of questions, which seemed to irritate Kera more and more, but Jack was quiet. He listened to what Kera and Jillian said to each other. Sometimes, days later, he would ask about something they had said. He was thinking, always. She loved that.

"I'm going to get some sweats on. You can change in the bathroom, if you need to."

She looked down at her sweat-shorts. They were extras she had never expected to wear. But when they'd gotten back to the cabin, soaked and chilled, Jack put their clothes in the washer. "You know what? I didn't bring anything. Just a tank top." To sleep in? To sleep in, where? In Chris's bed? Oh, what had she gotten herself into?

Jack held out his hand. "Come on, we'll find you something. Don't get me wrong, I like the shorts." She blushed. "And the tank top, that's still a good idea."

She kissed him on the cheek. "Right."

Together, they squeezed through the slider. They held hands, as if the efficiency kitchen and living area were a dangerous field they were passing through. He fumbled through the built-in dresser, looking for something she could wear, and she stayed in the doorway where he had planted her. Watching him hold up one ridiculously long pair of pants after another, she felt sorry for him. What was she going to do, make him coax her into bed, both of them pretending that's not what they were there for? He sized each pair, then made the same surprised judgment, "Too long. Nope, too long." She wasn't supposed to want him but she did, and she'd brought her drawstring shorts on purpose. She'd imagined wearing them the next morning, knowing that her muscular legs looked best in loose, short-shorts, because, as Kera put it, they made her no-butt butt (it didn't stick out much) look good. Especially after months in the mountains. She grabbed the next pair of pants he held up and hurried to the bathroom.

Outside, with his jogging pants draped over her feet, they settled together in the chaise. Jillian leaned back into his chest with her knees up, supporting her drawings, feeling a little more in control with her face away from his. The brightest stars began to emerge and she pointed out each target she and Kera were studying, explaining how the masks on their telescopes screened the light so they could search the otherwise light-flooded orbital area around each star.

She thought about other men she'd been with: Clay, one of Kera's electrical engineering pals, and Paul, who would probably end up working in the Rockies or the Smokies or the Grand Canyon; how the two of them had sat in that very same way, gazing up at the stars or simply enjoying some quiet, outdoor space together. They didn't have sex often, but when they did it was warm and gentle. Paul was so careful, almost timid when he wanted her. But this, sitting with her back against Jack's body, Jack curving his body around hers, was not warm and gentle. It was hot and tumultuous and wickedly attractive.

Jack nestled his chin into her shoulder and brought his nose to her hair, taking a deep breath. "You smell like rain."

"Yeah. Acid rain." Only the most hostile comment could interrupt the current between them. She could feel the heat in his legs, in his groin. They'd talked about where they both were in terms of school and work—nowhere, not yet—and damn it, this was no time for distraction.

Jack gathered strands of her hair into his hand and inhaled. "God, you smell good. A whole lot better than Chris."

She sat up and turned, and only when she saw his crooked grin did she realize he was playing with her.

"It was the couples thing," he said. "The couple's cabin. I thought it was funny. What?"

Some faces washed out in the dark, but not his. Jillian fingered his mouth and when he bit down on her fingertip, she kissed him. She gulped and pulled and pressed all of her weight into him, flattening her chest against his, wanting all of her to be in contact with all of him.

He pulled back. "We should go inside."

"No." She shook her head. "No we shouldn't."

But she stood and pulled him up with her. She folded her arm under his and squeezed her body into his side. Kera and Chris were probably entwined in their cozy cabin. Perhaps Kera had taken Chris out to Cliff Top. The four of them were supposed to meet at the summit at sunset the next day, Jack's and Chris's last day in the park.

"This is stupid." She wanted a better word. "We're not going to see each other after tomorrow."

"We could." Again she was aware of how tall he was. She didn't like the feeling of looking up into his eyes, as if she were asking for something. "It's not like we're going to opposite coasts."

"Houghton *is* another coast, believe me."

They groped their way past the sparse furniture in the living area and into his bedroom. Lying next to each other and peeling off each other's clothes, Jillian realized she had carried her drawings with her. They were rolling on them.

"My drawings," she whispered.

He hoisted her up, pulling her star maps out of the way. When she looked after them, he hopped up, set them carefully on the floor, and dove back into bed.

She laughed and embraced him. The last thing she said, as she pulled him to her, lacing her feet behind him and squeezing her thighs into the length of his warm, warm sides, was, "You know what happens when Jack and Jill get together, don't you?"

Breathing into her hair as he rubbed his face along the side of hers, he said, "Fairy tale."

She woke with Jack's body curled behind hers and pulled the comforter over her shoulders. She allowed herself the time to wake slowly, let herself enjoy the feel of his large hand sliding over her hip. Their sex had not been gentle. It was stop and start, each of them taking turns pushing toward the other, then pulling back. They hadn't spoken, only moaned, and finally gasped and clutched at each other. Afterward, she had fallen asleep with her face pressed to his sternum.

Remembering the feel of his hands in her hair, the way he kept kissing her head as she fell asleep, she felt like soup all over again. Why did it have to be this way? Wanting something so badly but knowing it had to be put off. God, she hoped Kera was doing better than she was.

"Hey," she finally said.

"No," Jack whispered.

She turned and faced him, which was much harder to do with the yellow-white light of morning shining in the window. "What time is it?"

He opened one eye and shrugged. She stretched over him, toward the alarm clock, but his hands curled around her shoulders and pulled her back. She looked at him, confused. "It's after eight. We better get going."

He only shook his head.

Two days later Chris and Jack left. At least Jillian and Kera imagined them leaving. From high up on their ledge under Cliff Top, they commemorated the men's departure with a moment of silence.

"Well," Kera said, "that's it. Back to us and the mountain."

"That's right," Jillian affirmed. "Back to work."

"I'll have to tell you about it, sometime."

Jillian would talk, too. Later, when she didn't feel and think Jack, his smell and his eyes and that tuft of hair in the center of his bony chest.

"Resist all pairings," she said, as much to the universe as to her closest friend. "Right?" She let her head roll toward Kera and noticed a tear in the corner of Kera's eye.

"You bet," Kera said. "You bet."

10

Open Drawers

IT BEGAN WITH AN OPEN drawer. Actually, a bunch of open drawers.

Jack was at work, where he had been for close to three hours, Manny was an hour or so into his third-grade day, and Peia had just gotten on the bus that would take her to her kindergarten classroom. Jillian waved from the front porch and Peia waved back, smiling. It had required a load of self-talk, but Jillian held tight to a positive, upbeat creation, and she made it. She drew pictures with Peia and listened to her sing. They sat together, in one chair, through a gabby breakfast. And when it came time to get dressed, Jillian stayed out of the bathroom even though Peia spent more time fiddling with barrettes and making soap bubbles than she did brushing her hair or her teeth.

Peia had left for school, smiling. Standing on the porch long after the bus had gone, Jillian could still see it: Peia's happy red lips, her square, white teeth beaming from the bus window, her hand fluttering fast. She turned her face to the sky, asking morning's rose for an equally fresh start. After three hours of successive leave-takings: Jack, who didn't want to be talked to as he rehearsed, in his head, some new procedure in the lab; Manny, who wanted to chat, just the two of them; and finally Peia, who wanted nothing less than Jillian's eyes and ears trained; Jillian felt as if she had orchestrated all that she could in one day, and her workday had not yet begun.

But—no time to wallow. Time to think hydrogen, cooling, thermodynamics. The guys from thermodynamics were coming in. What had she gotten herself into? She hurried through the house, tossing pillows, folding an afghan, taking breakfast dishes to the sink. If Jim's dream orbiter for the new space race was going to rely on bursts of hydrogen combustion, followed by carefully executed lilts of floating—no one knew how to manage the lilt yet, perhaps with parachutes—timing would be everything. Everything! And she needed every bit of her mind to help simulate and test that timing, even if the end result—a privately launched fleet for space tourism—made her uneasy. It wasn't Jim's fault. NASA and the European Space Agency had already opened that door with their millionaire fantasy camp rides on proton rockets.

She brushed her teeth, checked her face (picking at excess mascara), straightened her blouse under her jacket and ran upstairs. As she rounded the top landing, Manny's dresser caught her eye. She'd have to sit him down again. He'd left several of his drawers wide open.

She hurried on to her room, found her bag near the bed and turned to leave, but then she noticed Jack's dresser, sitting in the corner with a ball of clothes wadded on top of it. The same clothes he'd piled on the bed (to fold!) were now strewn all over his dresser, right on top of his old basketball trophies. Only now, a sweatshirt stretched down as if he'd started to pull it out, then stopped, fearing the whole ball would come down.

She stepped into the hallway where she could see into all three rooms, standing where she often stood still at night, listening to make sure the kids were asleep before she turned out the lights. Manny's drawers were wide open. Jack's dresser had clothes spilling out of it. And in Peia's room, every drawer was either slightly open or pulled completely off its side rails, sticking half in and half out at various, impossible angles.

Did they all hate her? They knew how sloppiness bothered her, that "leave it for someone else" mentality. Who did they think they were leaving their messes for?

Some mornings, she charged through each room, slamming drawers shut. Other days, she left them as an after-school example, marching the kids upstairs and harping on them to shut their own drawers. Some nights, before dinner, she asked Jack to follow her to their bedroom. He grinned, expecting some sensual gesture, and she swept her arms from dresser to dresser, reminding him that she was not his mother. Didn't he know what a turn-off that was?

Hydrogen, her inner voice said. *Cooling.* She had to think about cooling and floating. She had to think! She sat for a minute, looking from room to room, feeling as if she'd been punched—again. Open drawers, shoes left in the doorway, coats dropped wherever they were taken off. Could anyone hate her better?

Perhaps it was the clarity of the juxtaposition: the Jillian who was working on a model for contained hydrogen combustion, and the Jillian who was left with these open drawers, dirty socks, plates left on end tables. This was what she was to her family. What she was *for*.

At work Jack was patient and thorough, absolutely meticulous. He had to be, to extract insights from tens of rows of petri dishes. Why, then, was this trained observer unable to see the food on the floor after a meal? The scum building up on the base of the toilet? That wiping off counters and closing drawers was not what she was trained to do? They hated her.

But of course, that too was her fault. She was supposed to see it coming. *What did you expect?*

When she and Jack were roommates, he washed dishes. They stood side by side, one would wash, the other dry, and they talked. They had fun! When they shared that first apartment, he closed his drawers. He must have. She certainly hadn't. Early in their marriage, Jack knew the toilet had a base and the shower had an upper half. Now she was supposed to consider herself lucky if he cleaned half a toilet. At least he cleaned. What a guy! Never mind that he left the hard-to-scrub muffin pans for her. He never washed those. Why were they so definitely hers?

This was not what had kept her close to home. Not dishes and socks and clean floors. That's when it happened. Not so much with Manny, not with just one, but definitely once they had two kids and a house.

Now, it didn't mattered what her inner voice said. It could scream *Fight! Fight! Fight!* It could rasp and intonate like Dylan Thomas, "Do Not Go Gentle Into That Good Night!", one of her favorites, applied to life among the stars rather than death by submission. What was she supposed to do? *Fight, fight, fight* her family?

She looked from room to room and hung her head, knowing the open drawers, the dirty socks, the dishes left lying around were not meant to taunt her. They were worse. They were meant to wear her down.

Jack would never admit that his sloppiness had developed over time—over marriage. He didn't notice. He forgot. He never could get those muffin pans as clean as she could. She was so tired of playing Mommy to the child-like way he pretended. He'd hang his head and endure washer-side scoldings rather than accept the responsibility to change. Was that manhood?

"If you see a stain like this," she'd hold up one of Peia's new school shirts, stained with chocolate milk, "you can't let it go. If you do, the shirt's ruined." She'd demonstrate (again and again and again) how to use the stain remover before he threw the shirt into the washer. But his stain-fighting days were short lived. After a few days, he'd start passing the stained clothes by. She'd find them untreated, hanging over the laundry rack or shoved to the bottom of the basket.

All she wanted, all she desperately wanted the kids to see and learn was a simple principle of math: reciprocation. Peia grasped it right away, it was a turn-around fact. You take two factors and rearrange them in all the possible ways: $2 \times 8 = 16$ just as $8 \times 2 = 16$, just as $16/2 = 8$. Sometimes Dad would scrub the toilet, sometimes Mom would. But no matter who accepted the task, the base of the toilet would get cleaned.

Jack would never say it, but she felt it, always, in his solid-blue eyes, his refusal to speak, in his fidgeting. Jack simply did not feel he should have to be *as* responsible. Didn't she know? Being a man meant it was in his nature to disregard the laundry, school lunches, the kids' after-school schedules. And boy, did he have back up.

There simply was no turn-around fact, no reciprocal situation that could place Jack where she was. If the house was left a mess, if the kids went to school in unwashed clothes, if they arrived without breakfast, no one would ask, "Where is their father?" The first question, sometimes the only question, was "Where on earth is their mother?"

The earth and sky pun didn't escape her.

Why, her head's in space!

She stood, looking from room to room. Would it help to yank out all their drawers and pile them in the landing?

No. This fight would only distract her from her true work. How late would she be today? She grabbed the soft leather handles of her bag, squeezing them for reassurance. Only at work were there people who believed she was more than she was, that she could, using her knowledge of stellar heat transfer and radiation, help to create a model spacecraft light enough to rely on mere bursts of hydrogen. Light enough to float.

Well, then, her inner voice said. *What's it going to be? Forgive?*
No. But she could erase.

She headed for the door. If she were going to stretch her mind into the realm of thermodynamics, which was no more her specialty than slamming drawers and picking up socks, she was going to have to erase. Backing out of the driveway, watching to make sure the garage door shut before she drove away, it occurred to her that Jack and Manny and Peia would define this as a good morning.

Jack had received his kiss. Manny had talked about the spring concert. And Peia had smiled. Of course they wouldn't understand.

All she had to do was slam a few drawers.

11

Day Four—South Manitou

JILLIAN STOPPED AT EACH STORE window, sipping coffee and yawning, waiting for the morning ferry to take her to South Manitou Island. She had left the tent before sunrise, about the time she could have fallen asleep. With the eastern sky streaked purple and then red-pink, eventually lighting up to orange over the tree tops, she had hiked to her car. Once she'd decided the stars over the island were just what she needed, a sense of peace had come over her. This was a journey; there was only so much thinking a person could do! She had followed the county road north to Leland, curving in and out of tiny bays and marinas, and with both the sand and the water throwing highlights of white and gold, she had felt something close to joy.

But now, walking from one shaker-shingled storefront to the next, she grew irritated with the sickeningly sweet sentiment that oozed from Leland's store windows. Books in every size, shape, and quality claimed to be the "original" *Legend of the Sleeping Bear Dunes.* The deluxe edition, displayed on a rack of carved pewter, lay open to a beautiful pastel. Mother Bear sat at the peak of the dunes, her dark coat alive with strokes of golden-wet fur, her black eyes fixed on the water. Jillian knew that fix. You didn't sit alone at the peak of a dune staring out over the water strictly out of love. No. Mother Bear felt love, yes, but she was gripped by a much stronger mix of longing and regret. And the colors, poor bear, foretold more disappointment. Low, over the lake, the turquoise sky was tinged with sad purples.

Year after year, tourists pined over Mishe-Mokwa, the Great Sleeping Bear, as a symbol of maternal sacrifice. They took the ferry to the islands to walk among her cubs. And then, struck by the beauty of the cliffs and the unspoiled wilderness, they rushed from the docks to buy hats, sweatshirts, books for themselves, books for their sisters, and books especially for their daughters. The colors, the oily chalks, the orangey glow that bathed the bear's hulking form in tenderness were meant to inspire sympathy, but people were missing the point, a simple truth Jillian saw as clearly as that realistic streak of mint on the book's pastel horizon: faced with the decision to sink or swim, Mother Bear saved herself.

The ten-to horn sounded as if to reprimand her for her thoughts, but before she headed down the hill to the dock, Jillian purchased a plain ink and paper book written in verse, one that claimed to be the original Native American version.

The metal ferry, painted white, was headed for the littlest of Mother Bear's cubs, South Manitou Island. The captain let down the metal boarding plank and it rippled and rang. If anyone had missed the ten-to horn, they'd certainly hear that sound. The teenage girl who had sold Jillian her ticket helped the captain untie the ropes.

"You got your coffee."

Jillian raised the huge Styrofoam cup. "Fresh ground is such a treat."

"I finally heard the forecast." Jillian had lingered in the ticket office, listening for the weather. "Clear skies through Friday, at least. The stars will be out all right."

Through Friday. What Day would that be? Day Seven? Eight? She walked to the back of the ferry trying to remember, was it Tuesday then? Which immediately brought thoughts of Day One's earliest hours, her standing over the kids and Jack, Jack's prominent forehead and cheekbones swelling to neanderthal proportions in the dark. She checked the calendar on her watch. Because of the ferry, she had allowed herself the watch. Yes. Tuesday, Day Four, and here she was in Leland with its pinks and yellows and the powder blues of old boarding houses poking out between the trees.

The ferry lurched and she stumbled, which the captain apparently thought funny. His voice chuckled from a speaker at the peak of the wheel house. "Hang on here folks. You'll want to sit while I spin her around." He paused to rev the engines. "As we head away from shore, keep your eyes south of town and you'll see the Great Sleeping Bear." His voice notched up in pitch, projecting over the thunking that shook the steel floor. "Halfway out, we'll coast above three hundred feet of fifty-six degree water. So keep the little ones close and we'll dock in ninety minutes."

Things were simple on the lakeshore: the water was always west, the trees east, with dunes to her right and dunes to her left. She stood with her face to the wind, imagining Jack and Manny and Peia (east, over the trees) where the wind was made of noise and commotion: the scramble to prepare a decent meal, get the laundry done, answer questions and run toward shouts and get to school. School! She'd forgotten about school shopping. She looked at the water when the captain told her to—"Be sure to keep your eyes on the water as we approach. We've got three shipwrecks in the shallows this year."— trying to imagine Jack shopping with Peia, the horribly dysfunctional apparel Peia could talk him into: skirts (not skorts), high-heeled shoes. They had a rule about the slope of the sole. What marketing ace had started peddling heels to growing girls? Jack would know: growing spines, bad posture, scoliosis, especially with Peia's tall, narrow frame.

The ferry settled into an even speed and Jillian propped her pack between her legs. It was a bright, sunny day, and she felt good energy. She wished she hadn't packed the rain tarp. All day she would feel its weight. She had her mini-tent, a tube of nylon that required only two stakes and one snap-out rod to raise. One of three water bottles was full, the other two she would fill at the ranger's station. She had flint-sticks and matches in a sealed bag, and two mini flashlights. Did they allow fires on the island? The wind gusted and she looked up, thinking someone had spoken.

The ferry was small and people closed into small groups: a couple with small children, a scout troop, perhaps, with metal tins and huge backpacks. A young couple lugging diving gear walked toward the open floor space near her spot at the endgate. In the last bag she counted eight high-protein bars and a tube of gel. The climber at the outdoor store had sold her on the gel: *Even if your jaw was somehow broken, you could squirt the gel down your throat.*

The divers plopped down on the bench next to her. "Margorie. We haven't missed anything." The man's voice sounded sing-songy, British. His nostrils flared as he exhaled. "Lovely day, isn't it?" His eyes were dark and close together, animal-ish until he smiled.

"It's a beautiful day," Jillian answered, rubbing the back of her neck where mist kicked up against her skin.

The young woman's freckled face poked in. "Do you know about the area? We arrived too late to take up pamphlets."

The woman's accent was thick, and Jillian found herself craning toward her. She'd become accustomed to being alone. Her own thoughts formed incredibly fast and loud and clearly, which surprised her. She had expected solitude to be slow.

The woman slapped the man's leg, playfully. "We've heard so much about the books. Have you read them?" Jillian started to nod, but the woman pressed on. "Do you know which one is the Sleeping Bear Dune?"

Jillian pointed south toward the colored dots that were Leland. "See that long dune? Above the ridge?" They nodded and scooched closer. "That's the Great Sleeping Bear."

"That's her?" The woman gazed across the water.

"Ah. The humps, see there?" He put his arm around her and guided her gaze. "There's a shoulder and quite a rounded backside."

Jillian traced the Sleeping Bear's shape in the air. "And that's her snout, low in the sand."

The man turned his flaring nostrils toward her again. "And her cubs, are those the islands?"

North and South Manitou islands looked like dark discs lying still even as the green-black water heaved. Jillian had wanted to take them in, smell the mist, shiver in the wind, alone.

"You're hiking then?"

Before she could answer, the woman leaned in. "The shipwrecks are said to be outstanding. There's an old, English wood-burner washed up in the sand, they say." She squeezed the man's arm and they smiled at each other. "Could you tell us the story?" She slid off the bench and sat cross legged in front of Jillian.

Tell them the story?

The man looked embarrassed. She was so forward. "We'll read about it later."

This was Day Four, New Adventure Day, and here was this stranger sitting cross legged in front of her, who, Jillian had noticed, had eyes nearly as green as Kera's. Kera, who had grown up so close to the story and its terrible lesson, whatever that lesson was, it was never clear. And now this child-bride—that's how Jillian was beginning to think of the woman, the man seemed so much older and more refined—wanted Jillian to *tell* the story?

The woman wrapped her hands around the man's calf, pressing her face to his leg, and it reminded Jillian of a time when she had grabbed Jack's leg in desperation: *Just tell me what you want. Please.* She was pregnant with Manny, unexpectedly, and some part of her had wanted someone to tell her what to do. She'd begged Jack to tell her. The sight embarrassed her, made her feel weak, and she wanted to move on, quickly.

"The story actually begins on the shores of Wisconsin." Jillian pointed across the lake, and as the couple gazed over the water, she dug into her backpack and pulled out the book.

"The book! You don't mind?"

"Mishe-Mokwa," Jillian replied. She wanted them to know the bear's name. No one in the bookstores seemed to know which tribe the tale originated with, Algonquin or Ojibwe, or the story's true meaning. In Native American animal medicine, the bear was a symbol of healing, which continued to strike Jillian as odd.

"Mishe-Mokwa," the young woman pronounced, and she began to read the book, out loud, for any and all to hear. "It was a very hot summer, with no rains to cool the beating sun." In some way, Jillian cared. She didn't want the story stripped of its beauty or its sadness. "Every day Mishe-Mokwa led her cubs along a birch-lined stream to the great blue waters."

This reading, floating up from the deck, felt oddly uncomfortable. It was a private story, and Jillian was still remembering pleading with Jack. But the couple couldn't go back to Great Britain with the pining tourist version. A young boy standing near the wheelhouse moved toward the storyteller's voice. His father was talking to the captain, his mother trying to get a toddler to drink some water. Neither of them noticed.

"A thunderstorm came and lightning started the great woods on fire. Soon, all of the animals were headed for the water. But a cloud of hot ash and a huge wall of fire rushed toward them."

The boy stood alone in the center of the boat's rubber-matted deck. A sudden wave could toss the ferry—and the child.

"Mishe-Mokwa told her cubs, 'You must swim, and keep swimming.' So they did. All day and into the night, they swam. But the storm followed and the great blue waters swelled, tossing the cubs about. The cubs called out, 'Mother! Mother! We are tired and can swim no more.'"

The ferry rose with a high wave, as if to dramatize the telling, and the boy shuffled toward them. He reached out for the woman's shoulder and she wound an arm around him. The young woman, Jillian, the boy's mother, all looked at each other and nodded. He was fine.

The woman smiled up at the boy, her voice repeating. "Mishe-Mokwa called to her cubs, 'You must be strong and keep swimming. We are close now, close.'"

"But by daybreak Mishe-Mokwa was far ahead, and her cubs could barely see her. She called back to the two tiny dots on the water. 'Be brave, my children. Be brave and keep swimming. Far across the great blue waters there are trees and berries and streams full of fish.'"

The young woman must have read ahead, for she looked up at the boy and then at Jillian as if to ask, *Shall I read on?*

"The cubs were tired, very tired, but they were brave. They had promised their mother they would keep swimming, and so they swam. But sometime before morning, when Mishe-Mokwa's wet, heavy body washed to shore and she dug her claws into the sand, her cubs, far behind her . . . went to sleep." The young woman had substituted key words: *Some time before morning the cubs disappeared under the waves of the great blue waters, because they were tired and they could swim no more.* "But they were not afraid, because they were cradled, forever, in the great blue waters."

Jillian and the boy shared a moment of knowing eye contact: *I know, the legend doesn't explain.* And he hadn't yet heard the end, where Mother Bear is forever punished yet strangely pitied for letting her children drown behind her. What a story, really, and yet it was beautiful, complicated. The man squeezed the young woman's shoulders and she continued.

"Heavy and wet, the Great Mother climbed to the top of the dunes and searched the water for her cubs. She was hungry, but she feared her cubs would return and find no one waiting, so Mishe-Mokwa remained through the summer, through the cold winds of fall, through winter's icy snows. And then, with spring approaching and new winds roaring off the lake, the Great Mother Bear was covered in sand."

In the distance, the dark mound of the Sleeping Bear rested on a cliff of sand. Jillian knew what that was like, to pine for her children. To picture their faces for months on end. To begin to forget what they smelled like. It didn't matter how much you told yourself it had to be. It hurt—and there was a kind of burial involved.

Jack's mother—immediately, when Jillian had arrived home with the baby—had come over with nursing bras and a lullaby tape to help Jillian and Manny relax. But everytime Jillian settled in to rock Manny to sleep with the lullabies playing, she'd cry. She'd sob until she got up and stopped the tape. Little by little, she played more and more of the tape without bawling, listening to its baby songs in the morning when she was rested and feeling strong. And it became her test. Eventually, she was able to rock Manny, put him to bed, and listen until the tape clicked itself off as she stood over the sink washing bottles for the next day. That's when she called Kera and told her it was time for them to get back to California, time to schedule their second run at the observatory.

The young woman was patting the boy and he was leaning over her as they snuggled like mother and child, with the boy's mother looking on, straining to hear. "The great spirit Manitou, seeing the love of the mother for her cubs, took pity on her and blanketed her in the dunes. Then, calling on the clouds, he raised the cubs in the form of two islands, just off shore, where Mishe-Mokwa could watch over them forever, all three of them together in the spirit world."

Sometimes, Jillian understood all of Peia's stomping. On those rare occasions when Peia and Jillian looked into each other's eyes for a good moment, they connected and did not need words. Peia was strong, and Jillian hoped that strength would remain when her body changed, when breasts and menstruation and the attention of men challenged her sense of self.

A touch surprised her—the first touch she had felt since she had hugged Manny and Peia goodbye. Of course Jack had picked him up. Why would he forget?

"That was lovely." The woman extended the book. The boy was back with his real mother now.

"Yes, lovely." The man said. "And you know. The legend isn't far from the geology of the islands. It's fascinating, really."

Peia was always spouting off facts about animals and their habitats. She loved animals and wanted to be a trainer and a vet. And a singer, and a goalie. But first, she was going to have to become a woman. Jillian smiled at the man, though she wanted to groan. "Really. How so?"

"The islands, they're quite peculiar. They don't have a rock or volcanic base. Just sediment, really. Layers upon layers of shifting sand. That's why there are so many shipwrecks. Fifty-eight of them lolling about."

She imagined an underwater skirmish of boats.

"The tale, you know, it has geological merit."

She stayed at the endgate, allowing the couple to drift away as she watched the water. The lake was amazingly dark. Even the suds trailing behind the boat were a deep blackish-green. At some point, she noticed the vibration of the engines cutting back and the captain called out, "Three masts!" He jumped from the wheelhouse. "Three you can see. All the rigging too, still intact." The diving couple returned, hanging over the endgate. The freckled face of the woman turned up as she pointed. "There! There!" Ferry riders crowded around them. The little boy appeared at Jillian's side and she steered him to the front, placing his hands on the rail. He started to jump and out of habit she held onto the back of his shirt.

The first mast rose as a blur of yellow-green, wiggling comically, like a busy fish, and then it sank away. The main mast thrust up with a punch of yellow-gold and the ferry riders let out a collective "Oh." Thick rope spiraled toward them, each twist climbing over the other in a dash toward the surface. And just when it looked as if the mast would pop through, the rope shook and spun away, greening back into the water. The last braid of gold wasn't much more than a shadow, leaving ferry riders searching for more as the lake itself turned to gold in the shallows.

She stopped in the only toilet on the island before walking across the yard to the Ranger's Station, a large wooden building that matched the ferry's white and gray. From the porch, she caught sight of the diving couple sitting on the dock. They struggled with their fins and talked, excitedly. The ranger behind the counter, a middle-aged man, motioned to her pack. "Need a permit?"

Jillian watched the divers kiss before wetting their mouthpieces. "Yes. One night."

She half-heard the ranger recite the waste rules—leave no trace; pack in, pack out. He tapped her permit on the counter. "Permits must be turned in before you leave the island. And watch the ferry schedule. It's four o'clock or nothing. Every once in a while, someone runs up late and ends up sleeping on the doorstep." Jillian looked into his face, perplexed, and he smiled. She smiled to herself sometimes, when she was out hiking or sitting alone, but not, she thought, so vividly.

"I guess they like my light bulb."

Outside, the shallows were expansive and glowing aqua-gold, and the diving couple had disappeared. The day hikers, too, had scattered into the woods. In the distance, the dark stripe of the mainland split the world in two, the water below and the sky above feeding each other with the same luminous blue. A vast, lonely blue, but a strong blue all the same.

She could be alone. Forever, if that's what she wanted.

The first mile or so was semi-cleared, remnants of commercial logging. Young cedar and pine saplings grew within inches of each other, shooting straight up with very little flare. In the open sunlight, they didn't need to spread out. But oh, in the future, the competition would be fierce.

She noticed plants she had never seen before. A red blossom that looked like a handful of worms. Bulbs of black fungus hung from bushes that resembled hemlock trees. Frogs, hundreds of tiny frogs, jumped across the path. Climbing higher, she was surrounded by giant white cedars, an old growth forest full of aged trees. Their trunks were reddish and frosted white, with deep, craggy grooves, some wide enough for her to place fingers between them. And the treetops, nearly two hundred feet above, spread out like the heads of giants watching her stroll the dark trail. As the air cooled, she bounded happily on the balls of her feet, expecting that she'd be too tired to bound later.

She reached a split in the trail and took out her trail map. The shipwreck was half a mile out, toward shore, and the Lake of Glass about the same distance in. She guzzled more water than she should have and headed higher, toward the tanker. But her mind replayed the scene she'd walked away from, a day trip long ago, when she used to drag her family to observatories and dark fields and museum exhibits on the photoelectric effect.

How could she have forgotten? Her family had come to the Lake of Glass with her. Glass wasn't the lake's real name, but that's how she remembered it, perfectly smooth. She and Kera had always wanted to camp on the island, stay for an entire dark phase, but that had never happened. They'd become too busy with their separate lives, so Jillian had taken Jack and Manny and Peia. Peia was only a toddler and Manny not more than six or seven. They'd come for the day to see the Perched Dunes.

Now, as Jillian walked, she remembered Manny and Peia crouching after the tiny frogs that hopped across the trail. And Manny—he'd made her heart rate jump as he walked along identifying plants and reached for a poison Hemlock.

And then their day hike fell apart.

Halfway up, Manny had to go to the bathroom. "It's not a stand up, Mom." So they all went off trail. Jack dug a hole while she was showing Manny how to squat over it, and Peia took off running through ground cover laced with poison ivy. They used their drinking water to wash her down with Fels Naptha—the soap had to be applied immediately, Jack said—and by the time they reached the Lake of Glass, it was too late to go on to the Perched Dunes.

She'd wanted to share the wonder of the Perched Dunes so badly. But her memory was not without its consolation. Manny and Peia had waded in the Lake of Glass, giggling at the guppies that swam around their ankles. With the air so still and with so much green and blue reflected on the water, Peia was convinced the lake held another land.

Toddler-faced Peia had patted the water. "Mama Bear is here."

"This is one of her cubs." Manny was careful not to sound dismissive. "Mama Bear is the big dune, remember? From the ferry?"

Peia had bent down directly in front of Manny, flattening her hands over the water. "This is her cub, and Mama Bear is right here."

The ridge overlooking the shipwrecked freighter dropped off so suddenly that Jillian almost walked over the edge. A lone tree—she put a hand on it and felt it move—marked the end of the ground and the beginning of open air. Below her, pines and a few white birches stood stripped of their leaves, blown to skeletons by the wind. The birches were as white as snow, dead, but still upright. A Ghost Forest—she'd read about the island's shifting sands—trees that were smothered in sand one year and stripped bare by the wind the next.

She sat with her legs dangling over the grassy lip, snacking and gazing at the tanker, aground on a sandbar a few hundred feet from shore. A motorized raft circled its rotting hull. Two divers surfaced and traded something with their driver, a camera probably, then dropped back into the water. Jillian watched their bright orange fins pause, kick, and disappear.

After a rest, she followed the narrow trail toward the outermost rim of the island, skirting the edge of the cliff. The trail disappeared in chunks, as if bites had been taken from the ground, and there, she grabbed tree trunks and swung herself to the next patch of ground. Bark and leaves gave way to solid blue, and she stood at the edge of the Perched Dunes.

She staggered, sighing. The whole western curve of the island, as far as she could see, fell in massive, four-hundred-foot slopes of sand. Here, there were no shallows. The sand plunged into the aqua-green, angled, like a slide. And the blues of the water, aqua and the deepest sapphire, were striated with dark, purple fingers. The contrast was breathtaking—aqua on sapphire—and the sky was as vibrant as the water.

She had passed an old logging outpost and read about the logging camp's demise. The official account claimed the logging operation folded when trains replaced ships. But the locals, in their journals, wrote of the ground rumbling and moaning when storms blew across the island. And every spring, when the ships returned, half the loggers would leave. The mill managed to stay in business as long as it did thanks to Manitou's shifting sands. Every fall there were shipwrecks, and stranded sailors were put to work until they got their chance to ship out.

Millions of tons of sand could moan, she thought, especially with the immense stretch of these dunes.

She walked along clumps of dune grass and sand cherry, remembering *sandslides!* highlighted on the hiking precautions list. Small stones, blown smooth by the wind and bleached by the sun, lay on the surface of the sand. She found a steady pad of grass and stood strong. The ultimate aloneness, this island. Even the dunes, standing stoically against the lake's roaring winds, stood alone. It was amazing, how strong the wind blew, even on a calm, clear day. She wished she had giant hands to pat the dunes.

She unlaced her boots and tucked them behind her, and into her boots she tucked her socks. The water below had only a rim of sand, just a few feet of beach. And what about rocks? Sure, those aqua swirls looked gentle from here, but there were structures below the surface she couldn't possibly see from hundreds of feet above. She ached for the drop. *Imagine the momentum!* The angle sloped downward at forty-five, maybe even thirty degrees. Could she control her speed?

LEAVE NO TRACE. That's what her hiking permit said. Hikers were supposed to leave the land and water exactly as they found it. Leave no trace of their presence behind. No one had more respect for this place than she did. Still, when would she get another chance? Off in the distance, she could hear the diver's boat. They were taking their own adventure, they wouldn't notice.

The water was deep, she knew that. And much rougher than it looked. And Perched, these were the Perched Dunes for a reason. These massive mounds sat atop pillars of glacial sediment. Sand above, sandstone below, like the long-nosed man had said, and it all fell away, suddenly, silently, into deep heaving water.

She'd take a dive at the last minute. She wasn't going to go that fast. It was sand. All she had to do was dig in. She stood up.

Dig in.

The ranger's highlighted, underlined, bold-faced letters, LEAVE NO TRACE. flashed in her mind, but only during the first few steps. She spread her arms out and howled into the wind, slaloming and jumping to keep from tumbling as her feet flew faster and faster. Hot sand whipped up all around her, in her eyes, in her mouth, but she kept going, she kept digging in. The run down the dune lasted longer than she had expected. She had time to think, to feel the depth of the sand, to hop around bigger and bigger boulders. Her knees felt as if they might snap and her toes rip apart, but she kept digging into the sand until finally, near the bottom, she slowed. Her feet slapped the shoreline's flatter sand, and as the aqua and sapphire of the water swelled, coloring all she could see, she stretched out in a lunge, unable to lift her feet for a dive.

The icy water sheered her skin. As the waves pulled her under, she tried to see what was really under the island, but an undertow, sudden and strong, yanked her away amid a cloud of sand. When she surfaced she was fifty feet out, her back to the island.

The idea of seven or eight hundred feet of water under her kicks, of her legs moving water that deep and dark, made her head swoon. She had to fight to tread back to where she could pull up on shore, a hundred yards or so from where she had jumped in, and there she flopped onto her back in the sand. She loved heights and the idea of endless space, but deep water made her feel small in a way she didn't appreciate. She could have been carried away from the island. But she hadn't been, and between short, steady gasps, she smiled. She lay flat, admiring the sky, and smiled. The sky over the lake held its blue.

She found the tracks she had created and began the climb. Pointing her feet, she dug into the sand. She balled her hands into fists and punched in, trying to be patient and wait for the sand to settle each time she punched and slipped. But the sand grew hotter and hotter as she climbed, forcing her to work quickly and sloppily.

At the top, she checked her watch. Two o'clock. She had spent two hours running down, splashing in, and climbing back. In two hours, the ferry would leave. Did she have time or the strength to do it again?

DogMan popped into her thoughts, not so much the picture, which had been brewing on the boat as she gazed at the long-nosed man, but that ridiculous hiking story Kera had told her. Kera and her stories! DogMan, vicious slaughterer of hikers and hunters alike, roamed the forests of the Upper Peninsula. DogMan looked human until he got close, and it was too late. And on DogMan's heels came the drowning cubs she had refused to attend to on the ferry: their struggle to keep their snouts above water; their heads overtaken with the highest waves as they watched their mother swim on. They must have known she wasn't coming back. Jillian had imagined their disbelieving eyes flooded with dark, stinging water. It was bad enough for a mother to see her kids eyes and noses covered by water in a swimming pool, let alone this huge, heaving lake. But it was their thoughts, the direct connection of their mother with the pain, that got to her. How did Mishe-Mokwa do it?

She felt that old liquid pain in her chest, a pain she'd always associated with swallowing water and later with her father, his inability to draw a clean breath, and now the thought of the ferry spinning around and leaving her made her long for her tent in Manistee. She pictured its green sheen on the dune cliff, the flap blowing in a gentle breeze. Hikers passed, she heard voices, she saw campfires in the distance.

At Manistee, she had possibilities. She could spend a day at the campground beach. Move into one of the campground loops and surround herself with people and their noise and their fires. But the stars, here on the island, *the stars would be so lovely*. She used the diver's word on purpose.

Here, there would be total and complete aloneness.

If Jack and the kids were here—even if it were just she and the kids—she could make it. Her chest might ache as island darkness fell, she might flinch and strain with hyper-awareness, but she would tuck fear aside, she most certainly would, because her children would need her. Why couldn't she do this for herself?

She looked down hundreds of feet of sand, into hundreds of feet of water.

And she heard Kera's voice: *Every new type of isolation, every challenge, brings its own bag of fears.* Fear invigorated, reinvented itself bigger and deeper each time. Always there was a new place to face an even deeper part of yourself.

DogMan couldn't get to her. Neither could the sounds or the shivers or those figures that flickered between glints of a fire. She could chase the sounds and the shadows away, any day. But here, with the island's four-hundred-foot dunes and diving couples and drowning cubs; here, where there was only one lightbulb, she was facing a new pull. In a sense, she had achieved something quite miraculous: she had made her own comfort. She had weathered herself into her dune chairs and her tent, and she wanted to go home to her two-hundred-foot dune and her aqua shallows without purple fingers.

No more testing herself. What did she have to prove? She snugged her hip belt and snapped it shut.

No more tests!

Heading away from the Perched Dunes, she swung her body, two trees at a time, around the bite marks on the ridge. Bounding down the steep grade, she came to the central island trail. She stopped to catch her breath and listen for others, but there wasn't a sound. What about her lake? How could she leave without seeing the Lake of Glass?

It was after three o'clock when she ran under the giant cedars. It had taken her close to an hour and a half to get in. She could make it, in reverse, in half that time. She could make it if she wanted it bad enough.

A well-trained physicist—astrophysicist (she and Kera had modified the saying)—*can do anything.* They'd earned it after years on those rugged, mean-spirited hills with Superior's frigid wind and all the looks and grumbling from the men. She was a well-trained *astro*physicist, and she could do anything.

Half a mile from the dock she heard the ten-to horn and kicked with all her might. Sweat drained from her head in rivulets and ran into her eyes. Heat throbbed from her forehead and cheeks. *No!* Feeling sorry for herself would use too much air. Her thoughts went only to controlling her breathing. She sprinted through the saplings. Her feet pounded the planks of the old logging village. Gasping for breath, most likely purple with excess heat, she ran into the clearing at the Ranger's Station and hailed the captain.

She gulped water from the faucet at the station, knowing a ferry load of people were watching her, but she had to get water. The ranger behind the desk took back her one-night permit and tried to joke, "Happens to the best of them," but she couldn't joke back. It was all she could do not to cough and gasp.

She crossed the metal boarding plank, breathing as steadily as she could as she passed the staring faces. She stood at the stern begging the breeze to cool her, and the four o'clock ferry made its exit at 4:10.

She felt a tap on her leg and looked down to see the little boy stretching a water bottle toward her. The boy's mother nodded. "We have plenty."

"Thank you," she said. "Thank you." And she turned back to the great blue waters, her throat too tight to drink.

Later, sitting at the back of the ferry, gazing at the islands, she held on to the feeling of flying down the Perched Dunes. For those few moments, she had flown. She had taken flight. LEAVE NO TRACE came to mind and she pictured the path of disturbance she had created. But the flying was worth it. That she had dared to try was worth all future twinges of guilt.

She, a well-trained astrophysicist, was bound for complete indistinction. If the only trace she was going to leave behind were her initials in a giant tree in Houghton, two children, and now, a four-foot-wide path in a sacred dune, then she might as well be glad she had the courage to enjoy every grain of sand that split the skin between her toes and stuck to her eyelids along the way.

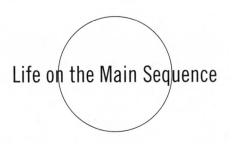

Life on the Main Sequence

ONCE A STAR IS STEADILY FUSING HYDROGEN TO HELIUM, IT is said to be a Main Sequence star at zero age. Of course, zero, as a point on the stellar life cycle, is a measure of one overarching quality: stability.

New stars form when gases and dust floating in the interstellar medium are slowly or suddenly disrupted: heated by the birth of a nearby star, stirred by the sweeping arms of a spiral galaxy, or compacted by the rush of a shockwave. Atoms and molecules that once floated in clouds the size of galaxies are slammed together, creating a dense, hot environment where gravity—the force of mass attracted to mass—takes over. Hydrogen, the simplest element of life, with its single proton nucleus and one orbiting electron, is the first to fuse. As gravity squeezes, hydrogen atoms are brought closer and closer together, bouncing and colliding with greater and greater force until their electrons are stripped away, leaving the proton nucleus without its protective electron shell. Gravity continues to squeeze, heat and pressure continue to rise, and deep down at the center of a ball of compacting gases, hydrogen nuclei are brought so close together that they begin to fuse. The stellar core reaches an important milestone—and the young star radiates the bold, hot light of nuclear fusion.

The time it takes for free-floating gases and dust to develop into protostars and eventually stars, ranges from fifty thousand to five hundred million years, depending upon mass. Massive protostars are compacted and rise to the extreme temperatures required for fusion, more quickly. Some protostars, too low in mass to generate the necessary squeeze of gravity, never reach the necessary temperature. Failed stars—Jupiter may be one of them—remain as giant balls of warmed gases, their huge cores glowing but never contracting enough to manufacture and release the bold heat and light of nuclear fusion.

The great majority of stars in the sky are lower-mass Main Sequence stars, such as our sun, formed over hundreds of millions of years. Because they're all burning hydrogen at roughly the same temperature, Main Sequence stars tend to look and act alike. Most emit a characteristic blue-white light, and with the steady squeeze of gravity and the internal push-back of gas pressure in balance, they maintain a uniform spherical appearance. Even on the inside, their anatomy is distinctly similar.

A Main Sequence star has a fusing core buried deep within an envelope of gases. Intense heat and energy created in the core spreads out into the stellar envelope, where gases are slowly, continually heated and readied for future use in the fusion cycle. In the process of passing through and interacting with gases in the envelope, the energy of nuclear fusion is converted into particles and lightwaves that continually move toward the surface. Finally, the star's outer layers, also gaseous, radiate the light we see.

Core, envelope, surface—every portion of the star regulates temperature, the key to balance.

Gravity is strongest at the core, where the weight of all outer layers comes to bear. The core must remain hot then, very hot, to generate enough gas pressure to resist gravity. Heat causes atoms within the core to zing and collide faster and faster, and this creates pressure. Without the support of gas pressure, the star would collapse, its outer layers imploding toward the center. Conversely, if the core generates too much heat, gas pressure overwhelms gravity. A too-hot core will inflate, expanding into and converting gases in the envelope at too high a rate to be contained. A star that expands too rapidly will eventually overheat, ignite, and explode.

Essentially, the need for balance comes down to this: stars radiate light, and in doing so, lose energy into space. Stability depends then, upon the composition and behavior of the stellar core. Ideally, for longevity's sake, the core must create just enough energy to replace the heat and light (luminosity) lost from its surface and no more.

The most successful stars make adjustments, gradually, over thousands and thousands and even millions of years.

Stars remain on the Main Sequence as long as the supply of hydrogen lasts. Once the star's original source of energy has been fused into helium, the predominantly helium-based core must endure a great jump in temperature if nuclear fusion is to continue. Helium, with two protons and therefore double the mass and positive charge of hydrogen, requires a hundred-fold increase in heat and pressure before it will fuse into the next heavier elements: most notably carbon, nitrogen, and oxygen, the building blocks of life as we know it.

12

The Call

MANNY WAS FOUR, IN KINDERGARTEN, when Jillian got the call. She and Jack had been married for two years, they'd purchased a house on a hill outside of Ann Arbor, and Jack was taking great care of the lawn. Having a second baby was an idea that had come up but was quickly put aside.

"Jilli, don't you get it?" Kera was so excited that Jillian had trouble following her. Maybe it was the rushing in her own ears. NASA wanted *her*? Kera did it? She did it. Convinced them to take a look at their back-to-the-benches coronagraph?

"I'm not saying astronaut school. That's the longest shot, but it always has been. But on the team. It's so déjà vu, you wouldn't believe it. They're talking about occluders and light nulling and something Hubble-sized."

"An orbital telescope?" She and Kera had dreamed of an orbital system: four mirrors equidistant from a central guide station with some kind of positioning controls, but after they'd experienced adaptive optics' many failure points and the headaches of keeping everything in alignment, they'd given up on space for awhile. Besides, Kera was the one who'd stayed on and kept up with the optics. Jillian had only rushed in when Kera's NASA application had been accepted and they'd pushed up the test date for the coronagraph.

"Kera. I haven't touched the coronagraph. Not since our last stint at Lick. You have all the background on the benches."

Once the Air Force had released its adaptive optics knowledge, astronomers flocked to the labs, working to put Reagan's Star Wars technology to work in the larger universe, and Kera had been part of that effort. She'd stayed on at Lawrence Livermore, testing masks and trying to get the computer and the optics and a myriad of mirrors to work together. Jillian had kept up, but from a distance. Everything between the time she and Kera were last at Lick and the reality she was now a part of seemed like a path that had dissipated into dust,

skills and knowledge that had faded away. Was there still an astronomer or an astrophysicist or an instrumentation specialist in her? "All I
can remember now, is what we tried to do. Prematurely at that."

"Hey. All we have to do is figure out what we'd need for a control
station, set up some graphics, and the boneheads on the floor will
figure it out."

"Careful there." Jillian's job had pretty much turned her into an
engineer. She was busy; she was earning decent money, but she was
no longer working with the stars. She was writing software and creating simulations for other researchers.

"Jilli. Every time I roll out one of your drawings, every time I list
one of our findings, I say this is Jillian Greer's, my partner's. We
worked together on the NIRV studies at Lick. And then I tell them
about tau Ceti."

Tau Ceti. That incredible arc of light that appeared and then
stayed, night after night as they clasped hands and bounced before the
imaging screen, getting closer and closer to proving that the dim outline of an object they had imaged wasn't some blip or error in alignment.

"I know. You've worked really hard to keep me in there."

"No. That's not what I'm saying here. You're in. I can feel it."

They had shown, with their terribly hurried coronagraph, their
VLC, how a visible light coronagraph *could* find a planet. But they
had never actually proven it. That would take years of back and forth
between the benches and the telescope, and Kera, just finishing her
first year of astronaut school, no longer had that option. Now it was
Jillian's turn.

"We're going to have to move fast though, Jilli."

And she knew what Kera meant. It was only a matter of time
before the promise of their radial velocity studies and their initial failures with the coronagraph became the fuel for someone else's planet-
finding success.

Jillian pictured herself in the long, two-story complex that sat in the
shadow of the towering Shuttle Bay, Kera's most recent workplace.
Kera had spent months in flight and docking simulators; now she was
working on the International Space Station prototype. Candidates for
future ISS missions were participating in the final assembly, so they
would understand every component.

"I'll catch up."

"I know you will."

"Oh, my god. Jack." A few weeks before, they were talking about having another baby. That, she wouldn't mention.

"Jack? He'll love it."

"He's different. You'd be surprised. He's planting shrubs and doing that diagonal mowing thing."

"You're kidding."

"Last week, he took out a pad of paper and made me sit down to make a list of what we were having for dinner each night. It's the house."

Kera sounded serious. "It's going to be tough, with Manny starting school. But maybe that's not such a bad thing, Jack getting all settled in at home."

Because this time, if they went for it, Jillian would be the one who would stay in the lab, get their coronagraph back on the benches and start chipping away at the alignment problems and the computer crashes and the pistons that wouldn't fire off in just the right sequence to deform the deformable mirror. She would have to be gone a lot, which gave her chest an instant heaviness. But they'd be dreaming again of actually seeing a planet, of testing some future version of their coronagraph in orbit. In space! She'd have to make it through astronaut school before they'd even consider letting her up there, of course, but first and foremost she had to get down to Kera, fast. Show them how committed she was.

"I can't wait to hear about Manny. He'll be so proud of you."

And then Kera was off, and Jillian didn't have time to worry about Manny. "You can stay at my apartment. Jack and Manny can fly down on weekends, and we'll fly up too. We'll dig through the initial spectral studies and go back to the first five or six targets that looked promising. Which means, with my schedule, you'll be doing most of the digging. But we'll be here together, Jilli. We can walk through the spacestation, even if it is a prototype parked in the garage. It still gets to me. You know, I bet we could find some support from SOHO. You should see the images of the sun they're getting with a simple occluding disk."

Jillian jotted down some notes, her head growing heavy with Kera's excitement. When Kera finally stopped and said, "What do

you think?" Jillian answered, "Everything. I'm thinking, everything."

"You're kidding! You're not kidding!" Jack stretched his long arms
across the table and grabbed both sides of her face. He kissed her and
was up, pacing around the table. "This is it, this is it. You did it. I
knew you would. I knew it."

Jack grabbed Manny's face too. "Mama's going to NASA, bud!"

Manny, eating a muffin and some apple slices in place of the dinner that neither she nor Jack had made, turned his eyes to Jillian.
"You are? When?"

Manny had no idea what that meant in terms of their living
arrangements. Neither did she, really. Jack could find a transfer position, eventually. Florida had research colleges. Most of their tissue
studies were in regeneration, nerves, they'd been through that before.
But she could end up in Massachusetts, California, down in Houston,
just about anywhere.

"It's not for sure yet." She rubbed Manny's shoulder. "But I'm
very excited. Remember when we went to see Kera? She wants me
to come down to Florida."

"Can I come?"

Jack ran interference. "We'll go down sometime, bud. Soon."

"I'll go too." Manny turned to his apples, digging them into a splat
of peanut butter. Jack was getting better at varying the food groups—
three with this plate: fruit, dairy, and protein. A significant amount of
fat too, which wasn't all bad for an almost five-year-old. Jack could
handle it. Manny, on the other hand, simply assumed he was coming
along. The old days were lurking in his memory too.

Jack shrugged and mouthed "later."

The rest of the evening Jillian repeated for Jack, each time he asked
her this question or that, the exact words of her conversation with
Kera.

"So, they want you to show them how the Suitcase could work on
the space station."

"How a coronagraph might be launched *from* the space station, as
Hubble was." Lately, she'd had been thinking of an even smaller solution, of a suitcase-sized unit that could take initial high-contrast photos of one star at a time. "Did I tell you that Sandy worked on

Hubble's optics?" Another point in their favor. Dr. Sandra Moore Faber, the astronomer who helped fix Hubble's fuzzy optics, knew of their work. She'd approved it herself. "But that's way down the line. First, we have to get the coronagraph working."

"Is Kera crazy? She wants you down there in two weeks?" Jack was planning and getting tense. "What about Jim?"

She hadn't called her boss. "I haven't said anything yet. Only to Arnie, at Tech. He's been doing some image-a-day thing with Hubble. I asked him to send me anything that might help." She held up her notes. "Kera's putting a library together at this point, recent space funding and speculation. The numbers NASA plays with are staggering."

Jack folded his hands around hers. "Wow. Tomorrow's not going to be what we expected, is it?"

"What will I say to Jim?" Jillian pictured Jim Burton, Uncle Jim as Kera called him, a private financier who had doubled the funding for her and Kera's last stint at Lick Observatory.

"Two weeks. Well, if that's all we've got, that's all we've got." Jack rose and returned with one of her graph pads and a pencil. "I believe a list is in order. Indulge me?"

"Do you realize how much we have to do?"

She had to read. She'd do that at night. She had to give notice at work, figure out how to give Manny some transition time. Manny had forgotten apart-time, but Jillian remembered: the begging in his voice, his toughness when he tried not to cry. He'd tell her, "Get some good stars" when it was time to hang up the phone. And then, the calls after Manny was in bed, when Jack would lay the receiver on Manny's pillow so Jillian could hear him breathing. Their breakdown order—that's what she and Jack had called it—first Manny, then Jillian, then Jack. Two thousand miles away, Jillian would hang her head and Kera would take over her imaging controls, rubbing circles over Jillian's back, telling her to get it all out. And back home, Jack would stretch out on Manny's floor, gazing into the face that looked so much like Jillian's.

They could fly down with her, once she figured things out, stay with her, wherever she ended up, so Manny could find her in his heart and in his mind. Around midnight, as they headed up to bed, Jack stopped her on the stairs. "You're back on the pill, right? Looks like we'll be a one-kid family after all."

Jillian sat across the desk from Jim Burton—Mystic Jim as she called him—holding one of his pyramids. If anyone deserved to look mystic, staring back at her with shelves of glass hovering near the wall behind him, it was Jim. He was such a dreamer. She remembered his excitement when the transparent Lucite mounts and screws had worked. The Lucite was her idea, designed for the effect. Jim had been so pleased he'd surprised her, in turn, with a huge print of The Pleiades, the same image that hung in Lick Observatory's circular gallery. She'd come into her office that morning, touching the punched-up purples, and every one of the hot periwinkle stars seemed to be pulsing: "You've done it, you've done it!"

Pyramid Corp (known simply as "Burton's" to people in astronomy and aeroscience circles) had supported Jillian and Kera's post-doctoral studies. And later, when no one seemed interested in their proposal to actually build a coronagraph, Jim put up the money for Kera's fellowship in adaptive optics. And his hunch was right. Adaptive optics were the latest rage—in astronomy, in medicine, even in surveillance.

He sat with his fingertips pressed together, concentrating on Jillian's face. Whenever one of his employees presented some urgency, Jim asked that they sit quietly and allow him to sense the issue. Pick it up on his own. "You've received some very important news."

"As important as it gets."

"Kera, of course."

"Well. That's a no-brainer."

"And so is the timing. The clowns are listening now, aren't they?"

Sometimes Jim was a bit dramatic with the mentor role—and his criticism of NASA—but Jillian had always respected him. He was convinced NASA was pushing the spacestation concept because they knew, after flying ninety-some shuttle missions, that humans were destroying Earth's natural resources too fast for us to recover. As far as Jim was concerned, Mars was the clowns' first step toward a spacestation-to-spacestation network for transporting humans to other planets. That's why NASA was so interested in "Planet Finding."

"I flew down over the weekend and we made a three week plan. Jack and I are going crazy."

"I figured it out yesterday, you know."

Jillian thought of the bigwigs in their starched shirts and dark suits gathered around Jim's conference table. She heard the names they called him later, saw them hunched on barstools, laughing, mimicking him.

"I'm sorry. I wanted to be sure of my timeline."

"I saw something." He was going to go mystic. There was nothing she could do but wait. "It's that same look I saw so many times as we sat around the conference table talking about a whole catalogue of new planets. Those were the days, weren't they? When it seemed so far out?"

It still was far out. Jillian directed her eyes to the jade pyramid she held.

"You've kept up, used your team well, haven't you?"

"Jim, if it wasn't for this position, I'd be so out of touch. And you getting me involved in some of the early talks about the new space race." She was feeling a little too raw. Her eyes were getting hot. "I'm glad we got a little wacky at times, you know?" If only the clowns knew how wacky! Orbiters without rocket fuel, space catapults, space elevators that would ride bands of carbon to space ports above Earth's atmosphere. "And, of course, the funding. Kera and I both, we will always appreciate that."

"Well. We both knew it was temporary, didn't we, a sputter in the big stream." He dropped his hands, ready to talk. "Are they putting you through the application process?"

"Kera says it's a formality."

"Damn fools."

She had to redirect, quickly. A chat on bureaucracy could consume the day. "I'm going to take some time to figure out what needs to be drawn up and what can be summarized. I should be ready, by the end of next week, to go over everything with you and Nikki."

Jillian felt a surprising flare of emotion. Yes, there had been "money" projects: her *Life of a Star* simulations for museums and planetariums, setting up a series of tests for future spacestation-to-spacestation transmissions. Jim's wise-cracking bigwigs were hoping to use the network to introduce space currency: a trading system to keep future space dwellers in touch with their earthly accounts. But there had also been the graphic interface for a space probe, and her flight simulations. Jim had been approached by a group of investors who wanted to put out a challenge, a modern-day space race between private companies to build a cost effective orbiter. Something that could conceivably replace the aging shuttles, though she knew, in corporate hands, space tourism was the ultimate goal.

Still, without Mystic Jim and the projects he pulled her into, she might not have had any science at all. The public assumed astronomers and astrophysicists were simply hired and funded by the government. That they had secure, multi-year contracts and were housed at numerous research stations. The truth was much grittier. The late eighties and early nineties nearly brought NASA and the National Science Foundation's research programs to their knees. It was only through private investors that research such as hers and Kera's—too unique to duplicate readily—went on.

"Jillian, you concentrate on showing that damned government of yours what idiots they were not to jump on this a few years ago. The rest will fall into place."

"I'll be sure to mention that, Jim. But not on my first day."

At home, Jack and Jillian returned repeatedly to a gap in Jack's list. With Jillian gone, Manny would be without daycare on Tuesday and Thursday mornings. She had been staying home with him.

"What do you mean, switch daycare?" Jillian couldn't believe how immediate, how automatic Jack's reaction was.

Jack sat up, pressing his shoulders back. "Just what I said."

"You're willing to put Manny through a whole series of drastic changes, in three weeks' time, and you haven't even tried?" Let him rearrange his work hours. It hadn't been pleasant for her either.

"No one's going to let me make those kind of arrangements."

"What's so extraordinary about a father reorganizing his workday to take care of his child?"

"What do you want me to do? Build a lab in the basement?"

"It'd be easier than moving a forty-five-ton telescope." He looked away. "You haven't mentioned the idea to anyone, have you. You have no reports? No lecture notes you could work on at home?"

Carol, Manny's daycare provider, was full on Tuesdays and Thursdays. With Manny in kindergarten those afternoons, Jillian had made arrangements to work from home on progress notes and specifications she and Nikki could coordinate from any computer. Jack had the same tasks embedded in his day. Sure, she ended up doing a lot of work on nights and weekends, but so could he.

"What do you think I've been doing?" She scraped a truth and waited.

"I'm not the one pushing all the change."

Oh. Of course it had to go this low. What a child he looked like, sitting there all stiff, making a show of his defiance. She was embarrassed by his obvious attempt to manipulate her with guilt. Ashamed of his instinct to strike out when she refused to go along. In a matter of seconds, her simple solution had been exalted to an outrageous demand.

"Oh, I see. I can leave. You've got no problem with that. I can leave, as long as I understand Manny's going to pay for it."

Jack sat with his jaw clenched, making dark scratches on their latest list of things to do.

"You know what Jack? Manny's right. I'll take him along. How about that? I'll pull him out of school, move him down to Florida or Houston or California and just not worry about whether I'll stay or not."

"Talk about here we go again. Go ahead, Jill, tell me what I'm thinking."

If she wasn't utterly frustrated at his inability to budge, his face—jaw thrust forward—would have made her laugh.

"Carol cannot take Manny on his school mornings, and I don't want him put through any more changes."

Manny loved Carol, and Carol loved Manny. She didn't try to act like a mom. She was a friend who enjoyed Manny's humor. She goofed around with him. Manny couldn't lose Carol and his Mama too.

"Jack. Earlier this year when I changed my hours, we were in complete agreement that Manny needed to stay at Carol's."

Jack scribbled at his list. "No one asked you to do that. You did that on your own."

"Tell me you can hear what you're saying."

He sat, scribbling harder.

"Come on. Is Manny somehow less important now?"

"No." Jack looked directly into her eyes, blaming her for something he was feeling. Then he shut down completely. He took their coffee cups to the sink, rinsed them out, and walked away.

Jillian followed him upstairs. "There's no way I'm going to have time to find a new daycare provider. Neither are you. Don't you remember what that was like?"

She did. Places with names like *Happy Hippo Daycare* used office dividers and sheets of masonite to wall off groups of six to twelve kids each with a haggard adult. And the elite organizations, the learning centers with fingerpainting and outdoor gym classes, had waiting lists two years long.

A few days later, Jack provided his solution.

Jillian knew from his presentation that he had come up with something she wasn't going to like. He talked up his efforts, all the calls he had made, the influence he had exerted.

"I called the bus garage. Hear me out before you say it won't work. Actually, I talked to the transportation supervisor. Normally, they don't transport kindergartners because of the half-days, but he said they'd try it. As long as Manny didn't act up. Which I told him was not going to be an issue."

"A bus ride from where?" Manny stuck on a crowded, noisy bus filled with older kids?

"From home."

"You're going to stay home with him, until the bus comes?"

"Before you say anything, hear me out."

Oh, great. Great! Jack's mommy was going to bail him out. The transportation supervisor, Jack's mother, who wouldn't help out? People were running to offer their services! Jack was tall, dark, good looking. If he had to, he could stand outside Manny's classroom for a few days with his labcoat on for effect. Smile and chat. Sooner or later, a classmate's mother or daycare provider would offer: *Drop Manny off at my house.* Would he? Drop Manny off with someone they hardly knew? Someone Manny hardly knew? God, she wasn't sure he wouldn't!

"My parents are going to come over on Tuesdays and Thursdays for a while."

"For a while."

"Hear me out. I okayed it with Carol too."

Oh! Even Carol could bend the rules for Jack!

"She'll take Manny after school, as long as the bus drops him off right in front of her house. Which is all set. He won't have to walk anywhere, alone." His grin faltered. He knew all this talk about what was in Manny's best interest wasn't fooling her.

"You never approached it at work, did you?"

Silence. Of course, silence.

"How many hours did you spend on the phone? And how many hours after school do you expect Manny to sit at Carol's, waiting for you to pick him up?" She wanted Manny to be able to come home after school, not to have to go to another place where time and activities were structured. What were we doing to children's imaginations? None of his buddies would be there, only the babies. He liked helping, but was that his place? He was so proud when Carol let him push the stroller or keep the babies busy with one of his song and dance shows. Still.

"He'll be fine, Jill." Jack pulled at her elbows. "Come on. You can't fault me for trying."

She could, and she couldn't.

"You're lucky I don't have time."

13

To the Roof

JILLIAN HEARD MANNY AND JACK IN the bathroom, but the thought of seeing them together, identical grins warm and wet and red, was too much. She stood, drawing breaths of soapy humidity through the open slit in the doorway. Another baby. Another baby—now?—when Kera, when their chance, was really truly waiting? On the other side of the door, she knew, Manny was belly-deep in bathwater, making foam snakes and snowpeople in the water. But she couldn't go in, not even for his moist little face.

Upstairs in her room, she stared at the flashing red light on the answering machine, and she let the tears fall. *Message one: ten seventeen am.* Right about the time the nurse had said *Congratulations* and Jillian had gone too long without taking a breath.

"Jilli!" Of course it was Kera. Excited, impatient Kera. "I checked with review and they said your application's all set except for your doctor's report."

Twelve hundred miles of wire couldn't stop it. Jillian smiled at Kera's excitement and tears streamed into the corner of her mouth. Salty—overly salty—she could taste pregnancy.

"Knowing you, though, you probably haven't seen a doctor in ages." Kera's breath whooshed out the speakers.

She hadn't dared to. Not since she had woken up days before and her stomach had retched at the smell and the sight of her coffee, dark and swirling with oils.

"Okay. It's about ten a.m., I'll try back. Hey! I did a remote today. It wasn't real. I was underwater. But I felt like I was floating in space. Amazing. I'll see if I can send you the tape. I'll try back."

Jillian replayed the message, perhaps to make it real, maybe simply to feel the pain again, she wasn't sure. She and Jack, they had invited this possibility. Kera's voice repeated, "Hey! I did a remote today. . . ."

The nurse had said *Congratulations* a second time and Jillian said, "No."

Why did they always say *Congratulations?* Even the first time, when she had sat on a cracked plastic chair at the health center at Michigan Tech, certain it could not be so—she had been on the pill, the chances were too slim to believe—the LPN that performed Jillian's blood test had walked over to her and said, *Yes, I'm sure, it's congratulations.*

The message light flashed 2-2-2-2. She pressed play.

"Me again." They'd spoken at least once each day since Jillian had returned from their planning week in Florida. "It's about noon. Where are you? I'm dying to talk. I know you have a million things to do, but it'll all be worth it. For Jack too, I know it will. And Manny. I can't wait to see him. Okay, off track, way off track. I was thinking about Mount LeConte for some reason. The Llama train. We have to get back there someday. Oops. Sacred word. Not to be used lightly. Shit. There was something I really needed to tell you."

At noon, Jillian had been sitting on the bank of a polluted creek, not a river. When the nurse said again, louder, *Congratulations!* as if Jillian had not understood, she had left the doctor's office with the nurse chasing after her, *We haven't scheduled your next appointment!*

"Kera," she whispered into a long pause.

The Mulick River—Hah! Michigan knew its lakes, but the Mulick was no river!—flowed straight under a roadside park, diverted by a drain to the other side of the street. She had called Jack from a pay phone to tell him the pregnancy test was positive, but she never did get any words out. She'd been watching the muddy Mulick and thinking about driving away, simply driving off. But Kera and Jack, everyone was watching her, counting the days and the minutes until she left for Florida, they'd all know something was wrong. What would she do, really? Stop in Savannah or Jacksonville, have a secret abortion and drive on?

The minute Jack picked up the phone, she had cried. And he moaned, "Oh, babe." And when she couldn't stop crying, he'd said, "Stay put. I'll come and get you."

Kera's second message continued.

"So I'm daydreaming, and I screwed up a transmission. Totally fried a wire. You should have heard everybody, all at once in my headset. 'Sully, get your act together!' Not a great day. Well, actually, it was. That's it! I saw Hal today. He's going to have Arnie get our file from the Space Consortium. There's interest, Jilli. There is. It's perfect timing."

A man's voice razzed Kera in the background, making buzzing, electrical noises.

Jillian heard a thunk and the man's voice said, "Ow!" Kera laughed. "Sorry, we're all a—" The message beeped, cutting Kera off, which was not perfect timing.

It was awful to be standing there, her answering machine and Kera pregnant with what the next year might have held, while she had already been pulled away by a smaller, closer love. Hers and Jack's and everything it should have been able to be but couldn't, some-how, in their lives. People always said a home's value was all about location, location, location, but with her and Jack, they could never reconcile what they each needed home to be: his a big city hospital, hers a remote observatory.

That first time, at the Michigan Tech health center, Jillian had immediately inquired about abortion. And the same nurse who had said *Congratulations* minutes before handed her a pamphlet with step-by-step drawings of a vacuum aspiration: shots to numb the cervix; dilation rods to open it up; the tube that would suction everything out. For days, Jillian had been conducting home pregnancy tests, cer-tain that each test was flawed. But the strips kept turning clear-blue yes. And the dark cloud in the bottom of the test tube assembled itself into a bright red yes ring. Even when she watched that damned ring hold itself together as it washed down the drain, she didn't believe it. She was on the pill, what more could she do? She had gone to the health center, insisting on a blood test. And when the blood test came up positive—*Congratulations!*—she had left her car down below and walked up Agate hill. She turned on the star lights—gaudy, star-shaped lights they'd hung around their picture window—and she waited for Kera.

"One of those, huh?" Kera walked to the refrigerator, grabbed two Salt City Sluggers—their Manistee beer—and sat on the floor next to her. "Hit me."

Once the words were out of her mouth: "pregnancy test" and "positive," they weren't as injurious as Jillian had thought they would be. She had been tricked. It wasn't real. And when Kera said "No way," Jillian started to believe.

Kera once dropped a single birth control pill down a cold air register, and rather than buy a new pack and waste close to twenty dollars, they had removed the register cover and dug it out. Kera knew. What more could they do than dig a four-millimeter pill out from a four-foot-wide duct and then dust it off and swallow it?

Kera had clinked the string of stars, trying to humor Jillian. "Boy, I don't know if these things are heavy-duty enough for this." But Kera was still assuming, and Jillian was too, that they'd deal with it together and move on.

Jillian could barely see the answering machine's blinking 3-3-3-3.

"Sorry." Kera's voice was muffled. "We're all a little giddy. Hal had us mounting and remounting the connector strips between pods until midnight last night. And then, back at it first thing this morning."

Connectors, pods, midnight. *God, she wasn't going to be there! She wasn't going to be there!*

"Ow!" Kera paused, laughing. "I'm sorry. It's one big frazzle party down here. You're gonna love it. I'm gonna love it. I better go, though. The boneheads are throwing things at me. I think we're wrapping up. We've got some Hubble films to watch, then I should be home about seven. Call me Jilli! What's going on?!"

It was eight o'clock and Kera had no idea what Jillian had done to their plans.

She had gotten caught up in the house, and Manny starting school, the shrubs. She and Jack had painted each other's faces with dirt as they planted them, laughing about a weekend taken up with shrubs. She had called Jack *Mr. Jones* and they had wrestled, with Manny jumping on top of them and giggling. And later, as they sat in lawn chairs watching Manny perform a dance-rap, she had watched Jack dancing in his chair, flirting with Manny's gestures and special moves, and she had felt deeply sorry that their separate lives had kept them apart for so long. Alone, apart, they'd had a child. And she began to feel something she'd felt so strongly during her pregnancy with Manny: she felt weak with love.

She asked Jack if it bothered him, still, that he had missed Manny's birth. But he wouldn't admit it. Jack was such a soother.

Back then, she and Kera had agreed. Having your uterus vacuumed out sounded awful, but what was the worst that could happen? A perforated uterus, and then what? A hysterectomy? Would never being able to have children be as awful as spending the most productive years of their lives trying to prevent it?

But alone, in her room at night, Jillian was feeling confused. It was such an odd thing to do: *I love you. Let's vacuum it out.* And then, her grand mistake. She invited Jack into the decision and that made everything different. He had driven up after a huge board exam. When she saw his face, his eyes so blue and so red, she knew she was in trouble. With him far away, she could tell herself they weren't coming at this from the same angle. He was a man, she was a woman, the difference between them was insurmountable.

They had climbed the ski hill and Jack had remained quiet. Too quiet. She smirked to show she was okay. Picking at the grass, she told him about the procedure. He knew surprisingly little, abortion was a specialty covered only in gynecology. He rested his hands in hers and listened to her reasons: she had years of research ahead; she'd always figured she wouldn't have children; and then, of course (she must have pointed up) they both knew where she was headed.

But then, finally, she couldn't take it anymore. He wasn't struggling like she was. He wasn't pregnant. His mind was holding the idea, but her body was. Her body was!

They had talked all night, and with the sun rising, Jack stood, saying they'd better get some sleep. Sleep?! They hadn't made a decision! They hadn't put an end to her constant self-questioning: *I can't have a baby, can I?* Her exhaustive self-monitoring: *Why was she feeling so wishy-washy?* If there were moments when your life changed, moments that tested what you were really made of, *that* had to have been one of them. She had grabbed Jack's leg, reached out and held on with her eyes closed and said, "Tell me. Please. Tell me what you want to do."

He had bent down and wrapped himself around her, rocked her. He didn't want her to think he didn't care, so he was going to tell her the truth. Yes, he'd always figured he would have children. But not until later. Still, they loved each other, and they weren't teenagers. That made things complicated. At one point, he had whined in frustration, "I'm pretty stable. I could take the baby." And later, as he sat next to her, clutching the sides of his head, she had watched his tears fall into the grass. "Don't worry," he said. "I'm just fried."

At that moment, Jillian understood. She could have this man— gentle and strong and determined and confused—forever, if that's what she wanted. Or, she could have the abortion and they would be through.

She'd had opportunities, though, to break things off. *That's when you do it*, Kera had said, *Break things off, as soon as you start swooning. Together they had joked and despaired. This is war. We go in with a good pair of binoculars and a hefty roll pack, but no man. A man is too damned heavy to pack!*

Earlier, in the spring, Jillian had driven to Jack's world. To the University, the hospital, his apartment—the world she and Kera had been so eager to leave. The University of Michigan's Space Consortium had been fantastic. The physicists and astronomers and aerospace engineers she had studied with were all highly experienced and eager to help Jillian and Kera put together a new Astronomy minor at Tech. Jillian had worked with Dr. Powell, one of several women in the department, on a reclassification of Annie Cannon Jump's original spectrographs. The originals! It had been thrilling to touch Annie's notebooks, to reinterpret the same stars—feeling Annie's presence— but using much more sophisticated instruments. But with one twelve-inch mirror on the roof of a dormitory in the center of the light-flooded campus, she had pined for the Point, where the stars sprinkled down from the blackness and wheeled into Lake Superior. That's where she'd gotten pregnant, she was sure of it.

Jack had come to her world, to her and Kera's beautiful August world, and they'd driven out to the Point. She had driven Kera's Jeep, though she hadn't mentioned to Jack that Kera always drove. It had taken every bit of her concentration to keep the Jeep from getting stuck in those rutty, two-track roads, but they'd made it. With the sun about to set, they had walked to the furthest point of land as it curled into Lake Superior. She had scraped her boot over the ground to show Jack how thin the dirt was, how under the powder there was nothing but a stone plate. That's what she loved about the place. Both the earth and the sky were thin, designed to favor the stars.

They had said the "L" word, though they'd previously agreed during months of tense phone calls, not to say it. But once it was out, it was out. And later, as they watched the sky recede until only the stars seemed real and solid and true, they took off their clothes and dragged one sleeping bag to the edge of the water. They melded, skin to skin, as the Point's planetarium show wheeled around them. Jack had taken her hand and swept it across the sky, asking her to love him as she loved the stars, from a distance, and she'd felt a new sense of being.

Later, she would tell Kera it was the colors, the bright orange mosses and those tiny blue flowers that grew right from the mauve-colored rocks, and Superior's unnamable blue, at once so deep and dark but glowing with the purple of its rocky bottom. Because she'd stood there, holding Jack's hand, thinking: *So. This is love.*

It wasn't guilt that plagued her, not the guilt people assumed came with abortion. She could have gone through with it. She had pictured herself ghostly-white afterward, tired and relieved, Kera holding her hand. It was early. There was nothing more than a ball of cells, a blastocyte, embedded in the uterine lining. But—she would have to get away from Jack's hands and his eyes and her feelings, let the experience be her drive to keep going without him, because she never would have gotten over the resentment. She never would have been able to forgive Jack for being able to sit apart, waiting, while she made the decision.

Jillian didn't realize she was rocking until she heard Jack's voice.

"Babe?"

She looked away, fingering the answering machine.

"Manny's in the tub. I thought, if you went down and talked to him, I could get him to leave you alone."

She looked at Jack's eyes, their color heightened by all the emotion. She was pregnant and he was sorry—again. How had all their thoughts of togetherness brought them here, again, to a pregnancy that was wanted and unwanted, to a pregnancy that couldn't have been more ill-timed. She tried to walk around him but he caught her, and his touch pumped her full of "Sorry." His head on her shoulder, his arm across her chest. Why couldn't he see how it was hurting her? She stood stiff, bracing against his need.

Leave me alone. She burrowed it into his eyes. *Please, please, leave me alone.*

The bathroom air was warm and wet and hard to breathe. She knelt down beside the bathtub where Manny sat surrounded by floats of foam. He scooped one up and spread a glob on her arm. "Are you working?"

"Something like that."

He pulled her arm into the water. "Better wash it off. It gets itchy if it dries."

She put her arms around his wet body and hung on. She loved him so much. She knew Jack had come in and was watching them, watching her hang on to Manny, but she couldn't give Jack the same. She should never have wanted anything from him.

Upstairs, she removed the screen from the dormer window and crawled out onto the roof. She was sold on the house as soon as she saw the roofline, the dormer, and the possibility of adding a deck off the short slope in the back. They could sit at the high point of the neighborhood, sit above the suburbs gazing up at the stars, their night view edged by the trees.

She climbed to the peak and laid her back against the humped joiner shingles that softened the apex. It wasn't dangerous. All she had to do was relax, let the line of the roof peak settle into the flesh of her back, one side or the other, around her spine.

Stars, more and more of them, were beginning to poke through the hazy purple darkness. Albireo, the head of the swan, flashed yellow and blue, in its early fall position. The Pleiades would not be visible for hours. Perhaps not at all with the street lights blazing. A shiver ran through her. Her shirt was drenched from Manny's hug.

"Babe?" Jack's voice rose from the dormer window. "Jillian?"

"I'm up here."

"Maybe you shouldn't be. On that incline."

How quickly things changed. It was fine for her to be up there stringing Christmas lights, walking upright on cold, slippery shingles in November. But now, now that she was no longer herself, alone, the roof was too steep.

"Come in."

Leave me alone.

"Please?"

Leave me alone.

"Come on, babe."

"I will be wherever I want to be." She heard the statement—overly dramatic and once and for all untrue—and she wished Jack would go away. Go away so she could stop speaking, quit thinking in such melodramatic gestures. "Go be with Manny."

She looked toward the dormer, found the front of its peak, and drew with her mind a line down to Manny, in the tub. She hadn't been taken over or turned instantly maternal when she became Manny's mother. She simply loved him. She loved the funny little person he was becoming. When she and Kera were in California and Jack was back home with Manny, Jack used to call her during Manny's late-night bottle. The two of them, Jack always said, were watching west coast baseball. And she would turn on the same game.

Sometimes she yearned for the three of them to have been together, for togetherness to have been in their past. How could she say to this baby, *No, I've decided not to let you become?* She and Manny and Jack, they'd all made it.

How could she have known, when she decided to go off the pill, that all these possibilities would collide? NASA and Kera and Sorry and Congratulations, with Jack standing by. But was that really the issue? Or, was it: Sorry, Jack will never move with you. It will never be okay to have this baby and move on.

There were other memories. Memories of Jack letting his parents take care of Manny when she was gone. She would call home and his mother would answer the phone. She was constantly at their apartment, cleaning or doing the laundry. "So Jack can spend good time with the baby," his mother would say. As if Jack being bothered with the same things she would have been bothered with, had she been there, was such a shame. Jack caring for a baby and picking up the house and scrubbing bottles would be such a hardship. But she wasn't there, and that gave Jack and his mother all the room in the world to expect her to accept so much.

She looked up at the stars. *Does it look any different from there?*

She had gotten caught up in it, for awhile. It was time for Manny to start school. Time to let him settle down. *Is there something more I'm supposed to know? Tell me. Please.*

She heard Jack's voice from a distance and Manny's growing louder. She heard their footsteps and realized that the mourning doves that nested on their roof every year must hear them all moving around the house, just as she could hear the bird's spoked feet plunking over the dormer.

Manny was whining. "I want Mama to tuck me in."

"Mom's watching the stars," Jack said.

"I want to too." Jillian could hear Manny's feet running under her. He was headed for the dormer. Jack's steps, below, vibrated to the peak. "Not tonight."

Manny's voice thinned with a breeze. "I can help. I'll go get my kit."

Manny still had the little sextant kit Kera had rigged for him. She heard both Manny and Jack's footsteps move to the back of the house, to Manny's room, and Manny's bedroom window opened.

"Mom? Can I come up?"

Jillian wanted to answer, but she cried instead. Hot water streamed from her eyes, trickling into her ears. She couldn't move.

"Come on, bud. Mom's working on something."

"Sometimes I help."

Jillian pictured those nights on Mount Hamilton, that second fall when she and Kera and Manny were together. To keep him busy, they gave him graph paper to help chart the stars until Jillian would tuck him in for the night on his very own cot. He loved their graph paper. He knew he had the real stuff.

Jack's voice rose, louder. "Babe? Can you say good night?"

"Aren't you going to tuck me in?" Manny asked.

She imagined the two of them, leaning out the window, both of them silhouetted by the soft light of the bear lamp on Manny's dresser.

"Mom? What's wrong? Why can't I come up?" Little sobs floated up to her.

"Manny?" She directed her voice down toward his window.

She heard his bed squeak and Manny thumped against the window. "Mama? Will you come tuck me in?"

"I'm going to stay up here for awhile, bud. I'm right above you, hear?" She sat up and pounded.

Manny giggled. "You're right there? Right on my roof?"

She crab-walked down the back slope and stretched her body over Manny's bedroom, pounding again. "Right above you. You get into bed and I'll kiss you goodnight a little later."

"Everything okay?"

He sounded so adult-like sometimes, honest, and she couldn't lie to him. "I'll be right up here."

"Okay. Me too." He pounded on his window sill. "I'll be right down here."

"Good night, bud."

She heard Manny settle into bed and with a click, the spray of light that fanned out into the woods from his window went dark. In the silence, she pictured Manny, smiling as he dug into his pillow below her. Jack was probably making a list of things they should talk about, think about, work out. She knew he was hurting, but she had nothing to give. She was out, completely out. She looked up at the sky, with so many more stars appearing, and remembered Kera. Kera who was unknowingly fighting for their partnership, for their research to go on, to get them on the ISS together. No matter what she and Kera promised to make each other believe, someone else would get the job. Someone who could start and finish, now.

She located Albireo, a double star, one of the success stories. A binary couple that didn't demand too much of each other. Gravitationally paired, but they didn't exchange mass. Jillian always thought of her mother and her father when she saw Albireo's two distinct colors: a pale orangey-yellow and a minty blue. Gayle, the hippy who had been hauled away from more than one anti-war demonstration, and Manford, the president of the mathematics club, who had come out to his first demonstration after Einstein's impassioned call for peace. The universe was an expansive place, more expansive and complex than any one human could possibly understand. But there was one thing Jillian was sure of: love was part of it.

She believed in love. Was that so awful? She believed love was meant to be.

She had imagined, before Kera's call, a second baby's Manny-like face, but with Jack's darker skin. Even now, as she touched her stomach and told this new baby it would be loved, no matter what, she pictured Jack's searing blue eyes. They could make this work. They could.

Tears flooded her eyes and she appealed to blurry stars. "All I did was love."

With night cooling, she watched her words float away, hoping her breath would somehow rise and expand and make her good intentions clear, that the universe would hear and all would be right.

14

Something and Nothing to Prove

THEY WERE SITTING IN THE cafeteria, in the recessed floor area at the center of the huge Huskie gold room, when Jillian realized that the seating sections and railings that rose in terraced levels all around them directly reflected the landscape outside. There she and Kera sat—the only two students at lake level, the only two women in sight—with hundreds of men rising around them on the rugged hills of Houghton/Hancock. And suddenly, everything about Houghton and Michigan Tech became oppressively visible: the mine vats left exposed on the hillside, the gas station built in front of them; the historical markers; the history of maleness in the naming and claiming. Even the cafeteria said history, mining, men.

Male shoulders, dense bodies, long limbs spread out, spilling out of chairs, pushing into each other and the space around them. Coarse voices jabbed in loud outbursts—in chorus, never alone. If only she could hear one of them, just one of them, speaking softly. Their voices, their shoulders, the way they spread out and took up space; the competition forever present in phrases such as the one formed by wooden letters nailed over the entry door—*Through these portals pass the best engineers in the world*; the historical significance of the Keweenaw Commons; the gold-plated markers everywhere, like the one she could see sticking up from a pile of snow. Everywhere there were constant reminders that this was a mining town and Michigan Tech was a school of and for men.

Kera, surrounded by books and binders and running equations on her new scientific calculator, seemed oblivious. But Kera was adjusting better than she was.

At first, Jillian thought it was the way she looked. Maybe there was something about her dark hair and her light skin that said *soft*. But if anyone were to choose one of them strictly on the basis of how feminine they looked, they'd pick Kera. Kera looked like one of those Swedish supermodels compared to Jillian's compact, muscular body.

And their clothes. Jillian went for warmth. She'd given in this winter and purchased flannel-lined jeans. Kera wore her cords and jeans tight, sometimes layering two pairs, not to show off, but because loose jeans sagged from her hips and ended up dragging on the floor.

Kera was the one who climbed the high ledge at Big Canyon Falls without trying the lower ledge first, and Jillian knew why. She knew, even when Kera didn't, why Kera went for the top: she wanted to make sure she would dare to do it again. And then there was the dredger, Kera's (supposedly!) final induction into manhood. That damned rusty old dredger leaning over the bank of Portage Lake with its long crane arm extended out over the water, and Kera letting those yahoos from the Electrical Engineering fraternity talk her into jumping from it. Jillian would never forget watching Kera hanging upside down, her arms and legs wrapped around that rickety damned crane, inching her way out to the end of the ladder over deeper and deeper water. And when Jillian climbed after her—What else was she supposed to do?—her chest had filled with an awful fear. Not the good kind that prepares you to take a great risk, but the bad kind that swells up in your chest just before you do something really stupid. The kind that forever replays in your mind as you sit in a wheelchair, or worse, as your best friend sits in a wheelchair and you move on via the pedal power of your still-functioning feet. Jillian had followed along, hissing, "Kera! What do you have to prove?" And Kera had curled her body to eye Jillian directly, her upside-down face puffed with blood flow and her green eyes looking absolutely evil with desire. "This. Okay? This."

That's why they liked her. The wild bunch Kera hung out with liked her drive to compete. Even in her tight jeans and her weekend eyelashes—Jillian wasn't the only one who wore mascara now and then—Kera had proven herself one of the guys. The guys all said it: Kera's got balls. The professors knew it too: That girl's got balls.

"Can you hear that?" Jillian whispered.

Kera, hunched over their calculus pretests, grunted. She was running Jillian's numbers, trying to figure out why Anderson had scratched angry, red comments "Use formula!" "Where's the statement in the equation?!" on Jillian's test, underlined so fiercely that her paper was torn.

Every science had to have a foundation, its guiding principles. Jillian knew that. And she knew how to use formulas. Anderson was holding onto something that had nothing to do with physics. She put her hand over the test paper to get Kera's attention.

"Seriously, listen. The rest of our lives are going to be like this." Chemistry, biology, the new liberal arts college—some lecture halls and classrooms boasted close to 30 percent women. But not physics. Day by day there were only five or six women in Fisher Hall.

Kera's look suggested she knew Jillian was in trouble, but she was also annoyed. "Our lives?" Jillian was bringing up life when their calculus midterm was minutes away?

Only Kera's voice, two-toned and tremulous, was remotely mas-culine—sexy, really. People turned when Kera spoke, curious to see the face and the body that held her voice.

Jillian gestured around the room. "Don't you ever get sick of it? Their bodies, their voices, the way they look at us everytime we move?"

Several men at tables—the guy with the buzz-cut going over a midterm with his professor; three guys in Huskie jerseys at a table up one level from them—chewed and stared.

"So what? What's new?"

"Anderson stopped me on the way out of lab." Jillian let out a sigh and it almost squealed. Her throat was dangerously tight. She packed her books in her bag as fast as she could. Crying didn't go over too well in the School of Mines.

"Hey," Kera rose with her, "I was kidding."

No, she wasn't. She thought Jillian was becoming a drag; Jillian knew she was. And they were attracting attention simply by standing. She waved Kera off. An entire room full of men could rise forcefully, kick their chairs back with teeth-vibrating screeches, and no one bothered to take notice. But she and Kera, they couldn't make a move without being watched.

"Jilli. What the hell happened?"

"He said I better drop the class. I could take it next semester." Her eyes started to heat up. What Anderson said had been much more dismissive. *Perhaps this type of laboratory thinking isn't for you. Your ques-tions, they point to a lack of understanding of the basics necessary to complete the labs.*

"I can't play the man game anymore. I gotta go."

She left Kera sitting alone and hurried out the door, banging into several men who were passing through as she pushed her way out.

Michigan Tech, in the winter, was a giant wind tunnel. Its square and rectangular buildings, lining the lake in two parallel rows, provided a thoroughfare for Lake Superior's wind. She stepped into a gust that tried to take her scarf and she snatched it back. Winding the scarf around her neck, she pressed her chin to her chest and started walking toward town. Only the engineering tower she and Kera called the penis (because the top expanded into a crown) sat in the middle of the tunnel, obstructing the wind. *The penis my friend, is blowing in the wind.* Their winter carnival song, another wild night with the guys from EE. They were fun, a lot of fun, especially outdoors. And she had to admit, watching Clay hanging from the success side of the dredger, watching him spray paint *Kera* and *Jilli* in bright pink letters among a wall of red and black *Bill*s and *Dave-E*s and *Kirby*s, immortalizing them as the first women to jump from the dredger, that was wonderful. Exhilarating. But it didn't make up for the longer stretches of feeling so alone. Kera could always do it—whatever "it" they threw at her. What she didn't seem to understand was that lately, a lot lately, Jillian was tired of fighting. They had to stake their own claim: We belong! It was one thing when they were together, but when they got split apart, all the tests in the world weren't making Jillian feel "in."

She lifted her head momentarily, as if looking up the path could propel her through the blowing snow faster. She could barely see the bridge.

Houghton was a ten or twelve or twenty hour drive from almost anywhere else in the world. That's why she had chosen it: for the outdoors, for the stars. She'd read about the winters. She'd witnessed the historical marker near Copper Harbor that rose up like a giant thermometer, reading three hundred and twenty-one inches as the record snowfall. But she'd never considered the wind that whipped your face until your skin felt sanded. And the snowmobiles and the short days and the long nights that made you feel isolated, so far from anything but the campus and the town and the history of this very ungentle place.

Anderson had been dogging her since she had presented her Women in Science paper. She had pointed out that the women he often referred to as the "Heroines of Star Cataloguing" weren't secretaries. They were scientists. They chose to investigate stars that had already been discovered precisely because their male colleagues did not want to. And, of course, because women weren't allowed to use the observatories. Men photographed hundreds and thousands of stars on glass plates, moving from star to star as quickly as possible, naming and claiming. It was a woman, Cecelia Payne, who first formally joined astronomy with physics, analyzing the temperatures and chemical compositions of stars and making suppositions about the stars' inner workings. Cecelia wasn't taking dictation. She observed and recorded her own spectral studies and came to understand that stars were made mainly of hydrogen, that the entire universe—all of life—might owe its root beginnings to hydrogen and helium. Her PhD thesis on the chemical composition of stars was sweeping and majestic. "Stellar Atmospheres" ignited the field of astrophysics, but Cecelia wasn't granted a doctorate. Her male mentor, Shapley, was given credit. And the catalogue composed by several other women—Annie and Henrietta and Willemina—was published under the name Henry Draper, the infamous HD.

At the close of her presentation, Jillian had proposed that the acronym physics students often used to remember the chemical classifications of stars—"Oh, Be A Fine Gal, Kiss Me"—where O signified the hottest stars and M the coolest, be more directly credited to Annie Cannon Jump and the women who made modern star cataloguing possible. And their saying would have been "Oh, Be A Fine *Guy*—G for *Guy*, not *Gal*—Kiss Me."

The wind lifted chunks of snow from the rocks along the lake, and Jillian turned to avoid catching icy pieces in the face. Huddled with her back to the water, waiting for the wind to die down, she heard a sound and peeled back her scarf to listen.

It was the bells of the carillon marking the noon hour.

She stood listening to the soft, reverberating tones and recalled the plaque she had read in the library. Flemish bells and harp bells and celeste bells, they called to her with a gentleness she'd almost forgotten. She and Kera had been working so hard that they had lost their late night talks to formulas and equations. They'd gotten up that morning at five o'clock to pore over their pretests one more time. Everyone knew what Anderson's job was: to weed out the weak.

Lake Superior's forcefulness, evident in the blowing snow, curled around her and streamed on to the Administration building, around the penis, and eventually to the square of Fisher Hall. Maybe the Women in Science Scholarship did leave her with something to prove. Fear, after all, was a positive force, if you understood its roots. The heart palpitations, the increased awareness of stimuli, the feeling that she was sinking into insignificance beside the battalions of men all around her. All of it was preparation. Fight or flight. It was her own nervous system readying its protective mechanisms.

Right now, all she could do was take the test or not, and there was no way she was going to run. She headed toward campus, stepping in time to the carillon's song.

Tradition, that's what was so weighty at MTU. Male tradition: male sounds, male need to overpower, male deodorant soap smells. That's what Kera didn't get sometimes. Jillian wasn't trying to become a man, she had every right to be a woman *and* be accepted as a scientist. Her questions didn't mean she didn't understand. She wanted to understand better, more, completely. How else was she going to experiment and test and apply? She understood Anderson's formulas, she just didn't believe in them absolutely. If Vera Rubin—the woman she had selected to study for next year's scholarship—was right, over 70 percent of the universe consisted of something other than atoms and matter and mass. In Vera's universe full of dark, exotic energy, traditional ideas about mass and gravity would have to be questioned.

The carillon's song ended as Jillian passed the library, just in time. Anderson would pass out the test at 12:10. And she was going to wear mascara whenever she liked and continue to ask "Why?" and "Why not?" She would stay on top of the work in the evening lab, when grad students who understood what she was questioning entered into a circle of discussion—sometimes heated, often frustrating, but open. And perhaps, as Kera had suggested, she would spend more time with one of the nature boys she had become good friends with. Perhaps Paul from Forestry could remind her why she liked men and their bodies and the way they talked and smelled.

Shaking the snow from her scarf and hat and double-layered gloves, she walked the dark hallway of Fisher Hall. When she entered the room, Kera and Anderson both looked up with expressions of surprise: Kera's full of worry; Anderson's followed by a taut grin. She was going to pay for not dropping his class on this last day to drop.

She concentrated on her breathing. She had nothing to prove. Nothing to prove to Anderson anyway. She might have something much more important to prove to herself.

She would never believe, not with blind adherence to tradition, in the ugly side of science—the drive to disprove, discredit. And she certainly didn't want to grow balls.

She didn't have to do either to belong.

15

Day Five—The Old Man

SHE WAS SLEEPING IN HER BEACH chair, journals piled in her lap, when a cold wave washed over her ankles and she started upright. She was in a strange place; she shouldn't have left the tent. Every time she left it she felt uneasy.

A man was walking toward her from the north, far off to her right, following the slow curve of the campground beach (she remembered: she'd hiked to the campground beach) and she was certain, instantly, that it was the old man she'd seen following day hikers on Day Three. Surrounded by the lake's sparkling silver, his silver hair blended into the water so that his head appeared to be only a slight, dark dot.

She'd been dozing all day after running away from South Manitou Island the day before, and after the hike back through the woods in near darkness that evening. She'd been so riled by the snaps and the dark shadows and the possibility of meeting up with a bear that she'd plunged down to the lakeshore and walked on the sand all the way back. Her four mile sprint across the island coupled with four more miles in the sand had left her so tired she'd actually slept.

The old man waved and she waved back. Damn it, she wanted to sulk alone. If he hadn't caught her looking at him she would have folded her chair and disappeared into the bowl between the dunes. But not waving, one on one as they were, would have been rude, perhaps even hurtful.

She'd gotten herself all jazzed up that morning, flipping through astrophysics journals. The big journals always made her feel inadequate. Who were these people who devoted years to extensive research projects and still managed to pump out papers every other month? "Rotation Curves in Active Galactic Nuclei." "Hubble Spies Puzzling Pariahs, Planet-Sized Objects in M22." "Cepheid Variables and Quasars, The Next Standard Candles for Cosmology?" She scanned the contributor notes: eleven men, two women, and that's when she'd really gotten angry. No matter what the colleges or job surveys or economic statisticians claimed, the pipeline to scientific success was leaking—horribly. Men and women entered graduate school in equal proportions, but year by year, more and more women were siphoned off by the phenomenon schools referred to as "personal/family interruptions." And once you'd been siphoned off, it was tough to get back in.

Day Five: halfway. That's why she'd gone to the island, to avoid the slump. There was nothing wrong with the idea. Seeing the Perseids skid across the dome at a rate of forty or more per hour certainly would have refreshed her. Even here, she'd seen a few streaks fizzle by through the gauze of her tent top, but she'd been so tired and so disappointed at not being on the Perched Dunes where the light would have tailed green and gold and burned with a flare of purple-blue at the end, that she'd zipped the roof flap shut to punish herself. She'd hung the lantern several feet away on one of the trees that held her food cable, telling herself to be brave, and she'd whimpered herself to sleep. She couldn't hurt herself anymore than she already had by running away from the stars on South Manitou Island or by giving into Jack's schedule when hers should have been equally important.

The old man wasn't as old as Jillian expected him to be, and his hair, up close, was more yellow. White and silver and yellow melded together by the sun. He called out as he neared. "Another beauty. You camping?"

She gestured down the beach where the far reaches of the ridge seemed to join with the lake, where scruffy brush and waving dune grass mellowed into a green-black haze. "You too?"

"Yup. Have for twenty-nine years." He dropped his head when the cold water washed over his toes. "Almost didn't make it this year. Which loop are you in?"

He hadn't understood about her tent, her dune spot, her bravery. She'd come to the campground beach hoping to relax among a crowd of strangers, but when she'd arrived this beach looked the same as hers: empty. She rose from her chair and pointed far south. "I'm right about there, where that last dune juts out. How about you?"

"Not the Hemlock."

Jillian laughed—too loud. After days and nights of silence, her body had become an instrument for receiving sound. Even her own Mantra, repeated silently in her head—*Day Five. Five. Five.*—was beginning to blend with external sound, and she wondered if the vibrations in her mind were being sent out into the world. "So, you're roughing it," she said, modulating her sound. Only the Hemlock, precious and new and closest to the lake, had running water and flush toilets. She wanted to joke: *Roughing it was digging a hole and trying to relax with the black flies swarming!*

"Should have gotten here earlier. I hemmed and hawed, getting packed. Came in over the weekend. It's getting so you have to be here early in the week to get a good spot."

She was sweaty and slimy from falling asleep in the sun. Hopefully, the seeing would be decent; she'd be awake all night after napping.

"Me and my wife and all four of our boys used to come every year. From the east side, north of Flint."

She resisted following his gesture. She'd given that up, looking southeast, over the trees, wondering how they were doing at home. Though she couldn't stop thinking about Peia.

"A small town with a funny name. Flushing."

Jillian eased out a "Hm." She knew exactly where Flushing was.

"We came out that once, and we just kept coming back."

She took in the whole of the lake, letting its immense, sustaining rhythm calm her as she wiped sweat from her arms and her neck. Just as she had vowed to take the Smokies sun with her forever, she would always remember the lake's silver: the oily purple grace of morning, the silver-white highlights of midday, the hot-silver aquas and oranges just after sunset. And finally, late at night the lake and the sky blended into their most beautiful—the silvery purple-black that echoed the stars. "There's something about this place, isn't there? You get hooked."

"Yup. We got hooked." He stooped to pick up a stone, and though Jillian had settled in for a moment of gazing, hoping he might move on, the old man moved into conversing. "Well, look at that. A petosky. Years ago, the boys would find hundreds of them." He held out the pebble, rough on one side, smooth on the other, patterned with glossy, web-like shapes.

Jillian took the stone, comparing its sides, while the old man went on. She let his voice narrate some of the same facts Kate Sullivan had once told her. Used to be, the rocks were abundant in the Bay of Petosky, an hour to the north. Now, it took a keen eye and a strong surf to find them. "You ever polish them? Every once in a while one of the boys would get one going. But I never could get more than half a stone to shine. Mine were always waxy looking." Bubbles sprang from tiny air pockets as the water pulled back from the sand, and the old man dug after the bubbles with his toes. "The boys used to make Ada the most god-awful jewelry. She'd wear it though. She'd wear it."

"Ada. What a nice name." Jillian pictured Ada: short, stout, motherly. Peia wanted to be Cassie because her name sounded like something you do in the bathroom. And of course, the Jack and Jill jokes abounded. *Hey Jack, where's the crown? Jill, what are you doin' with a guy like Jack? Don't you know where he's headed?*

The old man skipped a stone. He was good—it bounced four times. "How about you? You from around here?"

He would recognize the town, might picture her neighborhood, and she didn't want to talk home. "You know that lone house that sits near the state park entrance?"

"The old railroad depot? With the train cars sitting out front?"

"That's Sully's Depot."

His mouth curled up in a grin. "We used to go swimming at the Beach House, and every time we passed that old place we'd dream about buying it. Even the kids. So that's where you live, huh?"

To agree she'd have to negate the farm house and the river, her own mother and father. That hard liquid pain struck her lungs. Still, Sully's Depot was a second home, a heart-home. "I spent summers there, with a friend from college. The Sullivans, they've owned the place since the state decided to clean up the old rail yard."

"Quite a story, isn't it." He moved his arms, chugging like a locomotive. "The way that storm buried the old engine, and they never could get those other two cars pulled out."

Jillian laughed. He was funny. "They were planning to log here, until the tracks drifted over. It was too expensive to lay new track so they kept going north."

"Good old Mother Nature." The old man winked. "You mind walking? These old legs don't like to stand still for too long."

Jillian took the high sand, letting the old man slosh along the gentler slope of the shallows. His skin sagged away from his chest and stomach, but there was obvious musculature underneath. And nothing about his legs looked old. He could be a retired military man or an astronaut.

"You and your friend. Did you go to college around here?"

"Michigan Tech." Jillian waited for the typical reaction: *Way up there?*

"You don't say."

"We started some research in astronomy, right here at the lighthouse, and it grew into a big project out West."

She remembered Kera's giddiness that first time they sat in the control room, feeling the rumble of the telescope's motor—*Holy shit Jilli! Holy fricking shit. Giddyup!* Jillian had pinned a drawing above the imaging station of Kera straddling the barrel, riding it like a rocket.

"You know about all that, huh? Stars and space and all?"

"My own little bit." Jillian was seven months pregnant with Manny when they first went to California. Kera had drawn her on the rocket too, but not pregnant.

"You don't say. Well, that's fantastic. Will you get to go up, then?"

She thought of Evelyn Young, the Space Shuttle Commander, and Evelyn's friend Patty Hall, the biologist doing slide transfer studies. She imagined Kera in the Vomit Comet, trying to hold on. Jillian could do it. She could ride the comet, any day, anytime.

"It all depends. If I get enough training time."

The truth was, she'd come and gone too many times and now NASA wouldn't have her. In a few months, she'd be forty, too old ever again to be considered for astronaut training.

"Well. I've never met an astronaut."

"Yeah."

"So you're with NASA then."

She nodded and shrugged, something between a yes and a no, and she blushed. She'd never been a good liar. She and Jim and Nikki could submit an infinite number of contractor's proposals to supply designs, optics, simulations, but she'd never go up. "We're getting ready to set up a science lab. A big one. As big as a bus." Kera was training for the all-science mission, and the two of them were hoping Jillian might end up supplying light-nulling masks for Hubble, as a trial. Funny, how she'd always felt she had years ahead of her. There was no official age limit, but it was well known that getting in *after* forty was nearly impossible. Kera was turning forty too, but Kera was in. What had ever made Jillian think she was special? She wanted to laugh. Time had defeated her after all. Simple, straight forward, point A to point B time.

"I bet you work with computers a lot. One of my sons, the oldest, he's been in computers for years. He's got mine all set to log in to the news and weather, but that's about all I do. I just never got the hang of it. Ada, she could do pretty much anything."

"I do a lot of simulations and modeling." Always a modeler, never a doer. That was the truth.

The old man stopped, shielding his eyes and looking out over the lake. "Sometimes you can see the Badger, the old passenger ferry."

"I saw it a few days ago, going out for a night cruise." Jillian sensed that the old man was far away, so she waited.

"You have kids?" he asked.

"No." The meanness of it surprised her, but why should it? Women astronauts didn't have kids. Not until after, like Evelyn Young. Peia's foot stomped into Jillian's mind, but it was Manny who came to her fully. (She couldn't have handled Peia's insistence. Hail the human mind for knowing what it could and could not take!) Gayle was drawing Manny and Jillian together, Manny as a toddler in her lap. Her mother had taken out Jillian's kindergarten picture, put her fingers over Jillian's pigtails and pointed to Manny. "Look, baby. Without the hairdo, he looks just like you." Except for Jack's crooked smile.

"No. I don't suppose you could have kids, could you," the old man said. "Probably no husband either."

Jillian wondered if Kera felt defensive when she answered these questions, or did she fill with pride—a woman alone, an astronaut.

"Oh," Jillian mimicked Kera's chuckle, "I had one of those once."

The old man looked carefully at her. "You don't need some old geezer asking you nosy questions."

"I'm used to it." She tossed her head, feeling perhaps for the first time that she truly understood Kera's head tosses and that swipe of her hand. Kera didn't let anyone make her feel wrong.

Alone, apart, she and Kera would always feel angry and isolated. Together they simply accepted and understood each other's abilities and limits. Kera was sometimes too quick, too single-sighted. Jillian often slowed down, getting herself tangled in all sorts of details. But the drive to protect each other—to keep each other *in*—that had always been their fuel.

So she told the old man about NASA's new Planet Finder project, a mission they (as if she were directly involved) hoped to launch in a few years. They would start with an orbital telescope about the size of Hubble. Even if one of the masks didn't work, they'd simply rotate the disks out of the way and the space telescope institute would have a second two-meter mirror above the atmosphere, a Hubble twin. But to find close planets, the best way to nullify starlight would be a system of linked mirrors. That's what NASA would be interested in, a wide-field view into the habitable zone around the closest stars. NASA was always interested in finding new planets. And deep down at the core of her story, deep down where the old man could not possibly detect it, a kernel of truth still burned: Researchers began cataloguing new planets just three years after she and Kera thought they had discovered the first. And Jillian would never, ever forget that feeling.

She and Kera had jumped up and down when they first saw it, a faint edge of light off to the side of tau Ceti. Then they'd gotten serious. They imaged and reimaged tau Ceti and their control star, comparing the empty area of darkness on their control image to the faint object they had imaged with tau Ceti, to verify that there was no similar bump or ripple that would point to misaligned optics or problems with the camera or simply a scratch on the lens. But on exposure after exposure, that incredible curve of new light stayed. They did everything they could to prove that their crude boxy coronagraph had failed, but after three nights of scrutiny, they knew it hadn't. The faint round object they could see within the scattered light of tau Ceti's halo was real.

They ran a final set of exposures using J and K band filters to determine the object's temperature and realized that what they had photographed was probably a faint companion star, too cool to see without more advanced adaptive optics, but too hot to be a planet. Tau Ceti appeared to have a faint close old friend, beautiful in her own right, but to announce their discovery, they'd have to rule out a line of sight error, the light of a faraway star that had reached the image, and that would take intensive study and time, which they didn't have.

They had built their coronagraph too early, that was all, but they knew way back in 1991, when they'd imaged the cool round shape of a companion in tau Ceti's slightly nullified halo, that it would only be a matter of time before planets outside of our solar system would be discovered. Someday, those planets would be *seen*.

The problem was, their ideas weren't new anymore. Now, at the upcoming fall conference where she and Jim and Nikki were scheduled to present, another team would be presenting a similar idea. A team from Princeton, a long-time NASA collaborator. It didn't matter that the seeds for the original idea had been planted over ten years ago. It didn't even matter, now, that The University of California had gotten their planet-finding program funded a few years after she and Kera had left. Nulling light in the visible range had been too complicated when she and Kera had first investigated the possibility. But now, everyone was looking back to visible light and mirrors. Now, in response to NASA's call for the latest ideas in planet-finding technologies, two men from Princeton had pushed through a decade of her own on-again off-again attempts, with a simulated telescope, a mask, and a beam of laser light. Using lasers projected through their masks, they had found a way to *prove* they could combine the tiny troughs of darkness and cancel out the peaks of visible light. And now, they, too, were shooting for space.

"So you're all the way out there by yourself." The old man smiled up at Jillian, looking like a proud father. "I wish I had that kind of guts. Hell. I wish my boys had that kind of guts."

To hell with guts. She wished she could leave her chair and her bag of journals and keep heading south. Pretend she was being walked home by an old friend. There were so many ways to care for someone, to support them, believe in them. Out there, alone, she was growing weak and tired. She needed care, even in the smallest way. "It's not so bad. There was a young couple nearby for a few days."

The old man stopped and so did she. Her mouth didn't want to work either. The silver of the lake's dinnertime calm brought her near tears, and she wondered if the silver old man and the lake had somehow melded together, colored each other after all these years. Would she silver too? She hoped so.

"I guess we should turn around," he said. She thought she saw a frown tug at the old man's face. "You've got to get all the way back."

Jillian moved into the shallows for the return trip. No beach ankles this time. "I go back and forth on the Dune Ridge trail. My car's in the parking lot."

"Me and Ada used to backpack. But after it got hard for her to get around, we bought the trailer. A big fifth wheel. A lot more comfortable."

Comfortable—Jillian imagined the word as a strip of clouds. She closed her eyes for a second and imagined one of those wallpapered rooms at the Depot; sinking into cool, dry sheets without sand. It wasn't the kids' fault, it was hers, really, and Jack's for refusing to see what he was asking her to do. Doctors didn't follow their scientist-wives. What was that quote: *Every good doctor needs a wife?* They had the same quote when it came to work at the observatories: *What every astronomer needs is a wife.* Why couldn't people understand? No matter how much she loved her children, they would never be a trade-off for what she didn't do. And "never" was a parasitic word. She'd seen "never" eat away at others: at her mother, though Gayle always tried to hide it. Why else would she cry, standing in front of a Chagall or a Pollock? Of course, after losing her father, nothing in their lives seemed worthy of complaint. She had to be thankful for family, always.

There suddenly, out on the lakeshore, she wanted Kera more than anyone. Kera, who was still trying to protect her. But she had to do this alone. Ten Days. *This* she would stick to.

"Boy, has the town changed, Manistee. Used to be the channel, a few restaurants and pubs. Now there's condominiums, a park, a whole new downtown. I'll tell you. The best time to go is Fourth of July. There's a great parade. And the Clown Band. The kids used to love them."

Jillian was silent. She tried to smile. And the old man filled the space again.

"Yup. I'm pretty old these days. We used to hike the trails, me and Ada. She loved the trees. Knew the names of all of them..."

After Peia was born, she joked with Jack that she had entered a dark time, purposefully avoiding the journals and the conferences and NASA updates because they hurt too much. *You'll get back to it,* he said, as if her life could be lived in spurts. She had begged him, so many times, to imagine doing half his work. What would his research amount to if he stopped, slowed down, rearranged his schedule every few days, weeks, years? But he always stood quiet, with the same blank look. He couldn't imagine.

"And rocks. She'd have me out there for hours looking for petoskies. But agates, agates were her favorites."

Ada was gone, of that Jillian was sure. The old man's recollections, the way he identified every landmark as a part of their past—he was nostalgic. Maybe Ada was that good. Maybe she had packed the old man's and her four boys' lunches and smiled. Maybe Ada loved being needed. Maybe the old man was wishing Ada still needed him to carry her from the trailer to the deck, or to wrap her up in something warm.

She could see her chair and the bag of journals that sat waiting for her to fold them up and lug them over four more miles of trail, back to her spot of aloneness.

"But that was one of the last times we went all the way past Nordhouse. We used to walk all the way to the big light."

Jillian wiped her eyes. She was constantly digging sand out of her eyes. "Well, that's eight miles one way." How she knew those eight miles! Her ankles still ached in the morning.

"I don't think a one of my boys would do it." He turned, looking at her arms. "You, on the other hand, you look like you could knock off a hundred push-ups."

"Maybe in stages." Jillian had passed the lighthouse twice on Day Two, but there were too many people. When she climbed its scrolly stairs and lifted herself through the trap door, she wanted the top to herself. "Have you been to Big Sable?"

"Yup. Did that earlier this week. They're tying her right down, aren't they. I guess tying her's cheaper than fixing her."

Boy, did that sound familiar. The old man would fit right in with Kate: *In the old days, the state kept the lights in decent shape.*

The old man half-turned a few times but stayed close as Jillian packed her things. "Time to head back, huh?"

"Yeah. I love the woods, but not in the dark."

They walked the dune bowl together, where the air was always still. After being baked all day the sand released stores of heat.

"I'll bet you know a lot about the stars. Maybe I'll take a gander on the deck tonight." The old man looked as restless as she was feeling.

"Sometimes, I walk along the beach with my lantern planted half-way up the dune." She had no idea why that seemed important to say.

"You too, huh?"

"The water looks eerie, doesn't it?" Jillian asked. "So thick and black."

The old man tapped her arm as they reached the big wooden deck. "I'll be down on the beach tonight, so you think about that if you want to."

She stood with her sandals pinched between her fingers, ready to go. "I will." She wanted to say more. *Why don't we meet on the deck tonight? I'll show you the constellations.* But what would she do when it came to one o'clock in the morning and she was four miles from her tent? Follow the old man to his campsite and curl up behind his trailer? She heard Kera's voice: *Why the hell would you come all the way out to the Manistee National Forest to get away from one man, to take care of another?*

If only Kera knew, today, how deeply she needed someone to care for her.

"You have a good night." She nodded and headed into the trees, thankful for the forest's cooling vapor. She was in the middle, that was all, weak and tired and stretched. But that's how the middle of any problem was: a soup of effort and doubt you eventually had to leave behind, acknowledge as some part of the process and move on. She stopped a few feet up and turned around, feeling as if she hadn't properly concluded the conversation. She saw him sitting alone on the deck.

"Hey. Will you be here long?"

He stood, smiling. "I'll be here all week."

"I've got some great maps of the constellations. If you're out on the deck tomorrow or the next night, look at the ranger's board. I'll leave one there for you."

"Well." He huffed but looked pleased. "You can't come all that way on my account."

"I have to load up tomorrow or the next day anyway."

The old man looked as if he were going to cry. "Well, that would be fine. That'd be fine." He held out his hands and clasped them quickly around hers. "You be careful now."

She turned, feeling much better, and headed up the path that would take her into and out of the woods; past the campground loops; across platforms the rangers had constructed as overlooks. She would stop and draw deep breaths but keep going. This—Day Five, Day Six, all the way to Ten—*this* she would stick to. For ten years her research had been pocked with interruptions, and she wasn't about to hide that hurt from anyone—not Jack, not the kids, not anyone, anymore. Why should it surprise her that coming and going from solitude hurt?

It was nearing dusk and the black flies swarmed her hairline, after the sweat that still dripped into her ears and ran down her neck. What a place, this universe. No hiding. Every organism, the silver on the lake and the silver in the old man's hair, even stars and galaxies and now pariah planets, feeding off each other.

Later, hours later, after she'd gazed up at the stars and watched a few of the Perseids sizzle across the night sky, Jillian woke, listening for the waves. Once she found their pattern she assured herself she'd been dreaming. There was no voice.

Did space have a voice, like the waves?

She stared at the damp inner lining of her tent, green and moist and lantern-lit, the old man's *You don't say* echoing in her mind. He had clicked too, clicked his tongue and shook his head whenever he looked out over the water. She imagined the old man on the campground beach, walking the shore with his lantern planted in the sand.

She shut her eyes and Jack's voice came to her, wrapped in a soft chuckle, teasing away her toughness. *Jill.*

No.

Yesterday, just yesterday, she had made it through the night with her lantern hanging twenty feet away. So much back and forth. Gain and loss, gain and loss. Jillian heard its rhythm in the water, far below. She pulled her nylon vest over the lantern. Tomorrow. Tomorrow, she'd send the lantern back outside.

16

Bad Mornings

JACK ROSE FROM THE BED AND walked, a shadowy automaton, to the alarm on the dresser. The night before, Jillian had said to him, "Don't leave the room unless I'm up, okay? And try to say something nice."

Every morning his alarm went off at 4:50. He showered, ate a bagel and a bowl of cereal, left his dishes at the side of the sink because the clean dishes from the night before were still in the dishwasher—he made way too much noise unloading them—and then he came up at 5:25 to kiss Jillian goodbye.

This morning he changed his routine by one sentence. "Are you up, or do you want your alarm set for 5:30?"

Jillian used to feel hurt, even punished, by the lack of joy—at least affection—in his morning voice. But after years of these mornings she knew it was just Jack. He was looking forward to the work of the day and he wanted the straightest route to it. He got ready and he left. That was all.

"I'm up," she said, and Jack left for his shower. She put on the exercise bra and bike shorts she had laid next to the bed and tiptoed into the upstairs bathroom to plug in the old baby monitor, which now served as a workout monitor. Manny and Peia's bedrooms were on the second floor. Her exercise equipment was two floors away.

In the basement, she stretched to the hiss of shower noise blaring from the monitor, then jumped on the Lifecycle. Thirty minutes on the bike, set on random—an interval workout that simulated natural hills—was almost as taxing as a good run, which she couldn't leave the house to do.

Jack came down after his bagel and cereal, which she heard him toast and pour. "I'm leaving." He leaned in to kiss her cheek.

"Hey." She motioned with her head for him to come back, closer. Some mornings they barely touched. But this morning she was feeling good. She leaned into him, kissing him fully. He hugged her and smiled, blowing her a kiss as he left.

The yellow dots that signified hills started to rise on the screen, and Jillian missed Jack's smile. She wished she could make that simple effort to be pleasant to him every morning. Let him know it was okay to leave, okay to leave her there with the kids. She would never agree that this was their only option. For now, until he figured out how many classes he was going to hang onto, now that they'd made him Department Chair, Jack needed the extra time, mornings in his lab. And what good did it do once morning was here and it had to progress, to mumble and scowl with resentment? They'd balance things out.

The yellow dots shot up, sustaining a three minute peak, and she started to sweat profusely. Her forearms were coated and glossy, her head was drenched. Streams of sweat trickled down her back and chest. She was fourteen minutes into the ride, getting into the meatiest hills, when she heard Manny's voice.

"Mom? Mom?" With his bed right next to his bedroom door, his face was only a few feet from the monitor.

Jillian pushed hard on the pedals. Her whole body galloped a bit off the seat to make the grade of another three minute climb. *Go back to sleep. Please.*

"Mom? Are you up here?"

She felt her chest clog with a palpitating surge.

Manny's bed creaked. She heard him walk across the hall and into her room. His voice sounded worried. "Mom? Mom?"

Ah! She was at the top of the hill. *Come down. Come down.* She used to work out every morning. Years ago, when Manny woke early, he would pad into her room and finding her gone, he would lean close to the monitor and try to scare her with an evil whisper, or simply reassure: *Mom, I'm going back to bed, wake me up when you're done.*

Today, he was caught off guard. It had been so long, so long since she'd worked out in the morning. "Mom? Where are you?"

Then Peia whined. "Be quiet. You woke me up."

With both of them awake, it was worth a holler. "I'm downstairs, working out! Manny! I'm downstairs!" If he would just come down, check, without any more talking.

"Mom? Mom?" He was talking all the way down the stairs.

"Be quiet!" Peia shouted.

Jillian swung off the bike, meeting Manny in the kitchen. "I'm working out, bud."

His face relaxed. "Oh. Sorry."

"Why don't you lie on the couch." Manny pursed his lips for a kiss, she tucked a throw around him. "Go back to sleep. I'll be up in about fifteen."

Downstairs, she pedaled until the screen lit back up and she set the resistance level at a solid five. The random program would revert back to warm-up and she wanted at least ten more minutes at a tough pace. The Lifecycle timer was at 53 seconds when Peia hollered out. "Hey! Isn't anybody going to get me?"

Manny sometimes liked to wake Peia before he left for school. He ruffled her mattress, tossing her about as if the bed were a boat. Bed tremors he called them. Peia would giggle so hard she'd get Manny laughing and he'd run out of strength. But this morning Manny knew better. When Peia was jostled from sleep too early, she was grumpy. "She's up, Mom."

"Mom!" Peia shouted.

"She's working out," Manny hollered. "Go back to sleep. It's way too early."

The timer read 1:20. Jillian sighed. Her heart was pounding. It was one of many mornings, a first attempt. There would be others, more successful.

"I want to get up," Peia whined.

"Then come down." Manny said.

Jillian knew what kind of morning they would all have if Peia didn't go back to sleep. She hopped off the bike.

Upstairs, in Peia's room, Jillian rubbed Peia's back and kissed her cheek.

"Ew. Sweaty."

Jillian went back downstairs and rolled out on the living room floor to stretch. Manny watched sports highlights with the sound off, something they agreed to with hand signals. Just before six, she signaled Manny that she was going into the shower.

Peia called. "Mom! Can I come down?"

She should have stayed on the bike. "If you lay on the couch."

"Come and get me."

"I can't honey, I've got to get into the shower."

"I'll get her." Manny and Jillian went up the stairs together.

Jillian gave Peia a quick kiss. "Manny's going to bring you down." She went to her room to get her work clothes.

"No!" Peia hollered. "No Manny. I want Mama!"

For such a bright, creative child, Peia could be incredibly babyish. Jack said it was her kind of separation anxiety. Why wasn't Jack around then? Peia hated to get ready for school and be hurried out the door.

Manny jumped on Jillian's bed. "She won't let me." His feelings were hurt.

Jillian kissed him on the head. "You get in the shower. I'll get her."

"Will you come right down?"

It was a few minutes after six, normal shower time for Manny. "Yes. Now get going." Manny was a little spooked lately. He showered and peed with the door open.

"Come on. Let's get you to the potty." Jillian pulled Peia's covers back.

Peia clung to her covers, winding up in them. "Fuzz?" Fuzz, a scraggly stuffed bear, slept with her every night. If Peia got ready without a fight, Jillian would talk "Fuzzy-talk."

"Fuzz isn't going to say a word until you get up and get dressed."

Peia rolled over on her stomach and tucked up on her knees. "One." She began her count. Peia had run out of math in the classroom, Jillian taught her fractions. "One and a half." Each increment was followed by some painstakingly slow movement toward the eventual stand. "One and a quarter . . . one and a half."

"Come on, speed it up."

"One and three fourths . . . one and five sixths . . . "

Jillian's calf muscles started to twitch. She rocked her weight from side to side.

"One and seven eighths . . . one and eleven twelfths . . . "

The year before it had been quite remarkable that seven-year-old Peia had figured out what fractions came after three quarters. Now, it was excruciating to wait through the sixteenths and thirty-seconds.

"Three!" Peia jumped on Jillian's back, and Jillian carried her to the bathroom. She waited several minutes for Peia to go to the bath-

room, then gave her another piggy back ride downstairs. They struck
a deal: Peia would get dressed as soon as Manny left.

Peia sat at the kitchen table, drawing and cutting, and Jillian started
in on the lunches.

"Mom?"

Jillian was laying out six slices of bread. "Yeah?"

"How do you make a ship? I forgot how."

Peia was trying to fold newspapers into a ship or a sailor's hat. "We
can't do that right now. I have to get lunches made." Jillian grabbed
the turkey and ham and mozzarella out of the refrigerator, keeping it
open with one foot while she reached for the mayonnaise and mustard.

"You tell me then. Tell me how to fold it."

Manny called from the bathroom. "Hey, Mom!"

"It's kind of hard to explain." Jillian answered Peia, then called to
Manny. "You have to come to the kitchen. I'm making lunches."

She was trying to teach the kids a simple communication tech-
nique. Every time they wanted to talk, they should look around, see
if Mom or Dad were in the room. If not, they needed to get up and
walk to where their parents were. Not holler from room to room or
floor to floor. For the last two mornings, Jillian had stuck to the system, refusing to move toward them.

"Try." Peia said. "What do I do with this part? It's supposed to
make a triangle, but it's not. See?"

Jillian sighed. It was hard enough to figure out which slice of bread
needed mustard and cheese, which needed mayo, and which to leave
bare. She left the middle bread bare and put a few slices of ham on it.

"I just wanted to tell you, we're out of gel." Manny, in seventh
grade, never went to school without a firmly-gelled, spiky hairdo Jillian called the Statue of Liberty.

Peia held up a glob of newspaper. "I can't get it! I know it has to
fold back, but I can't get it. It rips. Everytime, it just rips."

Jillian sliced the plain ham, bagged it, then put together Manny's
turkey and mayo. "You're going to have to wait, Peia. You can see
what I'm doing." Another part of their sensitivity training: If you see
Mom packing your lunch or putting the dishes away, you need to
wait.

"Oh! I can't do it!" Peia jerked her head, hitting it on the table.

Jillian stuffed the turkey and mayo into a sandwich bag and after putting it in Manny's lunch box, walked over to Peia to give her a quick hug. "I know you like to make things. And you can, if you do it with a little better attitude."

Peia's eyes were teary and red. "I just need a little help. Can't you show me? Just for a minute?"

The kids never understood. Every little help turned into ten or fifteen minutes. Jillian went back to the fridge to put the mayo away. "Not right now. Draw a picture or go get your keyboard until we get Manny off to school."

Peia crawled down the hallway.

Back at the counter, Jillian made her own ham, cheese, and mustard sandwich. Upstairs, Peia played songs. Every few seconds, Jillian could hear her sing something, then attempt to repeat the sequence on the keyboard.

Mornings had always been Jillian's best time too—to think, to work, to come up with those once-a-year correlations between sets of data and a new idea. She used to wake up and run, letting her consciousness breathe and roam. After a shower and with a fresh cup of coffee in hand, she could accomplish great amounts of work. She didn't want to stifle Peia's urge to create. But it was hard.

"Hey." Manny reappeared. "Can you make eggs this morning?" His expression was lively, absolutely joyful.

Jillian looked at the clock: six forty. "I don't know, bud. I still haven't gotten into the shower."

Manny frowned, but didn't complain. He pulled his backpack from his shelf, making sure his homework was in order. For three years, since fourth grade, Manny barely needed her. Once a week or so, he asked for a two-minute back rub to help him fall asleep. Recently, he had developed an intense craving for scrambled eggs—protein and iron, Jack said.

"Tell you what. You wash the apples, get chips bagged for you and Peia, and I'll make eggs."

Manny slid across the wood floor in his stocking feet, banging into her. He gave her big, smacking kisses on the cheek. "Thank you. Thank you. Thank you."

It was a rush, but she made it. Manny ate scrambled eggs and a bagel while Jillian washed out the skillet and wiped off the counter.

He stacked his dishes on the counter and went to brush his teeth while she finished packing her lunch.

The doorbell rang—Manny's friend Chad. It was seven-ten when she kissed Manny's forehead and they walked away, headed for the middle school.

Jillian ran upstairs. "Peia, come on. Time to get ready."

"Couple minutes." Peia was arranging beanie babies in a whole new way in her bookcase, a process there wasn't time for. It was seven-fifteen and Jillian still needed a shower.

"Peia." No response. "Peia."

"What!"

Jillian's heart was thumping, but she kept her voice calm. "Turn around and listen a minute."

"I'm listening. What do you think, I have to look at you to listen? It's the same thing you always tell me. I ask you to look, and you say, 'I don't have to look to listen.'"

Jillian gathered Peia's school clothes from several drawers. "You can stay up here while I make coffee. But only if you get yourself dressed. Now."

"Okay, okay," Peia said, too quickly. She hadn't heard a word.

"Peia."

"What!"

Peia was crescendoing. Jillian stepped close, placing a hand on her shoulder. Sometimes Peia needed direct physical touch as well as obvious and continuous eye contact. "I'm going downstairs to grind some coffee beans." She hadn't even had her coffee yet! "And you need to get dressed. Got it? Either you do it, or I'll do it. Right now."

Peia took her clothes. "I got it."

A minute later, Peia's voice hollered over the noise of the grinder, unrecognizable words. Jillian drew a deep breath and walked to the stairway. "You need to come down to talk to me."

Peia groaned. "Uhhh! I'll do it myself!"

If the kids were going to learn to move their bodies close enough to talk to her, she had to turn around. She walked back to the grinder, scooped the coffee into the basket, poured the water, and pressed the brew button. She watched the light go red and heard Peia scream.

"Ow! Ow-ow-ow-ow!"

Peia was constantly hurting herself in some way. Once, as a toddler, Peia had bruised her cheekbones trying to run her scooter up the
wall. It was that kind of impact, the deep purple bruises, Jillian pictured as she ran up the stairs.

Peia had moved the bookcase tight to her bed, pinning one hand
behind it. Jillian slid it back, letting out a frustrated—and relieved—
growl.

"I didn't do it on purpose!" Peia walked around her school
clothes—thrown on the floor—licking her pinched palm like a
wounded animal. Her hand was scraped.

"Come on. We need to wash this out and get you dressed."

Jillian held Peia's hands under the faucet. Her mouth watered at
the thought of a cup of coffee. Had she turned the pot on? Yes. She
visualized the button going red.

The phone rang and Peia ran for it before Jillian could catch her.

"It's Daddy." Peia said, turning away as Jillian tried to reach for the
phone.

Fine. Let your Dad handle it. "Tell Daddy you're not dressed yet.
You have to go." Seven-fifty. Peia's bus would be there in twenty-
five minutes and she wasn't dressed, hadn't eaten, no teeth brushing,
no hair combing.

"We're having a slow morning." Peia's voice was sweet and soft.

"Hah!" Jillian couldn't help it. "Give me that phone." She yanked
it away from Peia. "We're having a slow morning because toots here
got up early, got me off the bike—"

"I didn't do that, Manny did!"

"Now, we're washing her scraped hand and trying to get breakfast
before the bus comes." She said to Peia, "Get dressed, now, or I'll put
you on that bus exactly as you are."

"Mom! You can't put a kid on the bus in their underwear!"

"I guess we learned a lesson," Jack said. His supposedly inclusive
"we" made Jillian boil. "No matter how much fun we're having, we
need to get that one to bed, every night, by eight."

The evening before they had taken the kids to the park to let Peia
try out a new pair of roller blades. Peia was amazing on skates, a daredevil. She jumped the six-inch curbs, then the twelve, then crashed
over the eighteens. Jillian and Manny had skated around and around
while Jack picked Peia up and rubbed her, over and over. Jack babied

her too much. Peia needed to know she could pick herself up. She should always pick herself up.

"We?" Jillian tried to control her tone. "You showered. You ate. You're already at work. Who's we?" Peia ran out of the room. "Peia! Get back here!"

Jillian stared at Peia's clothes, still on the bed. She hated how her voice was continually raised from the time Manny left for school until Peia got on the bus. It wasn't all Peia's fault. Yes, she was hard to channel, but part of it was in the duration. So much time! Peia's day in elementary school started two full hours behind Manny's, while Jillian's day waited at the starting line. Day after day, she was stuck on the starting blocks, jittering, the last to shove off.

Jack's call made her immediately aware that he was in first: *This is first, calling last.*

"Sorry," Jack said. Somehow, he always managed to get out the door first.

"I'm putting on different clothes!" Peia hollered.

"It's lack of sleep. We'll get them to bed early tonight."

Tonight? How wonderful that he could think that far ahead. She still needed a shower, had to get Peia fed, had to get her on the bus. And all she wanted was a cup of coffee. But, like the coffee she could smell downstairs, waiting, the anger she didn't have time for percolated in her chest. Only someone in first could hear the tone of her voice and still chuckle.

"You have never, ever been where I am." Her voice was trembling, and she hated the sound. "All I want is a shower, a shower and a cup of coffee. Where do I get off, huh?" She waited for a response she could tear apart, but he said nothing. Nothing! "Why did you call?"

"Nothing, really."

"What nothing?"

"Nothing. That was a nice kiss this morning."

She hated the way she sounded. Hated Jack for not hearing and for being so easily moved by a kiss. Every picture she had of parenthood had the two of them sharing, not this. First out the door, last one home; he missed all the transitions. He showed up with their lives already in motion. Why were they always doing this separately? There she was, alone, consumed by transition-time.

"You know what? I can't chit-chat now." She hung up the phone on Jack's second "Sorry." And she sat, imagining him at his desk, holding onto the phone for a minute, saying "Bye, Babe" to keep the biologist or the chemist or the lab assistants around him from suspecting that he was being shamed.

Jillian held Peia's shoulders and steered her into the bathroom, where Jillian sat on the covered toilet and Peia obediently placed one leg after another into her jeans. Peia took off her own shirt and Jillian pulled the fresh shirt over her head. They walked down the stairs and Jillian brushed her hair. When Peia cried out, letting her head bounce back with exaggerated, reactive gestures, Jillian still said nothing. She seated Peia at the table with a bowl of cereal, walked into the bathroom, shut the door, and turned on the shower.

She rinsed her hair as fast as she could and towel dried with her heart pumping. She brushed her teeth while poking her head out from the bathroom door, prompting Peia to sit and eat. Twice, Peia got out of her chair, going back to the newspapers to cut and glue pieces together.

When Peia asked for a new bowl of cereal, Jillian said no, and made her sit, crying, while she ate soggy raisin bran. "And you better stop that crying before you choke."

Jillian hated the sound of her voice. She hated how these mornings of waking and lunch packing and dressing and feeding attacked her and left her with nothing but anger. Anger she somehow needed to survive.

At eight-seventeen, Peia ran to the bus in tears. What a way to send a kid off to school! And Jillian went to the coffee pot and sighed out loud. She moaned, growled, turned her head to the ceiling, fighting the urge to call Jack. What good would it do? Tomorrow, she'd have to kiss him goodbye and try not to hate him as he drove off for his half hour of music in the car, followed by his first three hours at work, uninterrupted unless he chose to pick up the phone or schedule an early meeting.

She poured a cup of coffee, went into the bathroom to check to make sure her blouse was entirely buttoned, which it wasn't. She had brushed mascara on so fast it was all over her eye sockets.

At eight twenty-two she sat at the kitchen table, looking out at the woods behind her house, trying to put herself back together.

She sat and she took in the trees.

The poplars and silver maples and cherries, wetland trees with shallow roots that knotted above the mossy ground, made her feel calm. The trees were old and wise. And the sassafras, with their deeply grooved bark and twisting branches had so much character. She loved their leaves—three shapes: the mitten, the hand, the football—and in the fall they turned blood red. If you rolled one in your hand and held it under your nose, it smelled like root beer.

Without this view, Jillian might be lost. If the view from her windows—of vinyl-clad houses on her left and her right—were all she had, if all she could see were Ann Arbor's endless subdivisions, she didn't know if she could survive each day.

Each day her brain came to consciousness, fairly screaming with ideas. And every day she shut it off, closed it down, protected it from the morning's onslaught. Some days it took hours to coax her thoughts back.

As she gazed into the woods from her seat at the table, she felt the circular, moist, fibrous wood absorbing her anger and absolving her guilt. She could love her husband and her children and hate the way their lives controlled hers. She did a fine job of that, every day.

17

Day Six—The Lighthouse

JILLIAN WALKED SOUTH ALONG THE lake shore, splashing in the water, enjoying the feel of the current tugging at her legs. Sometimes thigh deep, sometimes just webbing her toes through the bubbles as the water receded. She'd been paying close attention to the bubbles since meeting the old man, though she did not try to catch them. There was something about the way he scraped at the sand, knowing he couldn't stop the bubbles from sliding back into the water, that was entirely too sad.

She'd promised herself when she left the tent that she wouldn't let the old man's loneliness turn her into a nostalgic bubble-chaser. Today she was free. Unfettered. And she had a purpose. Today, Day Six, was all about the present, all about the lake and the sky and the breeze, a different kind of breeze.

Though she understood the pull. There was something about the lake with its waves and waves and waves that encouraged the past, dredging up the deepest sediment and carrying all forms of rot back to shore, as if shredded plants and petrified tree trunks and old plastic cushions could somehow re-thrive. That's when the bubbles got to her. When the lake seemed to be churning up the past and would not *let* her let go. The lake seemed to be telling her that these opportunities, these gifts—a pooling of chopped weeds, a plank from an old ship with iron nails curling outward like worms, a piece of a pink balloon—did not last forever. Reminding her: she'd let this very special place and all the gifts it had offered slip away. She'd done her best to keep in touch with the stars over the years, but there was never enough night time, not with the kids, and she had to accept that. She was on her way to the lighthouse to gaze up into that brilliant turquoise rectangle and let go. There was peace in putting the past in its place. She had felt it, walking along with the old man. He was there, too, to let the past wash over him and to move on.

Today, she would let the lake and the sky and that something deep and dark that rolled below the surface roll up and take the past—if it would. The lake had a way of changing course in an instant, and if there was one lesson she had to learn, once and for all, this was it: the present was always up for grabs.

So she opened herself to every portion of the present: the sudden slaps of water, the water pressing against her ears when she dove under a wave, the rush of air and the smell of cool moisture when she sprang to the surface. And the water, the sand, the sky welcomed her yearning. She wasn't there to harness or hoard or dam or syphon. All she wanted was to feel every part of her in complete communion with her surroundings. She was present. For today, that was enough.

Seagulls watched her, stopping when she stopped, sometimes flapping over her, curious. They squawked at each other: *Has she found a school of fish?*

No, I'm just playing! Swimming and playing and feeling. Because all of me is here.

She blushed, instantly. Walking along with the old man she had said "No" she had no children. Wasn't solitude supposed to inspire honesty? The thoughts and the worries and the love she felt for Manny and Peia had become a flesh of its own, an inner body that wiggled around inside her when she tried to ignore it, making her uncomfortably aware of its presence. Perhaps once a child had grown inside you, your very cells were forever changed—charged with a deep need to connect and to keep connecting. Perhaps life left a sort of living-memory behind. But then, that wasn't the kind of truth you could share with a stranger.

She passed a woman with a weathered face and a walking stick, a knotty wooden stick and a bouncing hat, and Jillian smiled without restraint. Because all she could do, now, was smile. She was capable of great love, and love was enriched in its own way when it lived side-by-side with sadness.

On the sandbar, in water just above her ankles, she jumped over ripples that looked like sound waves spreading over the sand at regular intervals—an ongoing dialogue between Earth's core and its surface. She ran after the longest ripples, following them over the edge of the sandbar, and stretching out over them as they turned to waves, she hurled her body into the whitecaps. She had to understand it all: the waves of longing and the waves of regret. The stars calling her to fight and her own desire to forget. The smiles that brought her close to tears and this new nervousness that was building. She could feel it in the waves. The air, far off, was changing. She'd felt it immediately upon waking. Something was hovering, still, in the lulls between breezes. The lake pressure, if there was such a thing, was building.

She'd become a barometer and everything around her—the sky, the sun, the water, and space—seemed to be waiting. Full of possibility. So she jumped when her muscles twitched, ran after ripples broken by gusts of wind, walked backward in the low sand, watching the lake wash away her impact. And when thoughts of Jack and Manny and Peia threatened to invade the wide-open spaces in her mind, she dove under the water and blew bubbles, bubbles that exploded with a rumble and dissipated as they scrambled toward the sun. Perhaps it was a particularly female elixir to admit that doing what was best for her children was the only way. After all, a person could not live, day after day after day, always doing things the hardest possible way. Exhaling a whale-like moan, she blew bubbles and stuck her face in them. The lake would understand.

When she rounded the three-humped dune, Big Sable, the lighthouse where it all began rose from the sand, looking stoic under the whitening heat of the sun. She was feeling stoic, too, after trodding for six days under that same hot sun. Stoic and worthy of forgiveness, wasn't she? She hadn't done it all, but she'd *done*, always, even if she hadn't always done her best.

She had hiked to the light before—that first morning, on Day Two—but finding people sitting on the benches and milling around the keeper's house, she had walked on. Today the grounds were nearly deserted. The old man was right. *Go tomorrow*, he had told her. *Middle of the week, when everyone's packing up or just getting in.*

She touched Big Sable's original stone base, now painted white. Levels of alternating black and white sheet metal had been welded over the hand-cut stones. About six feet up, the first circle of black was held to the stone with two rings and spring-mounted screws that looked like a huge embroidery hoop. She pushed her fingers under the hoop and tried to look behind it, but there was no space between old and new. No breathing room. The stone would suffocate and sweat. How was the old light supposed to expand and contract and survive? Only the first six feet of the hundred-foot light and maybe the top—she hoped the top!—was left open to breathe.

Esther, the current two-week keeper, was at the gift shop counter.

"You're back," Esther said. "Good day for it, too. There's just one batch of kids up right now, and Fred's closing the stairs for lunch."

She was going to get to climb, alone. Alone!

Jillian was reminded, again, of the desperation of Day Two, and she felt hot just remembering how she'd sank to her knees and worshipped Kera's Depot. She'd met Esther shortly after, and she was sure Esther has sensed her desperation. "So," Esther tried to sound calm. "How's your stay going?"

After her long hike back from the Depot, she had downed two bottles of water and had fallen asleep out on the breakwater. Esther had been there when she woke. She had shared her lunch with Jillian and told her about the new keeper program. And Jillian had gotten the feeling that Esther was making herself available, in case Jillian needed to talk. "People love the old lights. Why not give them a chance to save them?" Esther had talked and talked, and after a while it worked. Jillian had begun to listen. For two weeks volunteers ran the gift shop and gave lighthouse tours. They loved tending to the light and the grounds so much that the historic committee had a waiting list over a year long. Word had gotten out, Esther had said, about the stars at night, when those lucky enough to be keepers had the grounds and the house and the night to themselves.

Today Esther didn't look so enchanted. "The couple that was supposed to come Sunday, something with the kids, they aren't coming. We'll be staying on, I guess."

They turned to a rumble—the vibration of several pairs of feet coming down the staircase—and Fred's voice cautioned, "Watch out, now. There's fresh enamel on those stairs. They get slippery." From the sounds and the pounding of their feet, they didn't listen. The back screen door slapped shut and a jumble of feet and voices trailed outside.

Jillian held out two dollars for a ticket.

"Oh, go on." Esther waved Jillian's money aside. "You're as good as a local."

"Consider it a donation then."

Fred, his face taken up with thick glasses and one of those forever sunburned and lumpy noses, smiled when he recognized her. "You got her all to yourself. I'm going to close down for a good hour, so take your time."

Jillian ran the first few twists. From below Fred called, "Watch the slip, the enamel's a little glossy. And duck up at the door!"

The wrought-iron stairs with their scrolly, foliage pattern, were battleship gray—too clean, too fresh. She remembered them dark and rusty. And the old light was swaying more than she remembered. Outside, she had noticed cables draped from the tower and rodded down into cement blocks. Esther had assured her that the committee was keeping the light in good shape. They'd spent the summer refitting the metal bands. Fred had showed her where they drilled supports into the walls to reinforce the stairway. But breathing space for the stone, and what about air flow? She'd have to ask Fred about drainage.

Halfway up, a criss-cross of movement dizzied her head. The wind, high off the lake, sheered against the top, while the lower half, reinforced as it was, tried to hold its ground. She let go of the wall and stood with her knees unlocked, feeling the sway. Above, through the open trap door, she found that rectangle of brilliant blue-white sky.

"All right up there? Run too hard, did ya?"

She grabbed the rail to look down. "No. Just feeling the sway."

Fred's red face bobbled. "It's strong, right about midway."

"Yeah. It feels good."

"Most folks don't like it. Okay, I'll let you alone then."

She anchored the back of her heel against the vertical spire that ran along the stairway rungs, then took her hand from the railing. As long as her feet were stable, she wasn't going anywhere. She tipped her head back and watched the square of blue-white slide back and forth, to and fro. From the sand to the stairway to the tip of the tower, she could feel the rhythm of the water. The rhythm of the universe: of light, of magnetism, perhaps even gravity and dark space.

Jillian remembered being surprised by the Milky Way, that first time Kera had taken her up at night. She had been filled with energy, inspired by the depth of the stars and the way the stellar dust seemed to hold them together. In that very place, she had sat staring at a blanket of stars more dense yet somehow more focused than she had ever seen. The original masking concept had come from her work at the print shop. "We use cameras with really intense, focused light, to burn images into printing plates," she had explained to Kera. "Sometimes I have to shoot two or three plates to crisp up the image and then choke it back." That was the beauty of living in the present: being open to the oddest, most lucrative impulses and associations.

At the top, the tower swayed without guise of being stable. She leaned over the railing and saw thick cables looped through rings that had been drilled into the stone and metal sides, about halfway down. It was stability the old light fought against. Jillian sat with her legs dangling from the deck, her head resting against the railing, listening to the loop rings creak as the cables tightened in the wind. The old light would pull away, eventually.

Down the beach, she saw couples and families straggling south, making their way in little clumps toward the Ludington Beach House and its water-field of old pillars. Why hadn't she and Jack and the kids seen the Scotville Clown Band or climbed the light? Why couldn't they pack up and go to one of her places, the way they took off at sunrise with a cooler full of waters and snacks to spend a day at a basketball tournament, or to take a special trip to a new skate park? She had always imagined the four of them spending the night at the observatory. Joining the astronomy club. When they all piled out of the car, she'd say, "Look at the stars. They're beautiful tonight." But after they gave her stars a quick glance, she was left standing in the driveway, left wandering down the street alone.

Jack had once curled his long legs around her and pointed up to the stars and said, "Love me like you love them, from a distance," hoping their very different lives could coexist. But that was before kids. Now, Jack didn't want to remember the early years, those months of apart-time when she did her best to love them from a distance. The observatory was no place for a baby or a toddler, not unless they all stayed. She and Kera had always toyed with the idea of her accepting a position as one of the mountain's Support Astronomers. There were researchers, electricians, school teachers who lived on the mountain. But not Jack. No. Manny had turned into a two-year old the last time she came home, and her mind still built false memories of the events she could not have seen. But Jack didn't like to go that far back. It was more convenient to remember the Jillian who fit with their family life—the Jillian who worked close to home and got the kids off to school.

Jillian had asked Arnie once, a year or so after she'd gotten married, if marriages between two scientists, two researchers who had to live apart, ever worked.

"Some do," he said. "But it's hard."

"With kids?" she'd asked, and Arnie had given her the most honest answer she'd ever heard: "No."

She'd been puzzled. Arnie was married and he and his wife seemed to be doing okay. "How do you do it?"

Arnie's whole face had brightened and then turned dark, and finally, he had sighed. "We don't." His wife, he went on to tell Jillian, had a Master's degree in biology, but when his post-doctoral studies kept them on the move for six years and their first child was born, it had been hard for her. She'd taken a job, when they settled in Houghton, as a reading aide at their daughter's school. Arnie's eyes had stayed right with hers. His wife's love was being eaten away by resentment, and he knew it. Yet there was something about the way Arnie looked at her that said he was hoping, with her marriage so young and her desire to get back to big time observing so strong, that Jillian would break free.

Sometimes she tried to tell herself she was creating the problem. She was imagining people looking at her and treating her differently. But they did. Except for Arnie, whose face had truly darkened, people looked at her and smiled as if they knew what would occupy the rest of her life. That her children would extinguish all other drives. Her drive hadn't slipped away, only her resolve to leave, over and over again. The stars, masking, orbital visible-light systems and working with Kera—none of those possibilities had ever left her. They cycled like an engine, always: when the kids are older, when Jack gets sick of being strapped to his lab, when he remembers how deeply she needed this. When he realizes, finally, that she cannot wait forever. Yet she waited, and she stayed. And she hated hearing Arnie's and his wife's excuses coming from her own mouth. Jack's job was the most stable and the kids were better off in one school. She hated, always, feeling as if she had to explain. *What happened to you?*

"Company's coming!"

An hour—she could use a thousand of them. She rose with Fred's voice, wanting to call "Thanks!" but she couldn't make her vocal cords do the work.

She had never had the heart to ask Arnie if the respect he received from his colleagues, if the ongoing projects with NASA and his position as Department Chair were enough to make up for his wife's resentment. Jillian had met Arnie's wife and she'd heard her excuses: Arnie's early moves, the kids had started school, Arnie's weeks and months away. But Jillian was sick of excuses, sick of the responsibility to make her failure okay for everyone else. Because, whether husbands or anyone else wanted to admit it, they were all waiting— cheering for and at the same time fearing the Jillians and the other wives who would eventually break away.

She gazed out at the lake, its sandbars making greenish strokes into the blue, whitecaps splashing over the lip of each sandbar. The wind was picking up, turning into the kind of day she loved. The wind and sun together beat on her face and roared in her ears.

Astronauts who go into space, walk out into nothing but space with their bodies wrapped in sun- and temperature- and air-regulating suits, float and brace themselves from object to object. Tethered but free, they spring from grab-hold to grab-hold. They say it makes them feel small, and they get hooked. They can't wait to go back to that something in space that surges with rhythm. They can't wait to be a part of it again, floating, weighty yet aloft.

Jillian leaned into the railing, letting the wind blow over her, feeling the fullness of the sun. She closed her eyes and tried to feel small. In the lake and in the wind, in the space all around her, there was a bit of wonder, and she was a part of it.

In her last few moments alone with the old light, she held her arms shoulder high and let her body sway with the wind. She opened herself to the kind of small that is space without time. The opposite of the smallness of home—time without space.

White Dwarf

A STAR FRESH OFF THE MAIN SEQUENCE IS A STAR OUT OF balance. Its pure helium core has exhausted its supply of hydrogen, and the star sits, losing heat and energy from the inside out. The helium core needs to get hot fast to avoid collapse, and so it does. Gravity steps in, squeezing, and with gravity temporarily in control, density and temperature rise by powers of ten. Helium atoms, zinging about in tighter and tighter spaces, are stripped of their electrons, and nuclei in the core begin to fuse. With the fusion of helium to carbon, the star has a stable source of energy once again.

But each time lighter elements fuse into heavier elements, some mass is lost. Four hydrogen atoms fuse into one helium; three helium atoms form only one carbon; and so, nuclear fusion results in a continuous depletion of the number of available particles. When the number of particles drops, so does pressure, and the same old problem remains: gravity must continually contract the core to keep it hot enough to fuse.

Helium fusion progresses, and newly formed carbon atoms begin to collide with helium, producing oxygen. The stellar core, now two steps away from hydrogen fusion, is steadily fusing helium into carbon and oxygen, steadily getting smaller and hotter. Once again, the star reaches a fuel crisis. If carbon and oxygen are to fuse into neon and magnesium, a much hotter, denser environment is required. Temperatures must soar. So gravity, doing what it does best, clamps down.

But some stars seem to be born to push back. Gases

within the White Dwarf's core, its atoms packed so tightly that electrons have no space to move, will not behave in the usual manner. Instead of compressing further, instead of heating up and slamming into each other, electrons in this core exert an exotic pressure all their own. These electrons push back. Filling any remaining spaces between its particles with the stiffness of steel, the stellar core resists gravity. All the way down to its atoms, the White Dwarf resists further change.

Dwarfed thousands of times over, its gases packed as densely as metal, the Dwarf's core sits idle, refusing to fuse. Of course, this does not mean gravity gives in or gives up.

The envelope and outer layers begin to pulsate, throbbing back and forth as gravity strives for forced equilibrium, and again the White Dwarf pushes back. The core's insistent wind heats and expands the star's outer layers, creating an outward stream of pent-up energy that bursts with incredible color. From the center of a nebula of reds, purples, blues, and greens, the White Dwarf emerges, naked and white-hot.

The small but extremely luminous point of light remains long after its colors have burst and faded away. Without fusion, the Dwarf's core cools and fades until billions of years later, a dim round of charcoal the size of Earth crumbles into dust—dust that will eventually give rise to the next generation of stars.

18

Any Woman

SHE WAS TOO FAR ALONG TO fly, that's what the obstetrician said, so she and Kera were going to drive to California. That's how she put it to Jack. She intercepted him at the door to his (theirs, supposedly) one bedroom apartment in a student complex, where she dragged twenty pounds of extra weight up and down three flights of stairs while lean people ran past her or jumped on bikes and pedaled away. Standing tall with her hands on her hips—which hadn't widened, neither had her backside, but her breasts were huge—she announced she and Kera would be leaving the following weekend.

"You can't drive! What would you do if you got caught out in the middle of nowhere?" Jack looked at her as if she'd gone crazy.

Maybe she had. But they had been granted a "Proof of Concept" study–five consecutive nights for three months in a row, during the best weather the year had to offer. The powers in control of the one-hundred-and-twenty-inch mirror at Lick Observatory weren't going to wait because she was seven months pregnant. Take it or leave it, they would say. Go back to the bottom of a stack of requests.

She tried humor. "Lie down in the mountains and have a completely natural birth I guess." Birth at this stage would be way too premature, anything but natural. Jack's eyes grew even wider. "I've got at least two months."

"If you go exactly 40 weeks, which hardly ever happens."

"I can't miss this. We got five nights, Jack. Five nights per month at the peak of the observing season. No one but Princeton, or U-Cal, or the most promising studies get that kind of time. I am not blowing this." The masked light patterns they'd achieved at Mount LeConte and later, back on the benches, had gotten the committee's attention. That, and a good plan. They'd proposed two spectral studies first, using the radial velocity method. They'd use Lick's new Spectrometer to survey the closest twenty or thirty stars, record spectra in near infrared. Then, if they found any significant red or blue shift that implied movement around a star, they'd go back to the most promising stars in a second study. Zoom in and see if they could plot an actual orbit. Eventually, with the right optics, they'd keep working toward masking and high contrast images in visible light, but for now, it was infrared. And they had to leave, now, to get their foot in the door.

It was late, almost ten o'clock, and Jack had left that morning at seven. She'd been communicating all day with Kera and the University of California's Astronomy department. They were both too tired for this, but none of this could wait.

Jack's eyes darted back and forth, searching for some solution. "You're right. You can't miss it. You can't." She relaxed. "I'll drive."

"You can't drive! How are you going to drive all the way to California and back before your residency starts?"

A secret, irrational hope flared. She'd already decided she and Kera could get through two sets of observations before her due date. With Jack along, they'd be guaranteed all three. She could have the baby and he'd be there. But of course, that was impossible. A medical student couldn't skip a rotation, not without starting all over. What good would it do for both of them to fall behind?

He exhaled and hung his head. "Imagine how simple this could be, if one of us was say . . . a janitor."

It was their current good-will game. *Imagine if we were . . .* and they'd insert occupations with more routine schedules. But there were always complications.

"It's going to get harder and harder. I can't let this stop me."

Maybe it was crazy, driving thousands of miles through the Rockies, but not going would be worse than crazy. It would be negligent, wasteful, disrespectful to all that was possible. She'd pull a Vera Rubin if she had to. Which she decided not to tell Jack, since Vera made her initial observations of elliptical galaxies with a one-month-old infant on her lap. Jillian would have two laps: hers and Kera's. Three if Jack would drop everything and come along.

He had options, and she didn't really. Not for long. And no matter how hard she tried not to, she always ended up attacking him because he had more. "I don't have some rotating schedule." This was her one shot. *One.* "This is it for me."

Jack stepped forward and took her hands from her hips. "You look so sad."

"I freaked out all afternoon." Her belly had popped and she couldn't get a full breath. Her nose seemed to be growing and her face was splotched and red. And it was all a precursor to losing so much more. Jack knew she was panicked. He had been sneaking glances at her and she scowled anytime she caught him.

"We'll make this okay." His voice, her weariness, they were work-ing on her. Why did she feel like giving up everytime he said, *It'll be okay?* She moved away but he followed.

He set his backpack on the counter and knelt close to her stomach, holding the sides of her belly. "You, little bowling ball, are going to stay put for another ten to twelve weeks. There's no hurry here."

It might be good to get away. Her mind, her heart, her job track-ing stars, all the reasons Jack had initially loved her, seemed to be sidelined. He was cooing at her belly.

"And you." He stood and pressed his hands around her face. She noted, silently, that she had come second. "You are going to make it to Lick and back with the bowling ball intact. I'll have to figure out a way to get out there. Just in case."

After several more discussions, the three of them—Jillian, Kera, and Jack—revised the plan. Jack and Jillian would drive to her parent's house, just west of Iowa City, and Kera would meet them there. All three of them would stay overnight at the farm. Come Sunday, Jack would head back to Ann Arbor to start his first rotation—he'd drawn emergency room duty—and she and Kera would head to Santa Cruz.

Jillian agreed to check in with a Santa Cruz doctor as soon as they arrived. She'd follow through with weekly appointments. And the minute there were signs: the mucus plug, dilation, excessive Braxton-Hicks contractions (He made her a list!) Jack would fly out. Hope-fully, such a sign wouldn't show up until after Jack's emergency room rotation. His second was Internal Medicine. The hospital would be much more understanding if he left them in a lurch with a few stom-ach problems and headaches versus heart attacks and gaping wounds. Jack made their hotel reservations, planning and replanning their stops. She shouldn't ride too long. It would be hard on her circula-tion. Yes! She cared about oxygen flow and exercising her limbs, but they needed to arrive at least five days before their first run. That was worth suffering for. The word suffering, of course, stood out.

Studying the atlas, Jack kept finding tiny towns and teasing: they could still get married. How about Peru, Illinois? What a place to call from and say, *Guess what? We're in Peru and we tied the knot.* "What for?" she'd scoff. Didn't he know a shotgun marriage was intended to keep the man around? She finally shut him up when she asked if his mother's comments—*Why can't her partner finish the work?*—were meant to be helpful, or, were they a show of contempt for Jillian's missing maternal compass?

Her compass wasn't missing; it simply had two equal and opposing poles. She didn't want to go away, not without Jack. He had become, with his hands and all the new time they were spending together and sleeping in the same bed, part of her body. But she had to. She had to do this or face losing everything she had been before she'd become whatever it was she and Jack were becoming. She was going to miss him terribly. But she had to focus on Lick, and radial velocity, and rising above the crazy notions of her body.

The night before their elaborately planned departure, Jillian tucked Jack's list into her overnight bag, unable to believe two things: in a few short days, she was going to be operating one of the most powerful telescopes in the country, and she was going to be doing it pregnant. She felt proud of pushing herself so hard, but at the same time, tired of having to do everything *before*.

"What about your bag?" Jack held up a tube sock stuffed with tennis balls, a Lamaze tool for kneading her lower back.

Jillian shrugged and looked away. Jack held the bag, awkwardly for a moment. Then, pretending he had forgotten something, he walked out of the bedroom and Jillian flopped on the bed.

The night before, they'd attended a birthing class and Jack had gotten annoyed with her for not taking it seriously. But she couldn't help it. It all seemed so phony: women sprawled out on the floor, working hard to make husbands and boyfriends feel involved. The looks on the men's faces: some proud, some scared, and some, like Jack, acting almost romantic. And all of the women, kneeling and lying and turning over and panting. Not a one of them looked happy, no matter how many times the nurse told them they were beautiful. She had stood above Jillian as she knelt on all fours and claimed she could still see her waist.

"Hey." Jack sat next to her.

"Sorry."

"For what. What's wrong?"

"Nothing feels right." She ached to stay close *and* to go. But the two aches were so different. One made her feel weak and dependent. The other made her want to prove she was strong. Going to Lick Observatory was what she was meant to do.

"I have to go."

"And you are." Jack fidgeted with her labor bag. He pulled the tennis balls out of the tube sock and dropped them, one by one, at some target.

She wished she could take his hands, place them on either side of her stomach and acknowledge his touch with full eye contact.

"You're looking at me differently."

Jack's hand, large and warm, covered the back of her skull. He kissed her forehead. "No I'm not."

"I can tell when you're lying."

"It's the growth all of a sudden. It's been amazing."

Sometimes, alone, she sat quietly and listened for the being inside her. But when she was with Jack, she felt prickly with resistance. "I can't breathe."

"Put your arms up." Jack pushed her arms upward and folded his own above his head—a trick to lift the diaphragm and expand her lungs. Her doctor was a bit worried that the baby hadn't moved into a head-down position yet. "Better?"

God, she was going to miss him.

"You're still you, Jill."

No. She was a pregnant woman with her arms folded over her head. She had spent the semester at U of M to be closer to Jack. Why? So he could touch her belly. She had left Kera in Houghton to organize the first official astronomy courses at Tech, while she made the final revisions on their thesis and taught an introductory course in Ann Arbor. The universe was shifting, and so was her position in it. And damn it, the way he touched her and coddled her and kept watch felt so good. She was beginning to feel part of a threesome.

"How can you enjoy this?" She tried to laugh and started to cry.

He pulled her close and stroked her back. "It's okay. It's all strange for you, and you've got so much going on. It's just—"

"What?" Whatever it was, the look on his face was the same one she'd been scowling at. "What?"

Of course Jack was excited and doting and everything any other pregnant woman would want him to be. His universe was made of cells and cell division and specialization. He was enthralled with the growth. And she was leaving, just when he was able to feel the baby, to experience some of what she was, with his hands.

"Don't take this wrong." He kept his eyes steady. "I want the baby to feel loved."

Love. Sometimes, she sat back and let love flow from her belly to Jack's hands. It was as if her body had become their conductor, his and his baby's. But this was not one of those times. She had to leave.

"I am not loving this."

Jack gathered up the tennis balls and stuffed them back in the tube sock. "Can we pretend, at least while we're with your parents, that we're in love?"

She nodded, watching her reflection in the mirror above the dresser. What was the sight of her going to do to her parents? How did she look promising now, with her swollen breasts and puffy eyes and thick face?

Something sharp—a fist?—pushed into her ribcage. Feet kicked away at her pelvis. Jack, of course, noticed. "Babe?"

"Maybe I won't be such a big deal, given my Dad's situation."

Her father was on oxygen. Her mother had called just that morning. A warning, Jillian figured, so she would know what to expect.

Jack tucked the tube sock full of tennis balls back in her labor bag. "Oh, you'll be a big deal, all right. But it'll be okay." He kissed the top of her head—she pulled him back and hugged him—and he took the bag away.

In the middle of the night Jillian bolted upright, feeling as if her ribs were being split apart. Jack convinced her to lay on her side, so she could breathe, and together they held onto her belly as it balled on one side, elongated across her abdomen, then tucked down low. Together, they felt the baby turn.

Jillian lay still, breathing more deeply than she'd been able to for weeks. "I think the head is down."

Jack pulled the blanket around her shoulders and snuggled tight to her back. "Good. Good. Now I know everything will be okay."

19

On the Star Deck

KERA'S YELLOW JEEP WAS IN the driveway. Jillian spotted it as soon as they turned off the main road. She had insisted on being in the driver's seat when they rolled up the long dirt drive.

"This is it," she said.

"This is it." Jack kissed her hand. "You ready?"

Ready? For her mother and Kera and, oh god, her father, to see her looking like this? With her bowling ball stomach?

"No." She wanted to laugh, but laughing was so close to crying. "But we can't exactly back up and spit gravel."

Kera and Jillian's mother were standing on the porch, but neither one of them moved. Had they discussed it? Planned to let themselves view her from a distance so their fears, their surprise, could be handled before they were all at close range?

"Sure we can," Jack said.

"We can?" For a second, she wondered if he had a plan.

But his sigh was resigned. "I for one am glad Kera's here."

And she realized Jack was the one on the hot seat. This was Greer country. It was Jack who had to prove he was worth this obvious detour, this risk she had taken.

"You know what?" She grabbed his hand. "I can do this. All my favorite people are here."

"I don't know about the Jeep. You're going to get bounced all over."

Kera hesitated on the stairs, then strode toward the car.

Jillian stopped to avoid lopping Kera's head off as she thrust her head into the car interior and kissed Jack on the cheek. "Holy shit." She was looking at Jillian's belly. "I pictured it when you told me, but oh my god, you're huge!"

Jillian swung out of the car. Kera didn't seem to be able to step toward her so Jillian made the first move. "I'm not contagious."

Standing in the yard, they wrapped their arms around each other.

"Shit, Jilli. Holy shit." Kera was doing what Jillian had been doing in the mirror for days, letting the shock wear off.

"Hey, hey." Jack opened his arms to Kera and she hugged him and patted his bony chest. Jillian liked the same spot. A thought passed quickly: how many other women had patted that spot? Jack's eyes communicated his encouragement as she turned toward the house. He was there for her. Jillian would be the last, forever; the last woman Jack would ever touch if she wanted it that way.

Jillian walked toward the house, her house, with Jack and Kera firing questions back and forth behind her. *So, California, huh? What an opportunity for you two. You have to start in ER on Monday? Man, that's rough.* She loved the low porch, the way the wooden planks ran down, slightly, to drain the summer rain. And the roll-out windows above that flanked both sides of her bed. Her windows and her star deck.

"Oh, baby." Her mother's feet plunked down the steps. "You are such a welcome sight."

Gayle was a sight, too. She had always been thin, but in her gauze dress, she seemed much taller, as tall as Kera. And her hair! She had cut her long hair. It fanned out, stiff with protest, at shoulder length.

Gayle held Jillian's hands and looked her over. "You're not as big as you think." She opened her hands toward Jillian's belly. Jillian nodded and both of their eyes grew dark with tears. "She was nothing more than a little pouch last time. Are you sure you're only twenty-eight weeks?"

"I hope so. Where's Dad?"

Her mother stood back and looked at her face. "He wanted me to wake him as soon as you got here. All morning, we've been talking about what it was like when you were a baby." Gayle let a tear run down her face. She never wiped tears away. "He's so sentimental."

That's what Jillian was afraid of. Her father had never been afraid to let his feelings show. Or to say exactly what he felt. She looked back at Jack. He and Kera walked slowly, arm in arm. Jack was losing something too, with her leaving. She saw it in the way he clung to Kera. She should let him cling to her, at least a little, before they parted.

She and Kera and Jack were standing like a wall, arm in arm, when her father opened the screen door. If it weren't for their interlocked arms, Jillian might have fallen.

He was so thin. Everyone was looking thin. Here she'd gone and gained twenty pounds and her mother and father, both of them, looked like they'd lost it.

"Well," he stood on the top step, purposefully surveying her, then he let go of a grin. "Hi-dee-ho, hot mamma!"

Her mother slapped his leg. "He's been practicing jabs all day."

He took the stairs slowly, watching his step. Jillian felt reinforcement from Jack's and Kera's arms.

"Holy cow!" he exclaimed.

Gayle whacked him again.

Manford had two modes in a crisis: humor or silence. They were going to deal with this one with humor, thankfully. Jillian rested her eyes behind a slow blink and thanked the universe. He smelled funny when she hugged him. "Okay. You got your digs in."

"I'm just messin' with you," he said. "Just messin'."

Gayle went to Jack. "Give me a hug, you."

Kera stood alone. "I'll pour some more lemonade." She patted Jillian's arm as she walked into the house. "It's so humid. How do you survive?"

"I'll get the lemons," Gayle said, chasing after Kera.

They had planned it all right—time for Jack and Manford to face off. Or, was it time for Jillian's first full look at her father? She noticed a red V creased beneath his nose.

"Jack." Manford extended his hand to Jack and they shook, both gripping each other firmly. "In residency come Monday, huh?"

Work talk. Good. Jack would find it easy to talk about work. She excused herself and went for her mother.

"He's a lot worse than you said, Mom. Why didn't you tell me?"

"It's all been a matter of timing. The biopsy report came back right after your last visit." Gayle's eyes started to water and she tried to hide it, focusing on the lemon she was pulverizing. "You were still trying to decide what to do about the baby. We didn't want to complicate things. Not right then."

Jillian sat on a barstool and Kera came and hugged her. "Pops looks great, I think. You're the one who's looking ragged. Are you sleeping?" Kera knew Jillian's insomniac patterns. She stopped sleeping whenever a big project was looming or something was bothering her. It was both, this time.

"Thanks, pal." Jillian huffed. "Who needs a sister?"

"We all do," Gayle said.

Jillian groaned. "Oh. I've been assaulting Jack for days. And then, at the I-80 truckstop, a gang of truckers tried to rescue me when he lifted up my shirt and I started screaming at him."

"What was he doing with your shirt?" Her mother looked perplexed.

"Palpating. It sounds like a stupid thing to get upset about, but he's incessant."

"I told you he was dangerous." Kera was joking, getting into the sarcastic spirit of Jillian's household. But there was an echo in her words. *That one's dangerous, he wants a lot more than sex.*

"I'm sorry, okay? I'm sorry." Jillian caught herself sighing again. She was doing an awful lot of sighing. "I noticed a mark, from the oxygen tube. Does he have a tank or what?"

"I'll show you later." Her mother waved her hand through the space between the three of them as if to shoo the tension away. "Tell me what you know about the observatory. Kera says you're going to try to stick it out."

Jillian turned to make sure Jack and Manford were still occupied.

"Your Dad already had at him the last time you two were here. Don't worry."

So Jillian turned back, surprised when her mind captioned the snapshot *two fathers.* If Jack was going to be a father, sooner or later she was going to cease being a pregnant woman and become a mother. None of them—not her, not Kera, that's for sure—had ever considered her having a baby. By sheer conviction, she had thought she was immune.

Gayle chuckled. "Hell. They're probably talking sports by now."

Late in the afternoon, Gayle told Jillian she'd love to draw her.

"Capture the rapture," Manford teased on his way to another nap. He showed Jillian the tank on a tiny cart, explaining how he preferred to lie down and think while he breathed. "Quite a deliberation," he paused for air. "Like running."

The two of them used to run together when she was into cross country. Memories of all those road races remained in a sound. His feet used to clump, hard, once for every three of her strides. Clump and she would breathe in-in-in, clump and let it out-out-out. It was still her rhythm. Well, it would be, after. Jack said he would run with her. They'd get a baby jogger.

"Why is he lying down so often?"

"He gets tired out." Gayle arranged pencils and charcoal sticks and glasses of water on her little supply table on wheels. "I was worried too, at first, but the doctor says his lungs are functioning at 80 percent, which is good. Humid days are the worst. More moisture for his lungs to work out of the air."

"So the oxygen's a boost." Jillian waited. "That's all."

"That's all."

Gayle's workroom faced the south. She never called it a studio, that was too sterile. She didn't exhibit there, she worked—hard. As her mother slipped further and further into a world of light and dark and shape, Jillian gazed out the wall of windows and found Kera and Jack. They had pulled lawn chairs under the sweet gum trees near the barn. Jack's hands moved rapidly and he smiled. His head dropped back and he and Kera were laughing. Was he telling the story of the truckers encircling them? How she had stood in the truckyard with her arms outstretched, feeling the cycling of hundreds of idling semis coursing through her body's water. She'd stood there, feeling purple with heat, trying to coax Jack. "Try it!" But then she'd felt faint. And Jack had started pulling her away: *You need to get away from the heat.* And she had screamed at him: *Leave me alone! For a minute! Leave me alone!* And that tall trucker with the cell phone: *You need some help, Miss?*

Outside, their faces grew serious; they huddled close. In the privacy of their nonpregnant conversation, were Jack and Kera admitting to each other that she might not make it?

"I need your face now, Sweetie."

Sweetie? "Since when am I sweetie?"

"Sure," her mother said, trance-like. "Sweetie, sweetie-babe."

Jillian grinned. Gayle had spent much of her university career on right-brain/left-brain research, drawing contours of people from memory, drawing with her eyes closed, drawing still lifes upside down. Doing anything to rattle the critic that cried for order.

Sweetie—Jillian remembered hearing it when she was young—*that brain of yours has been blessed with a mighty corpus callosum.* Back and forth, her mother had said. *You'll go back and forth with the best of them.* Gayle's strong arms waved, sometimes on the drawing pad she had propped on her easel, sometimes grabbing charcoal sticks and committing a thought to the canvas once she'd tried it out on newsprint.

When her mother revealed the images on her pad and canvas, Jillian saw light and shape and movement and something she hadn't seen in the mirror: hard, dark eyes. Gayle's work wasn't realistic, it was empathetic, an emotional rendering. Nervous hatchings of charcoal defined Jillian's shirt. Light and energy pushed against it.

Jillian squinted and her portrait was reduced to belly and eyes. Dark, mean eyes.

"My eyes."

"They're so dark now, aren't they?" Her mother stood back, squinting. She dipped her fingers in water and stroked a hard line on Jillian's shirt.

"They look mean."

"They look intense. They always have." Gayle began to put her things away. She watched Jillian and the drawing. "What a gift, to have you here now. All of you."

But all Jillian could think of, looking at the light on her belly and the worry in her eyes, was the word *all*, and her father's place in it. Her father and his oxygen tank and his *Capture the rapture*.

"Dad's such a clown."

She looked up and saw her mother crying. Great. So far, she was three for four. She had pushed Jack to tears at the Truckstop. She'd scared Kera in the driveway. And now, she'd managed to draw out her mother's sorrow—again. Everyone was thin and tired and crying.

Gayle motioned beyond the window.

Manford had joined Kera and Jack. Kera was standing and making masks with her hands, framing objects in the sky. Jillian felt a twinge of jealousy (and immediately felt ashamed) watching her father's and Jack's enthusiasm. Kera wasn't trying to take her place. She was simply out in the yard, doing exactly what Jillian would be doing if she were out there.

Gayle touched her shoulder and spoke softly. "It's okay to call her a baby."

Jillian shrugged.

"As an idea she might be overwhelming. But as a baby, you'll see. We'll all love her."

Jillian had never referred to the bowling ball as having a gender. "We call it the bowling ball."

Gayle howled. "Jack too? That's a baby. That's about the only thing I'm sure of."

"Let's go up on the deck, tonight. All of us."

Her mother gave her a quick hug and went back to her supplies.

"He's going to make it, Mom."

"Your Dad? Hell. He's so damned stubborn and self-important. You think he'd go without telling us when? He still thinks he's going to teach a full load in the fall."

Manford made it up to the deck, with Jillian in the lead and Jack behind him. "Watch his feet," Jillian told Jack, after dinner. "He's tentative."

Jack stepped over the top rung of the ladder. "So, this is the infamous star deck."

"It's great isn't it?" Kera stood with her arms outstretched. "Look at the fireflies."

The line of trees and bushes along the driveway sparkled with pulses of light, lightning bugs, people always called them fireflies, tiny flashes of green accompanied by a faint crackle. And in the distance, the banks of the Iowa River glowed.

Kera went back to the ladder. "Come on, doc. Gayle's making coffee. We should help."

Jack eyed Jillian as he descended. She gave him the okay sign. He still didn't get it. The only person she had ever needed protection from was him, from a love too strong to compartmentalize.

Manford settled on the south bench; she took the north. After a long silence—they scanned the skies for several minutes without a word—Jillian spoke.

"Dad. How are you feeling? Really."

"Hungry." He took a breath. "You know how your mind is always hungry? Hungry to dig through everything and get a hold of it? Well—" He took another breath and held it. "That's how I am. Hungry for air."

"God. It's bad enough when your head does that to you. Now you have to breathe like that too."

"Double whammy."

"No kidding."

"Damned pesticides." He took in another breath and she waited. "Anything that brings about that powerful of a positive effect—"

She finished it as he evened his breathing. "Must eventually bring about an equally strong negative reaction."

"You, you and your generation . . . " The lecture was coming after all. "You're going to have to fight like hell."

"Absolutely."

"Course. We all want plump yellow corn, without the little green worms, don't we?"

She wanted him healthy. Hungry in his mind, not his lungs. "Dad?"

"Yeah."

"Jack and I. We're going to make it. With a baby, I mean. We'll keep each other going."

"Yeah."

"Jack knows I'm not going to put my research aside. No more than I'd expect him to."

Manford looked at her quite seriously.

"I was on the pill, too. I'd never be that careless." Now she'd reached the level of pathetic. Talking birth control with her father? What on Earth was she looking for?

"That's what your mother said."

"I just didn't want you to think—"

He coughed. "Don't let anyone tell you how to get by. You just do it. And keep doing it." Cancer had softened him. "Jack." He paused to breathe. "He'll come through?" His eyes, as he concentrated on breathing, looked almost as hard and as worried as the eyes in her portrait. He had to know, right then, that she would make it.

"He'll come through." But she'd have to be careful. In her absence, Jack's mother's daily *You're not doing it right* could be toxic. "His mother is a little over the top."

"Uh-oh. Mama's boy?"

"A little, I guess. But he handles it."

They heard voices coming from below. Her father grabbed her arm and whispered. "Just messin." He waited until Jack, first up the ladder, was almost to the top, and he growled. "And if he doesn't come through, I'll kick his city boy ass."

Gayle's voice wavered up. "Man, would you quit?"

Jack must have been feeling quite comfortable. He looked down the ladder to Kera and Gayle. "Don't worry. I can outrun him."

Kera and Jillian pointed to the stars they were planning to track. Manford asked questions about the software and the process of imaging a star's spectrum at Lick compared to the masking they'd been testing in the engineering lab.

Jillian pictured the five of them from above—what the stars were seeing: Gayle lying with her legs dangling over the edge; Kera with her arms stretched overhead; her father lying as he always did, with his hands cupped under his head. She was on her side to keep the bowling ball from sinking into her abdominal aorta, and Jack was fidgeting, his knees knocking in and out like a kid's.

She touched her stomach, trying to conduct that sense of peace. More and more she was beginning to feel—in the baby's movements, in the way her stomach was leaving the rest of her body—the presence of an entirely separate being. Jack laid his hand on hers and she lifted her hand so that his was touching her belly.

"We need to find a star for the baby," she said.

They all started pointing and suggesting. Polaris was too nautical. Sirius too obvious. What about Vega in the Summer Triangle? It would be a fall baby.

"How about Arcturus?" Jack said. "Isn't that it? The bright orange one? Follow the arc to Arcturus?"

"Go star man," Kera teased.

Jack reached across and swatted the air above Kera.

"Taken." Jillian nudged her father. Arcturus was Manford's summer star. "What about Lyra? That sounds female."

Jack sat up. "You think it's a girl?"

"Mom seems to think so."

Kera sighed. "We can only hope."

Gayle's voice was soft in the dark. "Maybe we should give her one of the galaxies. What do you think, Man?"

Jillian loved it when her mother called him Man. Such a lasting joke on her old hippy days. Manford was nothing but uptight when he was young. Too serious, he always told Jillian. *Don't forget to have fun.*

"Me?" Manford said. "I think this is wonderful."

Later, after Kera and Jack sandwiched her father between them on the stairs and escorted him down, Kera and Gayle followed Manford into the house.

Jillian brought blankets out to the barn and she and Jack made love, slowly, gently, lying on their sides and touching all skin within reach. Jack, thankfully, did not touch her belly.

The next morning, all five of them stood around both cars trying to figure out who should back away first.

Jillian stood alone with her mother. "Let me know how Dad's doing."

"He's not going anywhere."

"I know." She hugged her mother fully. "I love you. I'm sorry."

"Sorry?"

"I'll be back, on the way home."

Jack saw Jillian crying and came over. "Me too. I guess we'll come back. Yikes! With a baby." He made a face of mock horror.

"Oh, come here, you big goon." Her mother hugged Jack, hard. "You be careful driving home. You got your coffee?"

Jack held up his thermos.

If this baby was a boy, Jillian vowed not to dote on him like her own mother was doting on Jack, right before her eyes.

Kera and her mother hugged for a long time, whispering and nodding. It made Jillian uncomfortable, watching her mother pass on to Kera the duties of watching over her.

Jack and her father saw it too. They stood together, looking a bit lost. Jillian went over to the two of them and threw her arms around them. To hell with proving her strength. If there was a time to love these two fathers, it was now.

Five for five, she thought, as their circle increased. All five of them came together and cried. Her father never said a word.

"We are so damned corny," her mother said.

"God, you guys are," Kera seconded.

A few miles down the road, Jack caught up with them and honked for them to pull over. "Your hotel list!" He waved a pad of paper in the air as he ran to Jillian.

She grabbed the hair over his ears and held on, breathing his smell.

"Oh! This is only going to get harder."

Kera patted both of them. "But do-able. We can do this."

Jack opened the car door and kissed Jillian's belly. "One more time. I think we got somewhere this weekend didn't we?"

She nodded. "No more bowling ball."

She remembered the quiet little peace sign her mother held up as they backed out of the drive. She had never asked her mother if she was planned.

Jack held her face and kissed her. "Okay. This is it." He shut the door. "Go kick some U-Cal ass."

Kera and Jillian waved their arms in the air until his car rolled over the last corn- and soybean-lined hill.

Finally, Jillian let her head fall back with a moan. "Damn it!"

"I know. I'm sure beginning to like that guy."

Jillian watched Kera's face, waiting for something to break the pain in her chest. Once again, when Kera couldn't make the move, Jillian did. "Help! I am so pregnant."

Kera broke out in song, mocking Jillian with a screaming rendition of "Having My Baby." It was funny—it was crazy!—and it was sad. But what the hell. Jillian joined her, though neither of them knew any of the words after that disgusting line about being a woman in love and loving what it was doing to her. They belted out what they knew and hummed the rest.

They were headed to California, regardless.

20

Evelyn Young

IT WAS EVELYN YOUNG'S "Edge of the Universe" presentation that drove Jillian to the roof—eventually, indirectly—but first she drove home, feeling like space junk.

Floating five hundred miles above Earth there were over eight thousand pieces of junk—metal, plastics, bagged biohazards—dating way back to Sputnik. So many items that agents of the government, privates in the Air Force, NASA specialists were assigned the task of monitoring their flotation. Why couldn't Jillian float? That's all she wanted: to drive, to change lanes, to exit the freeway, senselessly. But no. She drove home, her head full of lines and curves and Evelyn Young—and such conflict. The immediate, rousing heat of *You can do anything* and *Don't give up* left stranded and unusable because she knew, deep down where knowledge was older and colder, there would be no after.

What had ever made her believe she was special?

Evelyn Young, Air Force pilot, top in her astronaut class, the first and so far only female Space Shuttle Commander, had done everything *before*. And Jillian had taken the message to heart: no woman did it after.

She had taken the day off to attend Manny's field trip, a trip she had arranged after Kera had called to tell her astronaut Evelyn Young was going to speak in Lansing. Jillian had known—of course she had known—it would hurt, a little, but she also felt she had to do it, for the kids. She'd spent the morning in Manny's classroom, giving relatively unexcited (she'd thought) seventh graders background on the Hubble Space Telescope, and electromagnetic radiation, and how light came to us in different wavelengths, some visible and some not. Some so invisible they could only be imagined. Until Chandra, that is. NASA's x-ray telescope was producing images of faraway galaxies and quasars and tiny hot blurbs of brown and blue called dwarfs. And she had wanted to go further. What else might be lurking beyond what our light-gathering instruments could see? There, in the sup-posed emptiness between galaxies and clusters and clouds. Here, in the space between each of us. But Manny's class hadn't needed to be prepared. The minute Evelyn Young walked out on stage, Manny and Josh and especially the girls—the whole noisy, electrified audito-rium—had gone wild.

Standing slightly elevated before them, dressed in a NASA jumpsuit adorned with mission patches, Evelyn Young looked like a goddess. Her plainness only accentuated the excitement. This medium-tall, permed-haired woman with bright gray eyes had flown fighter jets and landed on aircraft carriers. She had docked the shuttle, not just once or twice but ten or twelve times. And all of them, Jillian included, had leaned forward in their seats, trying to get closer, even an inch closer, to the goddess above them. They fell in love, and who wouldn't? Standing in a circle of softening yellow light, Evelyn Young absolutely glowed with self-prophecy. She gave them only one piece of advice: "Keep learning," she said, "Love learning, and never give up."

With her bright eyes fixed, she beamed into them: *You can do it. You can.* Because she had. To admit she was special, to celebrate her as a fluke, even as a wonder, was to admit there were still so many obsta-cles. And why start with obstacles? "Everyone has to work at it," she told them. "Everyone."

She showed slides of the shuttle crew strapped in flight simulators, immersed in a near-zero-gravity pool, working on circuit boards in a classroom. "And just so you know, not everyone loves math." That had drawn a laugh.

She poked fun, showing a slide of crew biologist Patty Hall floating next to her space-bunk as she brushed her teeth, her hair rising from her shoulders and poking out in all directions like sharp-nosed snakes. Yes. Yes! Get the women on screen! She paused and said, in her gravest tone, "The only known hazard of long hair in space. Space hair."

Jillian had laughed—it was early in the presentation—but she won-dered, too, what hardships had Evelyn Young endured? Was she fly-ing in the late seventies when Air Force rumors claimed a woman's upper body musculature would go limp under the G-force of a mach-warp roll? She certainly wasn't old enough to have been put through the Viking experiments, when doctors—doctors!—injected icewater into female astronaut candidates' ears, then put them through a barrage of zero-gravity tests in an attempt to prove a woman's inner ear could not maintain balance under certain, anti-gravity conditions.

Did those tests matter anymore? Evelyn Young had endured. She'd become a lesson in her own time. Now, in the car, Jillian was feeling that urge to drive, to keep driving. But she didn't. Because her head was full of Evelyn Young. Because she was weak and indecisive and she and Jack were supposed to make Caesar salads for dinner, with the paprika and mustard-grilled chicken Manny liked, and they needed spinach and lettuce and tomatoes. And finally, truthfully, she drove home because she had to. No one else would be there for the kids.

At the grocery store, she put the bagged spinach and head lettuce and roma tomatoes on the belt with the tag board and colored index cards she'd picked up for Peia, and she thought about baseballs and saddles and flat pieces of paper, about positive and negative and zero curvatures and what each meant to the shape of space. She had positive's baseball: her sphere of lettuce. And negative's saddle—she depressed the spinach bag at its center so that it resembled, loosely, a saddle. And for zero, she had tag board and innumerable flat, planar index cards. One had only to imagine them going on and on forever, with nothing above or below.

She thought these thoughts and arranged groceries just so to protect herself, she figured. Why should she accept, in a universe so vast and pliable, a life reduced to only one point on such a crooked, crooked path? Before or after. Our position in the universe, whether we were spinning on a singular plane or stretching the skin of our cosmic balloon, was not so fixed.

Space had warps and grooves and distentions, even interruptions of sorts in the distribution of mass, but we didn't hold that against the universe. We were fascinated by fluctuation and variation. We saw creation in space and we were stunned. But here on Earth, we wanted to lock it down.

She carried her bags to the car, trying not to crease Peia's poster board, smelling the fresh parmesan, and her thoughts were punctuated by the slam of the car door. What good did it do to know the beginning? Life—*Slam!*—had no reverse.

She had sat there, with blonde-haired, medium-tall Evelyn Young standing alongside ten-foot-high images of galaxies and clusters and birth and death shrouds, trying to imagine the cosmic background as the very beginning. Perhaps this radiation was some left-over wall or far-flung skin that still existed as a remnant of the Big Bang, even as it continued to race away. But—and this was where she believed Einstein had distrusted the idea of a constant for expansion—if space were to expand forever, how could "forever" hold a shape?

We forgot, at times, that we were looking through instruments of our own making. Einstein had said something to that effect. *The theory decides what we look for.* We look for certain wavelengths of light, so we find them. We create a yardstick for measuring distance in space, so we find distance in space. We look for forever, so we find it.

She turned toward home. Home, where her heart was. Why then, was she always so conscious of the roads and the intersections and the buildings? Oh, how she wanted true darkness, the stillness of the Keweenaw Peninsula or the crunch of hollow corn stalks under a late fall sky. Her dormer was nice, with its windows high above the neighborhood. And the woods, she'd forever be grateful for those incredible old trees. But she'd never felt at home in Ann Arbor. It was the stillness that called to her most, like the stillness that descended today, in the middle of a presentation that seemed crafted to break her.

Always, she seemed to relearn: there were moments of great power in the lulls.

First, Evelyn had shown slides of her and her navigator strapped into the Space Shuttle Endeavour. "We all have our favorites," she'd said. She'd shown close-ups of the re-entry tiles that had given NASA so much trouble, and slides of bubbles. Bubbles! Huge, distended bubbles floating inside the shuttle as Patty Hall looked on, wearing monstrous telescopic goggles that magnified her eyes. Evelyn had joked again, putting everyone at ease. "I'll bet you can guess why Patty's nickname is Magoo." She showed slides from Hubble's daily pan across the universe: deep field views of spiral and elliptical and irregular-shaped galaxies. Dense clusters of hot, swirling stars. And where Hubble saw only visible light, illustrating distant structures as areas of vague blackness or haze, Chandra, with its x-ray eyes, was picking up gorgeous reds and purples. Wondrous shoots of colors streaming from what appeared to be a black hole.

And then Evelyn had stepped back, quietly, saying, "For these next few slides, I'm going to let you look without narrating. These images tend to speak for themselves."

It was the Orion nebula that started it all. Those plump, luscious, billowing pillars. And oh, how the pillars of Orion had spoken.

Great gaseous rounds of pinks and reds and purples swelled into two great pillars of dust, passageways formed from concentric rings of blues and greens, gasses and dust held together by some invisible force. And all of it sprinkled with tiny, hot dots. Even on Evelyn's slide, the heat of birth glowed. From deep within those neon pink nebular ovaries, new stars made the pink to orange to white-hot climb, emanating from the pillars one at a time, alone. Each birth occurring as much as one million years apart.

And somehow, deep down in the hush of wonder, breathing the colors of Orion's nebular ovaries with the rest of the audience, Jillian had felt hope. Chandra had photographed the maternal in space. Space was brewing more of itself, more of its own heavy, impossible glitter—and stars.

But at that very moment, hope faltered. Those pillars, with life passing through them, did the Orion feel it? The responsibility?

Motherhood should be like that, like warm, billowing, pink clouds of life. And it was, for seconds at a time. But day by day, she wasn't basking in an ovarian-pink glow. She was drowning in function.

All her life, she'd been taught to work—to work hard. Never to give up. Hadn't she said it herself, a million times? To Peia, to Manny, to his class, just that morning? *You can do anything.* But there, in the hush of wonder, she'd felt cold, heavy despair wrapping itself around her hope. Braiding itself, slowly, coolly; bonding like a helix to her hot, silly hope.

She had no idea how to give up.

She'd turned from the mesmerized faces of the kids in her row, to wipe tears away quickly, quietly. Because insights in the dark were like that. They didn't strike. They built up slowly, and they lasted.

The elderly women behind her had patted her, both of them nodding and whispering and pursing their bright-lipsticked lips. One of them had held out a tissue. "She's incredible, isn't she?" they whispered, as if they knew that Jillian had turned away from a woman too bold and too bright for her to look upon. So she'd turned back. *I am a mother, yes, but that does not make me less.*

She'd felt it, of course, for so long, everything about her life moving her toward giving up. Evelyn's and Kera's, even Jack's "Don't give up" mixed with the hush of "But you have children." She'd held her lips tightly, though they trembled, because she was proud, so proud of Kera and Evelyn and Sandy Faber and Vera Rubin, because they hadn't given up. Though neither had she, not exactly. Perhaps she'd been born missing something that Evelyn and Kera and Vera had, something strong enough to make life different, to hold out for special, but she would forever be glad to see a woman's curves in a NASA jumpsuit. For that, she could endure.

At the end, when it was only Jillian and Evelyn under the stage-lights, standing close enough to see that the highlights in Evelyn's hair were blonde, not graying—she was so young!—Jillian had tried to hang on. Evelyn must have felt it. She'd thought Evelyn was hanging on too, clasping Jillian's hands and with gray-eyed directness, telling her *Don't give up*. But now, sitting in the driveway with the smell of parmesan filling the car interior, Jillian wondered: Was Evelyn trying to shake her off?

Manny got off the bus and tapped on her car window. "Hey." Hey, after the two of them had shared such a wondrous, intimate afternoon. Hey, after Orion's billowing pillars. Then again, he was used to finding her at home, staring off into space. She raised her hand toward the back seat, pointing with her car keys, and he reached in to grab a bag.

She was leaning against the kitchen slider, staring out at the woods when Peia came crashing through the front door. "Mom! Mom! You gotta see this!"

Peia emptied her Friday Folder full of school work and Jillian touched each fill-in-the-blank paper as if she were entirely there. Because no one else was.

"See, they're neatness checks," Peia said and Jillian nodded.

Who could blame Peia for rushing? Sheet work. Sameness. Lines.

Peia took one sheet out of Jillian's hand and inserted another. "Everytime I finish an assignment, I look it over, erase any bad penmanship, and then I sign the back." Peia pointed to the penciled box. "See? Ms. Beals signs it too. I got a check-plus."

Check-plus. Jillian hugged Peia when Peia brought her body close—Check-plus—wishing she could tell Peia everything that was in her hug, all of the fear and the anger and the aching. Evelyn Young had days like these. Days when her four-year-old's peanut butter sandwich or whether or not she was happy in preschool took priority. Days when she didn't feel like a saint or a rebel or a hero. Days when she was a woman at home with her daughter and she wanted the world to stop testing them all the way through.

Peia wiggled away.

Later, Jillian and Jack stood side by side, occasionally bumping into each other as she spun the lettuce. (Positive curvature and gravitational potential in a closed universe.)

She longed to reach out, to grab Jack and say "I am not special!" Not one of them: not Jack, not Manny, not Peia, not even Kera, was going to be able to grant her some special motherhood reprieve, some extension or exception for love of the highest order.

But one of the kids would come running through. Manny paced around the kitchen island, winding them up in his thoughts. Peia came back with another sheet, back with another drawing, back with another story. And so what? Jack already knew. No matter what she said he would stand, frown once or twice, and then turn away.

At the dinner table, Peia gave the order for their nightly ritual: *Tell about your day.* They would go clockwise, starting with Peia (a mistake), then Manny, then Mom, then Dad. What could she tell? That she'd found hope and despair in a pair of neon pink space ovaries? It didn't matter, the universe had not let go—Jillian found herself watching her family through a flurry of subatomic activity.

Evelyn had told them how space, the sky, the air around us was rushing with neutrinos—particles that streamed from the stars and passed through everything: water, rock, humans. And Jillian had loved her for it. Most people figured kids couldn't handle it: the invisible, the indefinable. But that was the point, wasn't it? First, we must imagine. What was astounding about neutrinos was their shape-shifting abilities. As they hurled toward Earth, they seemed to rotate and spin, bouncing off something invisible, changing from one "flavor" to the next as they traveled through space.

But the particles assembling over the dinner table were quarks—not neutrinos. Jillian recognized them from the "Particles of Light" model she had been working on. No shape-shifting secrets revealed today. Today, her own turquoise, yellow, and fuchsia quarks hovered in a cloud over the dinner table.

Jack said to Peia, "Okay, you're first. Tell about your day."

Quarks shifted in a wave as Jillian changed her gaze, and she smirked at their mocking. Had she really believed the world would wait for her mind? Yes. Some part of her had been stupid enough to believe, because she'd given the universe these children.

"Well," Peia began, pulling the crust off her bread, making a hole in the center, using it as an eyepiece to scope out Jack. Jack made a circle with his fingers and eyed her back. And the quarks framed this for her: *this* was what she'd waited for. For this excruciatingly slow, small cycle of wakings and workdays and book orders and "Tell About Your Days" in which Peia reenacted her every move and Manny chewed on.

"Ask me things," Peia said. "Ask me about math."

"Okay." Jack reached for the rolls, sending quarks streaming like a nest of disturbed wasps. Tomorrow, she would try neutrinos. She knew enough to get started. She knew that neutrinos passed through the human hand at the rate of 1,500 trillion per second when that hand lay still. And that they had bigger, anti-particle cousins she hadn't kept up with.

Jack's hand withdrew and the wasp-like activity settled. "What did you do in math today?"

Jillian looked at Manny and Manny rolled his eyes. Quarks buzzed round his head and zoomed back to Peia. Letting Peia go first was a big mistake. She'd never finish a bite of food.

"Well." Peia elongated the word, making it last while she ripped another piece of bread into strands. She stood up from her chair and laid strips of bread—flower petals—around her spoon and the quarks danced above her flower.

Finish a sentence! "Sit down," Jillian said sharply, and the quarks scattered. To hell with nutrition! If the girl never ate another square meal in her life, but she followed her dreams, wasn't that what Jillian wanted?

Manny dug into his spaghetti and the quarks whooshed him by. "Sorry."

Jack touched her arm and the quarks that had been racing around the table slowed to swirl around her and Jack. Why didn't he see them? Why didn't he feel their tiny, busy pressure?

"Peia." Jack said her name firmly to get her attention. "Sit and eat."

"Okay, okay!" Peia sat. "But you have to ask me things."

Manny made his comment. "This'll only take forever." Lately,

Manny was unable to let any situation pass without tagging it with some smug summary. "Forget anyone else's day." *Pop, pop, pop-pop-pop.* Quarks bounced from Manny's side of the table, assaulting the rest of them and Jillian was tempted to duck, but she sat firm, taking Manny's energy beating while Jack asked Peia questions.

"How far are you in your multiplication tables?"

She'd surpassed the twelves. She'd come home with that story yesterday.

"Dad. I'm doing random facts."

"Wow. Past twelves, huh?"

Peia stuffed a piece of bread in her mouth. "Oh yeah. Ask me some."

Jack and Peia, ever doing, challenged each other with equations. Quarks encircled the two of them, turquoise and yellow and fuchsia moving in little pitches and swells, a border of scalloped lace. Manny chewed. And Jillian found her "Tell."

Let's be honest, she would say, if she were going to be honest. *I love you. I love you all. But I'm dying here.* (The quarks, in her vision, flattened themselves on the table and wobbled.) *From the day I married you* (Quarks lined up in front of Jack and pelted him.) *and then gave birth to you* (Quarks circled Manny's head, a few pulsed over his heart.) *and even with you, sweetie* (Quarks danced around Peia's eyes) *I have been slowly dying inside.* (Quarks fell to the table and played dead.) *Each time I give to you* (Quarks slinked toward Jillian, throbbing as they climbed her torso.) *there are pieces of me sent out* (Quarks streamed away in waves.) *but they never come back.*

The quarks hovered, scared, waiting.

I can't possibly exist without you, is that it? My mind has nothing but space for you?

This was what she could never impart to Jack. How being married and having children could make her feel so small—so not special. People beamed their expectation into her eyes, sometimes so forcefully she had to turn away. *Of course your children are your choice.*

The quarks moved from one corner of the table to the other, trying to find refuge. There seemed to be nothing Jack had not accomplished.

Your thoughts are my thoughts, huh? Your dreams mine too? Mine fall away, like petals of a flower because yours come pushing up through?

Faced with her hardened, honest face, seeing no smile—and no take-backs either!—the quarks plummeted, rolling from the table and onto the floor. Harmed. Weakened. Shimmying.

At the end of the presentation, Evelyn Young had invited the kids up on stage for a question and answer session. Manny's teacher had asked Jillian to make sure the girls, especially, "got something out of it." So Jillian had taken out her list, ready to facilitate. But one of those elderly ladies behind her had hollered out: "I noticed a ring on your finger. Are you married?" And the girls followed along: "Do you have children?" "Does your husband help out?" "I mean, does he take care of everything when you're gone?"

Jillian had sat there, hoping to get her chance to ask:

- *What courses did you take in college?*
- *Did you always know you wanted to go up in space?*
- *What was your favorite mission and why?*

She'd sat there, hope and despair turning to embarrassment and dismay as their honored guest, woman of space, endured their home and family questions. But before she'd gotten a chance to redirect, to ask the truly important questions—*What was your biggest challenge in school? Out in space?*—Evelyn's dark-suited, pale-faced congressional escort had shooed Jillian and the kids away.

And Evelyn had taken her hand. "I get asked about my family every time."

The girls hadn't meant to diminish Evelyn Young's accomplishments. They wanted to know, honestly, how she'd done it. Had any of their mothers done *it*, after all? Whatever *it* was? Broken the barrier, as the slide of Evelyn in the cockpit of an F-16 assured them? But they weren't assured. The girls had tightened their ring around the Commander, and in the privacy of that circle, they pressed her for the truth. They needed a model, a standard approach, the real way to become. And they knew no one but an expert, no one but Evelyn Young, could tell them.

Manny—"Oh, finally, I get to speak"—sat up, excited. "I got to play a new piece, this bluesy kind of thing. Twelve bar blues or something like that, on the bass."

Jack put his hands in the air, holding an imaginary bass neck and plucking. "Walkin' eight. I think that's called walkin' eight."

"Yeah! Yeah!"

They plucked, walking their voices up and down, and Peia strode to the piano and ponked. "I can do that."

And Jillian checked the floor: no quarks.

What was that her mother had always told her? She'd go back and forth with the best of them? Jack's and Manny's voices were rising, jockeying for position above Peia's ponking, and Peia played harder and faster. If this was back and forth, forget it! She'd rather bale hay.

A sudden, painful realization—one of those hot ones—struck her. She leaned over, checking under the table, but the quarks were gone. *This* was why her father had helped out on the Otterbein's farm all those summers. To quiet his mind. To keep math from driving him crazy.

Jack scooted Peia away from the piano, keeping his body between the two kids as he made them clear the table. And Jillian sat, struck by the chaos. How intuitive someone had been to call the chaotic, modern family *nuclear*. Could it be that the insides of an atom understood? That they stuck together out of some intricate, particulate sense of responsibility to the whole of matter?

"We went to that presentation on space." Manny looked at her funny as he stacked fruit bowls. (Peia hadn't touched her peaches.) Jillian knew he was looking at her, she felt it, though she didn't return the check. She was trying to figure out what it meant, that the corn— her father's noisy, dusty, physical salvation—had done him in.

She had to say something. "Evelyn Young." The name that had sounded like proud music, like a manifesto earlier in the day, came out as a scratch.

"She showed these slides about erosion," Manny tapped Jack, who was leaning against the sink, eating Peia's peaches. "You just can't believe what the rainforest rivers look like."

Evelyn's last few slides were a series of topographical surveys of Earth. She had talked about how everyone's time was well utilized; how the shuttle crew was made up of biologists, physicians, a pilot and others; how her job, once the shuttle was safely in orbit, was to photograph the world's largest forests and rivers. From way out in space, it was so obvious, what deforestation was doing to the planet's water supply. Comparison shots near the equator showed green, lush forests and blue rivers from her first mission, side-by-side with erosive mud-rivers where clean water and forests had once been.

"Man, they've got to stop cutting down trees."

Man, you've got to stop looking at your mother as some inexhaustible source.

Peia got away. Jillian watched her walk down the hallway and turn to head up the stairs. Jack and Manny didn't notice. Or maybe they did. Rinsing and loading dishes would be easier without her. Poor Peia. Jillian suspected Peia's mind was more like her grandfather's— and her mother's. That's why they couldn't possibly give each other enough time. Manny's mind was busy, always composing, but his music gave him order. Peace.

She hadn't made a ceremony out of it, out of giving up, but it had always been there—that simultaneous, two-corded hope and despair. Especially once Peia was born. Everytime she told herself, *A well-trained astrophysicist can do anything*, she was quick to remind herself that it was natural to aim for more than you could accomplish. Everyone aimed high.

But Jack, her mother, even Kera, her dear Kera, had embraced the ongoing lie. There was no after. After was an elixir, a haze, a bundle of excuses. Jack and Manny and Peia were forever going to be her excuse. *Hail to the future!*

"Evelyn Young has a daughter. A four-year-old."

Jack half-turned his shoulders to look her way as he bent to load the dishwasher.

"Her husband's an engineer, in Mission Control. He knows what it means, space."

Evelyn Young had faced the girls as they pressed her for answers, scanning their hungry, disbelieving eyes. "I think, what you want to know is, can you get married and have kids and do something as demanding as a career in space, right?"

The girls nodded, pressing tighter.

"Sure you can. As long as you do it in the right order."

Commander Young completed Astronaut School *before* she married. She flew the fastest jets and the most expensive spacecraft *before* she had a child. And once young Evelyn had put those accomplishments behind her, she became so valuable to NASA, they were willing to put up with those last few months of pregnancy when she would not train in simulators and those first few weeks of her newborn's life when she wanted to breastfeed to give her baby the best start.

That's all Jillian had ever wanted, for Manny and Peia to have the best possible start. But every day started, and it just kept going on and on.

"Evelyn and her husband. They didn't have a child until after she'd gotten through training."

Manny seemed to understand that an argument was brewing. He remembered a sign-up sheet for some basketball party and went to his room to find it. Peia, who had come back to the kitchen to hunt through her marker bin for scissors and tape pulled the bin from its shelf and hurried after Manny. Manny took care of Peia when Jillian couldn't. And that was okay. It was okay for them to learn to rely on each other.

That's how she had come to know them all so well, by listening to their fears and disappointments. Each a different set of ups and downs. Jack trying to train lab assistants who didn't share his passion for exactness. Peia who had no exactness, only a spiral of ideas and actions and never the freedom to follow them all. The music that ran in Manny's head, like a river, a river he ached for when he was held too long away.

It was a mistake, hiding her pain. She should let them all have it: her quarks, her thoughts, the pain that had filled her chest as she'd gripped Evelyn's warm dry hand and felt the warmth of her wedding band, the shine of a special marriage.

When she'd walked up to Manny and his friends after Evelyn had gone, asking if they wanted a ride back to school, Manny had said, too quickly, "Nah, we're going to take the bus." And he hurried Luanne and Josh to the bus with him. *Shoo, Mom.* He didn't want her to embarrass him with her stories of almost-space: of his mother walking him around and around the barrel of one of the most powerful telescopes in the world while he—colicky and too skinny for a baby—cried and cried; of her visit to the Space Station prototype, when she and Kera had suited up together in dust-free gear.

Mothers were supposed to screen out the bad. Her own mother, when Jillian had asked about childbirth, replied "I don't remember much. We were gassed at the end, you know?"

Jack, near the end of her labor with Peia, had gotten scared. Her uterus was contracting in waves the size of an ocean, sending that pressure down through her groin, and Jillian had doubted, watching her own legs shake uncontrollably, her ability to go on. She had watched Jack's certainty, his position in the delivery room and in the world, slip away. But then she'd been lifted to push. When she got to holler and shake and push—*that* was the good part. The part her mother had missed.

Manny was shooting his plastic basketball at the miniature hoop on the back of his door. The door thumped, above, as she stood over the sink. The garbage disposal's grinding assaulted her ears, adding one more layer of noise that she couldn't screen out.

Jack moved behind her and slipped his hands under her elbows, pulling her to his chest, and he pressed his face to hers. "Hey." Hey, so soft, so soothing.

Evelyn Young had not dismissed her, the congressman had.

Jillian and Evelyn and Kera, they'd all been e-mailing each other. NASA was about to announce a call for planet-finding technologies, and Evelyn thought they had a chance. Kera was hoping Jillian and Evelyn would find time to sneak away, just the two of them. But the congressman had pulled Evelyn away. "The Commander's on a very tight schedule." Jillian had wanted to remove his age-spotted hands from Evelyn's elbow. *Talk about a tight schedule. This is my last chance, pal!*

And Evelyn had remained. "You and Kera, you were ahead of your time, but NASA's catching up." She beamed *Don't give up.* "I'll send everything I know about the conference. Keep me informed." And the two of them—mother before and mother after—had stood facing each other, each eyeing what the other could have become.

She dropped her head back, resting in the hollow between Jack's shoulder and his chest. "I am barely managing."

"Tough day, huh?"

Peia called from the living room. "Mom! Dad! Come and listen to this!"

No! I need.

"In a minute, babe," Jack called out. "Mom and Dad need some time."

"She's three years younger than me, and everything, the whole universe is opening up for her. And it should, it should." Why was it so difficult, to say out loud, what she dreamed of, every day, in her head?

Jack sighed and lowered his chin to her shoulder. "So you're thirty-nine, and working your way into some incredible projects. What about that hydrogen model?"

Model, yes. But to go up in it? He just didn't get it. The Hydra-whatever-they-named-it would never be enough. She leaned back harder.

"You have to hear this, before I forget!" Peia called.

"Babe." Jack reached out to her, showing his desire to stay connected as he inched away. "It's all going to work out. Something's going to happen with your MAT. I'll be right back."

She and Kera had joked about how male the terms were: WIMPS and MACHOS, so they had called the Suitcase a MAT, for Masked Aperture Telescope, early on. The name had dropped away once they decided shaped masks worked best.

Throughout the evening, as she listened to Peia's songs and helped Manny with Algebraic equations; while Jack hustled the kids in and out of the shower and ran up and down the stairs for pajamas; she tried to communicate the urgency in her despair.

"I can't wait any longer, Jack. There are only so many opportunities." She watched him plod up the stairs, calling after him as he disappeared around the landing. "This really could be it for me." She hated the way she was always saying: this is it for me, as if she had to prove there was a crisis before she could put herself first. She wanted to scream, *I am sick of talking to your back!*

Bedtime came. It always came. But this day wasn't going down, Jillian could feel it.

Peia talked about how she and Lisa had found a way to catapult their bodies over the top of the crossbars and land on their feet, most of the time. Jillian cautioned Peia as she was supposed to. She sat semi-still on Manny's floor, trying to listen. His friends were wearing plaid shirts and slouching and all acting alike, even Chad. By the time she made it to her room and found Jack propped up on pillows and falling asleep as if nothing had happened—"Jack!"—she couldn't contain the pressure.

She had watched a fermi-sized model—"That's ten to the negative eighteenth power!"—spin over the table. Didn't he think that was a sign? Her viewing quantum whatevers while they talked about their days? Had he heard what she'd said? Evelyn Young had a child! Kind of took away the old excuse, didn't it? Or did that part pass him by, because, so what? Women had children! Did he hear the "had" part? Had he ever had a giant petri dish looming over his dinner?"

"That one's rhetorical, I take it."

There were times when his sassy little remarks reminded her that he was just another husband being harangued by his wife. But this was not one of those times.

"No one ever looks at you and makes you feel small, do they, for having kids." Perhaps it was the lack of peace in her eyes that made strangers so forceful: *You've made your choice.*

"What? Who?"

"Seriously. What do you do? Look at me and say, that's what happens to women when they have children? They want to organize the junk drawers?"

"What the hell happened today?"

"No!" She pulled away. "Don't do that—hey. Hey. You just don't get it, do you? I still want it. I still want all of it. To be in training with Kera. To be submerged in the pool. To be outside, on the mountain, sitting under all those wires and metal. But every time I try to talk about it, the only thing you seem to be able to do is help me accept less."

And there it was again, the sad, vulnerable, "sorry" look. The "Sorry, but don't take this any farther" look. Because Jack was tired. He was tired of having to look sorry.

"You don't think it was real." Neither did she, sometimes.

"That's not true."

"But hey. Who needs a telescope or a mountain or a strong pot of coffee in the middle of the night when you have two smart, healthy kids and a house on a hill, right?"

She avoided his eyes because this was the part when everything conspired to make her feel small—stupid, silly, over-her-head small. Jack didn't realize it, but his smirk dismissed her, chuckled at her. Jack and the dark-suited, pale-faced congressman and his flat, condescending smile. He'd watched Jillian file the kids in and count them, and she knew what he'd thought: *Shoo, housewife.* And Jack, with his soothing hands, trying to steer her away from the past. And the kids who came crashing through doors and into rooms always with their issues first.

"Why are you so—god, why am *I* so willing?—to accept that because I have kids, I have to give up? Even when I say it. Space. See? It sounds so false."

Jack knew, didn't he? Then why didn't he ever say it? *Yes, you had it in you. You could have done it.*

"Talk, Jack. Tell me, I could have done it."

He shut the door, quietly, trying to maintain eye contact as he moved. His eyes were still studying her, trying to gauge how serious a blow-up this might be.

"I'm listening. I just never know what to say here."

"How about, gee, you're right? My research never faltered and yours, well, yours stopped."

It didn't really matter, now, what either of them said. He was tired of hearing it, and so was she. This was an exercise, a necessary exercise in getting the time and space she needed to think.

"You think I'm washed up."

His eyes softened. "What?"

Not washed up, exactly, but tied up. "That's why you can't listen. Somewhere deep down inside, you figure I'm your wife and Manny and Peia's mother, so there's no way I'm going to do anything but be here. Right? Okay, she's thrown her fit, back to normal."

He took a step forward. "Jilli."

No. No Jilli. Not now. "I was trying to figure out the difference between you and me, the way we look at each others' jobs, our whole lives really. And you know what it comes down to? A lack of respect."

"Oh come on. You can't say I don't respect you."

"I love thinking of you in your lab, sniffing over a dish and holding it just so. Why don't you think of me like that?"

"I do. I love what you do."

"No you don't. I work at Burton's now, Jack. I make software for other researchers, and shows for planetariums, and heat and pressure models for someone else's next shuttle." While he was escorting the kids in and out of the shower she had gone to the dictionary for help. She'd looked up respect, love, integrity, even taken for granted, but granted is a funny word. Before you can be taken for granted, you have to have been granted something in the first place.

"I was looking up words."

Jack's arms and eyes dropped away and he groaned.

"What? Am I supposed to shut up? What?"

What did he want from her when he dropped away like that? For a second his eyes paled and she knew she could have demolished him, but he was right. The lecture was coming.

"You have been unfaithful to me."

He let out a cry of disbelief. "What?"

"Who's talking?" Peia's voice called from her bedroom.

Jillian recited, from *respicere*, the root of respect. "Believing in someone and doing everything in your power to honor her dreams. That's the deepest kind of fidelity."

"I love what you do and you know it."

"No. You love what I used to do, because now it can't get in your way."

"That's not fair."

"No?" He didn't want to help her figure out how to give up. He wanted to keep pretending. "Oh, that's right. Families don't move and husbands don't follow their wives and parents don't uproot their kids, do they?"

"Damn it, Jill. It's bedtime."

"Did you know? Did you see some point where I'd become too bogged down and you knew I couldn't handle it all? You had me?"

"I have never stopped you from taking any position you wanted."

"What? You never stopped me?"

"Who's talking?" Peia's voice called from her bedroom.

Jack automatically moved toward the door.

"Do you really believe that? You never stopped me?"

"Mom?" Manny's voice scratched into the room. "What's going on?"

Jack looked almost comical, standing near the door, twisting back and forth between her and Manny and Peia's voices. "Happy now?"

Happy? "No!" She didn't mean to shout. But she refused to be put on hold. She jumped after Jack as he headed for the door and their bodies jammed in the doorway. "No! This is at the root of everything. Everything. You, Jack. Not Manny, not Peia. You."

Jack peeled her fingers off his arm. "Fine. I've wrecked your life. Can we stop now?"

Peia ran to him. "Stop fighting."

"We will, babe." Jack soothed. "We're sorry."

I am not sorry! She wanted to tear Peia off him. The kids were always there for him, protecting him. Poor, gentle Jack. "Another shield, huh, Jack?"

"Mom." Manny's voice came from his bed. "That's a little harsh."

She growled and went back into the room.

"What's wrong?" Manny called. "Dad, what's wrong?"

She heard Jack tell Peia to stay put, but she didn't. Jack stomped in with Peia right behind him. "You guys have to stop!" she said.

"Go to bed." Jillian never took her eyes off Jack. "Go back to bed, sweetie." She spread her hands over Peia's shoulders and steered her toward the door.

"Will you stop?" Peia stood and waited.

Jillian nodded and Jack escorted Peia back to bed.

When he returned, he fumbled around the closet for a blanket.

"Classic, Jack."

"What? That I don't want to sit here and get berated? How long am I supposed to listen to your definitions of everything I've done wrong?"

"Until you face it."

"Face what? How I've wrecked your life? What else is there?" He yanked the covers off the bed. "Damn it Jillian. Why do we have to do this? Why do we have to keep doing this?"

How could anyone watch someone they loved stand before them, pining for themselves, and shut down. Completely shut down.

"Because, Jack. Because for ten years, no matter what changes we've gone through, you've gone from Assistant Professor to Lab Director to full tenure. Your work has gone on."

He pretended to separate blankets, balling one around his forearms.

"Great. Protect yourself, Jack. Quick, protect yourself."

Manny appeared in the doorway. "Can't you two just stop it?"

She heard Peia run back to her bed and Manny followed. But she couldn't stop pressing.

She cut Jack off as he headed for the door. "You have expected, since—" She could not say *since Peia was born*, but that was the truth. One kid: travel as long as Grandma's available. Two kids: too much for Grandma. "For years. For years, you've expected everything I need to do, to drop away. Just drop away! What do you tell yourself to make that okay?"

He stood, glaring at her for being honest, and said nothing. Nothing! Smirking.

"You are such a coward!" She pushed against his chest with both hands, and when he did not falter, she pushed harder. "Coward!"

The sudden jolt of energy displaced him and he stumbled back into the hallway. For the tiniest second she fought the urge to push again, to watch him thump and crumple down the stairs, helpless, even with the incredible anger he would feel all the way down. But Manny and Peia were watching, huddled on Peia's bed. Jillian caught sight of Manny cupping his hands over Peia's ears. They trusted her.

Jack's eyes were wild with bright blue. She wished he would push back and get it over with. Have it out. But he wouldn't.

She bumped him against the wall as she rounded the stairway, with Manny's voice calling after her. "Mom? Mom?"

Downstairs, kneeling on the furnace room floor, she tried to calm herself with deep breaths. God, what next? Wail on him, verbally and physically, while the kids looked on? She knew, from the outside, how bad this would look. She wasn't oppressed or neglected. She had it pretty good. Hah! *Pretty* good! Simple short-hand for not good enough.

Sometimes, when you got close, close enough that you knew what you wanted and you could see what you needed, see the possibility of it, that's when you had to fight the hardest. She went for the column of boxes in the corner, pulling them down, tearing flaps open. When she found only books and three-ring binders, she kicked them aside and tore into the next pile. Jack would never fight back. He'd stand there and take it. Stand like a man and make her look bad. The same guy who used to call her Einstein. They all did. He'd been proud of her ideas once. Now, he could barely stand to listen to them.

She was going to dig up the NIRV studies and the old masks and get the visible light coronagraph going again. No matter what. She was!

She found the box she was after, untouched at the bottom of the stack, and it occurred to her that much of her life was in boxes. There was her memory before children, and it still existed as a whole, a "box" stored away that was still a part of her, but she couldn't quite open it, not fully, not at any given time. Then, there was her memory after children—with significant gaps. Anything she'd learned during those first few years after the kids were born, she had to relearn, it seemed. She had to re-read and study papers, even those she'd written herself, to jostle the box lid again.

This was what Jack didn't understand. Having the children had changed her. And in some way, she was afraid to open up the old box again. Everything in that old box had been possible until she turned away. She was afraid of stirring it all up, of failing again.

Sometimes she wondered how much of a woman's supposedly menopausal moods and fits and heat was purely physical and how much emerged from years of bottled-up, unexpressed anger. Giving in slowly, in daily and sometimes hourly increments, until you couldn't put yourself back together in any meaningful way. No wonder women got angry!

She sat back on her heels, her box of binders and disks and notebooks waiting, and she realized Jack needed correcting. She hadn't followed in the footsteps of Einstein, she'd become his wife, Mileva Maric! Mileva, the original physicist turned wife-and-mother, spent her early years at the Swiss Polytechnic Institute, the only female in the school. Unfortunately, Albert was also in class. When she got pregnant, they threw her out and Mileva spent the rest of her life alternating between bouts of depression and fits of rage, while, of course, managing the house (however poorly) and taking care of their two, maybe three children, if there was truth to the story about the first baby being given up for adoption.

That's why Albert left. The house was too chaotic. He couldn't get any work done!

Jillian draped her binoculars and a pen-light around her neck, and kept digging for her clipboard, the one with hand triggers on either side that lit up tiny red lights so she could write in the dark.

She'd never really considered her life as a Maric-model. Then again, she'd never fully considered pulling an Einstein either.

Upstairs, she walked to the dormer and opened the window.

Jack, pretending to sleep—if that wasn't a sign of detachment—sat up.

"What are you doing?"

"Isn't it obvious?" She removed the screen and laid it inside.

"You can't go out there, it's January."

She looked up at the stars. Thank the universe, it was January and unseasonably warm. She guessed fifty degrees.

"Jill. Come on."

"Hey." She turned back. He still looked comical, sitting with the covers pulled halfway over his bare torso. What was he trying to do? Entice her into bed? "Remember how you used to call me Einstein? Don't call me that anymore. Call me Maric." She swung one leg through the open window and hoisted herself through. "Maybe someday you'll figure it out."

Jack stared from the bed as she shut the window. And she wished she could have punctuated it with the snap of a lock. A lock from the outside, to keep him away.

She crawled backwards to the peak, thinking this was no time to fall, because no one could help her now. No one could hope for or believe in her—not Evelyn or Kera, not her mother, certainly not Jack. That's what Mileva had learned, too late. The hopes of her parents and her friends had not kept her in school. Their belief hadn't done her any good, either, when she went back once, twice, three and four times, pregnant and then later post-partum, to take the grad- uate exam which would allow her to teach and to grow and to pursue what she'd always intended to pursue. But Mileva failed. Over and over she failed.

Some said she never had it in her. But Jillian knew. She'd lost hope and probably her sense of self, too. Pregnancy and shame, and the wishes and judgments of others had changed her forever while Albert worked on.

Jillian knew the quiet promise of peace in *Give up* and the hard- eyed fix of resistance in *Don't you dare*. A chance, an opportunity to make something of herself beyond motherhood, that was all she was asking for. And it was going to require a fresh start—alone. Alone.

She was thirty-nine, the mother of two bright and active children, sitting with the pointy ends of her pelvis straddling the peak of a sub- urban home in a town she never intended to stay in, on a night too warm and too moist for decent seeing, yet she couldn't help feeling there had to be a way. There had to be a way.

Funny, how a good fight could do that, clear up the haze.

She looked straight up where her own R Aurigae should be, a variable star within the Charioteer, the bringer of the dawn. *Don't let this be an exercise.*

Under wavering points of light, she organized her supplies. She laid her clipboard nearby with a fresh sheet of graph paper readied, flashed her pen light a few times, settled her binoculars just under her ribs. Finally, she lay back with her knees bent and her feet dug in to the shingles, concentrating on quieting her mind, breathing in for three, out for three, in for three, out for three, waiting for the clarity of thought she knew must come.

She had had it in her. She had.

21

Pictures

WALKING THROUGH THE ENTRY DOORS their first time at the observatory, it was love at first sight. As Kera's low voice whispered, it was "Rapture." The telescope sat motionless and visible through large rectangular viewing windows, its 60-foot-long barrel poised between the tines of a huge two-pronged fork, a giant U-shaped equatorial mount painted yellow-gold. They pressed their faces to the glass and followed the barrel upward, counting three levels of metal stairways and balconies and catwalks, where the upper floors glowed a faint green-blue, throwing a soft echo of sky up into the dome. Such color! And such humbling height. Four stories above, the domed ceiling was open just a few degrees and a slice of light fell from ceiling to floor, picking up blues and golds and mixing them into a beam of golden-green, a god-like presence of light.

They walked the circular hall, sighing and squeezing each other's hands and whispering back and forth, "How did we get here?" They looked closely at the walls, filled with photographs of deep sky objects from Lick's own lenses; drawings from the late 1800s when the original 36" Lick refractor and its dome were constructed; a written account of the entombment of James Lick's remains in the supporting tier of the telescope. And there were women—head shots of astronomers, old and new—women!

"Look." Jillian read from a bio. "It's Vera Rubin. She and Dr. Faber, they worked together."

"Oh, Jilli." Kera's voice trailed off around the circular hall. "The Hyades and The Pleiades imaged together."

Jillian called, reading from a plaque. "Remember how I told you they had to shorten the Lick refractor? Guess how?" She read as Kera walked toward her. "An error in the estimate of the focal length had caused the tube to be built too long. A hacksaw—"

"No!" Kera scanned the old photos. "How could they?"

"A hacksaw was sent for and the tube unceremoniously short-ened."

"Oh, but listen." Kera read from an observer's log. "The first image, of a blazing red sun, the bright star Aldebaran, came into focus."

Jillian remembered being on the star deck at home with Manford, Gayle, Kera, and Jack, all of them pointing out stars for the baby. Aldebaran. She had always loved its strong and mystical sound. Oh, but she had to put that away! This was no place for baby thoughts.

"Here for a tour?"

Jillian's stomach scraped the wall as she turned toward the docent. They'd passed his desk on the way in. Sometimes she actually forgot she was pregnant. "We're here for research."

"Dr. Faber," Kera said. "She's expecting us."

Sandra Moore Faber, the observatory's Lead Astronomer, had been a professor at the University of California since Kera and Jillian had entered school. It was Dr. Faber who had signed the cover of their application, stamped and returned with: *Proof of Concept Study Approved.* When Kera called that morning—Jillian's vocal cords had become paralyzed with awe—Dr. Faber had asked them to meet her in the conference room before their training session with Tim, Mount Hamilton's Support Astronomer.

On the stairway, out of the docent's sight, Jillian and Kera inter-locked arms.

"We're going to meet Sandra Moore Faber." Hearing it out loud, Jillian wondered, again, if she and Kera should have attended one of the astronomy power houses. Students at the University of California saw women like Dr. Faber daily. Vera Rubin had given lectures there. U-Cal seemed, suddenly, full of prominent women.

Teaching astronomy courses at Michigan, Jillian had been glad to get away from the maleness of Michigan Tech. But even at U of M, where she was supposed to ignore the lopsided ratios—8 to 1 at best in astronomy and physics—it was her pregnancy that made the differ-ence all too obvious. When she entered a classroom everyone knew: she'd be gone for awhile.

Sandra Moore Faber, tall and blonde with high cheekbones and shining eyes, couldn't conceal her surprise. At least she was honest about it. "Well, hello! It's not every day a pregnant astronomer walks into my office." She leaned across her desk, extending her hand to Jillian. "I was pregnant with my first child when I accepted my position here."

"You were?" Jillian had been researching this woman for weeks. "I feel like I'm the only one." On the street she occasionally passed another pregnant woman. But never, ever, had she passed a pregnant woman in the halls of Michigan Tech or Michigan or any of the observatories they'd visited.

Dr. Faber smiled. "Oh, I remember. I think I was, literally, the first pregnant woman on the mountain. Let's sit for a minute."

Jillian watched Kera's eyes begin to tear and she glanced, quickly, to the floor. Pregnant was okay, but pregnant plus emotional was pushing it.

Kera recovered immediately. "I've read your studies on elliptical galaxies."

"You have?"

"Me too." Jillian blushed. "I'm sorry." Kera gave her an odd look. "I'm just thrilled to be here." *And acting like an idiot.* "Sorry." Too many *Sorrys*.

"We're glad you're here, too. Now, let's talk about the masking you've been working on. After the first paper around 1940, there were follow-up papers in the sixties and on into the seventies, I believe, that furthered the idea of a coronagraph."

"A coronagraph," Kera echoed.

"A simple occluder?" Jillian felt it necessary to clarify. "To study the sun?" She wanted to know exactly what they were being told. "We tried that for awhile with the Suitcase, our test telescope, and then later in the lab."

"That's right. You mentioned that in your introduction."

This woman read hundreds of proposals and she remembered theirs?

"We thought occluding might work, or some combination, but we kept getting better results with the shaped masks."

"So, pupil masks. That's where you see the most promise?"

"We think so," Jillian nodded.

Kera extended her pinky into the conversation. "We tried a finger-tip occluder, early on, but we couldn't get a clean enough edge. That's the trick, to get a super-clean cut."

"Finding the right material too," Jillian added. "We want to test something other than metal, but we don't know what we're looking for yet."

"That's the challenge, isn't it," Dr. Faber nodded along, "when you're doing something new. How close are you to being able to demonstrate a measurable boost in contrast with the masks you've tested?" She must have read the panic on both of their faces. Close? Were they supposed to be close? "I'm asking because I think we may be able to help, in time. We've got an optics lab in the works, which won't happen for another year or two at least."

"That's exactly what we were hoping for," Kera said.

"Exactly," Jillian smiled. They were going to use the doppler method for now; look for red or blue shifts in each star's spectrum that might suggest the movement of a planet. Then, when the optics were ready, they'd go back and try to photograph, in high contrast black and white pictures, real, visible evidence. "We want to have the masking concept ready when the optics get there."

"Well," Dr. Faber split her time between the two of them. "Let's keep thinking about both issues while you're here: turning your masks into a full-blown coronagraph, and what kind of optics that would require. But first—" she paused to smile, inviting them to relax. They'd both tensed forward. "enjoy being here. You've earned this time. Get comfortable with the spectrograph and analyzing the spectra. In the meantime, we'll have to come up with a highly descriptive name for your survey, something catchy. Which is, of course, required." She smiled again, waiting for them to understand that she was teasing.

She talked about the second study they had proposed, cautioning them against feeling as if they had to find stars of promise so early. "You might have to open your survey up even wider," she said, "add a whole new list of stars for the second study." Jillian and Kera had worried about that possibility. That they, with their novice skills, might not leave with any definitive science. But Dr. Faber put them at ease. "You're on the right track. Eventually, the optics will get there and we'll be doing years of broad sky surveys. And there's plenty of sky to keep several telescopes busy." As they walked toward the control room, talk turned to pregnancy. "So, how far along are you?"

"Seven months."

Kera broke in. "We're hoping to complete all three phases."

"Even after the baby arrives?" Dr. Faber looked to Jillian for confirmation.

"I want to stay, if it's permissible. I won't have any childcare."

"No, we don't have that yet."

"But this is such an opportunity."

Dr. Faber sighed. "When I had my first child, I was teaching my first astronomy course and I didn't publish or complete a shred of research for three years. Now, unfortunately, that kind of lag can kill a career."

Only the youngest of her three children was still at home. She'd moved, originally, to follow her husband's job, but as it turned out, the move had been her lucky break. Back east, she'd been struggling to find her passion, but once she worked on the three-meter Shane telescope she became obsessed with elliptical galaxies and the varying speeds at which their stars orbited, which eventually led to theories on the formation of galaxies with cold dark matter. She'd taught graduate courses and spent evenings there on Mount Hamilton, studying hundreds of galaxies, all through her children's growing-up years.

She stretched her arm to Jillian, not quite touching her. "It's hard, you know, but I've found, working odd hours all my life, that I can do three things at once, reasonably well. Add a fourth and everything comes crashing down. Now, both of you," she said, as she handed Jillian and Kera off to Tim, "call me Sandy. Everyone does."

Tim, Mount Hamilton's Support Astronomer, was skinny and intense looking. Short, spiky hair accentuated his alertness. He shook their hands and motioned them back toward the stairway. "We'll head down first, to the camera room."

Down was a floor down, under the telescope, and when they stepped off the last gray metal stair, they turned into another pale green-yellow hall with stairways going every which way. She and Kera had been reading the manuals, of course, learning all they could about each component of the spectrograph, but as soon as they stepped into the Camera Room, Jillian realized she'd been thinking of each piece in isolation, one by one. The reality was much more crowded. All sorts of metallic boxes and pale-painted ducts and black cables hung from the ceiling, bolted onto huge I-beams that created the steeply sloped ceiling. They were standing inside a room-sized spectrograph: a deep, miniature lecture-hall-shaped room.

Both Tim and Kera looked back at Jillian. The stairs were steep. "Watch your head," Tim smiled. "I can't tell you how many times I've bumped something that I know full well is hanging here or there. It takes a while to get used to."

At the collimating mirror below, Jillian unhinged the metal clasps and slid the dust cover down to reveal the shallow parabola, a one-foot mirror where the optics were aligned and the light prepared to be separated. Every day, before and after observing, they would uncover and recover the equipment. Dust had to be carefully guarded against. Tim pointed to the upper corner of the room. "You can see the shutter from here. A four-inch round iris shutter, not much different from any camera." It was odd, looking up at the dark metal petals of the iris, to think that the shutter would open and close as they set it to.

Tim's nervous smile tightened as they walked past the bright red cover on the diffraction grating. "Never, ever touch it," he said. "Just brushing your finger across the grating could destroy it." Jillian gripped Kera's arm for balance. "In fact, if you ever walk into this room and the grating is uncovered, cover it before you make another move."

The prisms hung chest-high from the ceiling, about two-thirds of the way up the stairs. When Tim ducked under the heavy glass pyramids and moved on, Jillian motioned for Kera to follow. This would be Kera's job. She would be much faster.

The CCD camera lay inside a long metal cylinder surrounded by more metal and hoses and a braided silver coil that ran to the Dewar—the camera's cooling mechanism. Kera put on safety glasses and the elbow-length cryogloves that hung from a hook nearby.

"The idea is to keep the camera at liquid nitrogen temperatures, to reduce dark current. Keeps thermal electrons from collecting in the pixels." Tim placed the funnel in a tiny hole at the top of the cylinder and waited for Kera to fill a Dewar flask full of the frozen liquid. Carefully, she walked the thermos-like flask to the camera. "The hole's open, so just fill it until it spills over. It'll boil off when it hits the air. That's why you wear the gloves."

In the long narrow Slit Room, Jillian and Kera and Tim stood side-by-side, facing a sidewall covered with hanging fixtures of orange and blue and strands of cabling. Jillian removed the clips that held a plate over the port hole, where light from the telescope first entered the room. They moved to the aperture plate next, a rectangular metal plate that had a series of shaped slits in it, and Jillian and Kera both nodded. They needed to pay particular attention to the place they were at now: right where the light of the telescope was focused on the slit and sent through whatever shape and size of an opening the observer selected. If their future study utilized an occluding disc or finger, it would go directly where the aperture plate was. If they ended up working with shaped pupil masks, they'd focus the light just below the slit and send it through a complex series of optics, their masks, and the CCD camera. Their future coronagraph would fit right there.

"From the port hole then, the light is focused here, on the slit. You can use a wider slit for bad seeing conditions, but you give up resolution. I'd go with the smallest for your Radial Velocity studies. You're going to be hunting for the tiniest shifts in light, so you want the tightest focus on each star that you can get."

Again, they paid close attention.

Upstairs in the dome, they stood under the sixty-foot barrel of the telescope, the entirety of it reaching upward with the yellow-gold backside of the huge primary mirror hanging above their heads. "It's just huge," Kera said, spreading her arms under the bowl as if she could feel its span.

Tim showed them the Telescope Control Console, a large metal table with all sorts of floating dials and intakes and switches. "We used to have to do everything from out here in the dome. Every move. But now, with the new TelCo computer, the telescope operator can stay in the Control Room. For big moves we still come out here, to keep a close eye on the Shane."

"So we don't move the telescope ourselves at all," Kera half-asked.

Tim shook his head, and Jillian could see Kera's disappointment.

It would have been thrilling, no doubt about it, to have been there in the old days, when observers sat in a cage-like pod that hung from the very top of the telescope barrel. Astronomers used to ride the telescope all night, eye to the eyepiece. What a difference from the current setup. The underside of the Shane was covered with electrical boxes and wires that ran to modern digital devices, the telescope's new eyes.

"We have full-time Operators here. Electricians, which is nice. Keeps observers focused on getting good science." Entering the Control Room, Tim added, "I'll stick around tonight, to get you started. After that Dan will be your T.O."

The Control Desk extended out from a wall of electronics racks, and for a second, Jillian felt as overwhelmed as she had standing at the top ledge of the Camera Room. But Tim quickly assured them that the two computers and the printer and the television monitor were all they had to worry about. "Basically, you have two choices." He waved his hands toward the two chairs. "Seventies orange or seventies gold."

He laughed with them, which helped. His eyes brightened when he smiled, and Jillian noticed that Kera's head was tilting as she smiled back. Tim obviously loved the telescope.

"Since there's two of you, you could designate one person to do calibrations and coordinates, and the other person (he tapped the stained orange chair) could be more of an imaging person, the one who makes sure you're getting good science."

Automatically, they chose: Kera sat at the station Tim called D-Take for Data Taker, and Jillian sat down at the Imaging computer. Kera would drive and Jillian, in essence, would plot their way through starlists and make imaging adjustments.

From their orange and gold seats in the Control Room, they began to move the equipment they'd just been introduced to down below. With the Spectrometer's software menu up on Kera's screen, Tim showed them how to activate the calibration lamps and move the motors that slowly, carefully adjusted the diffraction grating. Every night they would calibrate to make sure they were getting the range of spectral wavelengths they wanted on their final images. And every morning they would calibrate again, take end-of-data readings for comparison.

"The Hamilton Eschelle's going to be perfect for what you're doing," he said. "You're probably going to want to record the whole range of wavelengths. Unless you're focusing on sun-like stars. Then you might set up more toward middle yellow."

He looked to them for confirmation and Jillian responded. "We'll stay broad spectrum. We're going to be looking at all kinds of stars."

"That's what the Eschelle is made for."

"Definitely," Kera nudged her. Jillian had said something that made them sound as if they knew what they were doing. They would, soon enough.

When their calibration spectrum showed up on screen—a black background full of horizontal white lines that represented visible light's wavelengths—Jillian and Kera both leaned forward, looking for uneven or unfocused lines, and Tim chuckled. "Everyone does that," he said, showing them the dialogue box that offered several focusing options. "But rarely can you actually see the difference. Unless you hit a really big temperature change or the weather's crazy and you've had to adjust your exposure times to compensate for bad seeing. Then you might need to stop and refocus."

"Okay," he said, sounding like they were getting close. "On to the flat fields to beat down the noise."

Using the menu on Kera's software screen, they took turns exposing the flat fields. The idea was to evenly illuminate the CCD chip in the camera, to keep re-exposing it to a stable amount of light so they could detect later, when they analyzed the images, any variations in sensitivity from one pixel to the next. They needed to know, when they recorded their spectra, which signals truly remained, time after time, so they could identify and subtract out any variations that might be due to dark current, or readout noise (from all of the equipment), or even stray photon noise.

With the Spectrometer calibrated and ten or so flat fields taken for reference, Tim turned to Jillian and asked for the coordinates for their first star. Jillian handed him a disk and hard copies of several lists: their initial list of twenty of the closest stars, with ten more in a bonus category she had labeled "Great Seeing," their wish-list for that rare night when the atmosphere was so clear that they could hop from star to star even faster than they'd planned; a medium-range list of ten to fifteen stars for the not-so-great nights, and finally, the "Don't Go There" list of only six stars she had prepared just in case they ran into really bad seeing. They needed to have a short list ready to go, jinxing or not.

"Tau Bootis," she said. "It's the first of twenty on our standard list."

"All right." Tim motioned for Kera to open the Data Taker. "Once the T.O. has your coordinates, you start getting ready for the actual exposure."

Kera entered the star's coordinates, its name "Exactly as it appears on your starlist," and a four minute exposure time, in seconds.

"You got extras ready to go?" Tim turned to Jillian and she nodded, quickly. "Good. Once you get into a rhythm, you'll get pretty fast."

They heard faint clicks from above and from deep below, the slow steady moan of the telescope's motor. They leaned around the racks to watch, in awe, as the barrel began to rotate on its bed of oil.

"I felt it," Jillian said.

"Oh, yeah." Tim chuckled. "When the Shane moves, you can feel it. You forget about it sometimes, but there's always clicks and moans and whirs going on."

He pulled up the Telescope Operator's view of the Guide Camera, and they watched on the television monitor as he focused their first star.

"It's so tiny," Kera whispered. Jillian felt her heart skipping and bumping along inside her chest as Tim made audible, incremental nudges in the telescope's position, and she remembered to breathe for the baby. How incredible it was to be watching as Tim focused the light of tau Bootis, tiny and sharp, directly within the slit they had selected. Not a bit of its light was spilling out over the aperture plate.

"Okay, you're all set. You guys are in for some great seeing."

When neither of them moved, Tim pointed to the Data Taker. "Time to start the actual exposure."

Kera hit the "R" to start, which she and Tim jokingly termed "Rev it up."

Six minutes later, they heard a *Beep!* and they were staring at tau Bootis's spectra: a series of successively closer and bolder white lines that corresponded to wavelengths of the star's light, spread horizontally across a crisp black background. Tim, Kera, and Jillian examined the image together, assessing the strength of the lines and whether or not the absorption lines (small blocks of darkness missing from certain lines) matched the placement and range of what was expected from the star.

"Looks like you're going to be fine for tonight," Tim breathed from above.

Yes, the seeing, the Shane, the stained orange control desk chair, everything was going to be fine, and Jillian knew Kera was feeling the same. As they exposed tau Bootis for five minutes and then six to compare the strength of the spectral lines, Kera's green eyes were glowing and her grin was wide.

They had arrived, and this was a place that made everyone's eyes shine.

22

Time in Heaven

"FINE." JILLIAN ROSE FROM THE imaging seat. "Fine." She was speaking more to the faint lines of the spectrum they'd just processed than to Kera. "You take a look."

They were two nights into their second phase and the seeing was steadily declining. It was nearly three a.m. and they were still struggling to get decent lines from 61 Cygni. Three stars, that's as far as they'd gotten.

Jillian plunked into Kera's chair at the Data Taker and nearly fell backward. "God, this thing leans way too far back!" But Kera hardly took notice. She was staring at the same faint lines Jillian had been, trying to figure out what to do next: recalibrate and start over? Move on to the next target? Or, increase the exposure time (again!), which could prove to be a total waste of time.

Dan, their Telescope Operator, had retreated to the dome early in the evening, excusing himself when they didn't get a single, decent spectrum after the first hour. Tau Bootis and rho Coronae were too close to the horizon, so they'd jumped to the numbered stars near Draco and Cygnus, trying to maximize time with any star they could catch at meridian, way up high where they had the best chance of getting viable science data on this night of murk. Dan knew they were in for a night of scrambling, of potentially big moves for the Shane. Who could blame him for moving away from the tension?

The image program sounded off with its high-pitched *Beep!*. The same shrill *Beep!* that had drawn her and Kera and Dan and even Tim on the first few nights to the imaging screen, as they watched spectrum after spectrum come up crisp and clean with a beautiful degree of contrast between blacks and whites. By their fourth and fifth nights in the control room, Kera was entering coordinates for their next target before the telltale "save to disk" *Beep* had sounded. Now they were sitting still.

Lines started to come down in front of Kera and Jillian flapped her arm toward the screen, already sure that it wasn't a decent image. "And that's thirty minutes. Thirty!"

All she could think of was Tim's *First Principal of Big Time Observing: Keep the telescope busy at all times.* She went back to their big list. The Shane couldn't sit idle while they made up their minds.

Kera's mouth flattened. "What do you think? Combine them later?"

Before midnight the weather had changed abruptly. Winds had picked up, the temperature had dropped twenty-some degrees, and the seeing had gone from two-arcsecond to three-arcsecond seeing, which increased exposure times by a factor of nine. "Give it another twenty minutes and recalibrate I guess. Maybe we should open up the aperture, too."

Kera leaned toward the two-way speaker button, sighing. All night they'd been watching as Dan, out in the dome, turned dials in tiny increments, and the Shane's motor grunted as he tried to focus huge, fuzzy, wiggling stars over the slit. "Hey Dan. We're going to add twenty minutes here and then recalibrate."

"Yeah." Even Dan sounded defeated. "Move east after that?"

Jillian held her ruler under upsilon Andromedae, letting Kera give the coordinates. With Kera's hand still on the button, Jillian confirmed, "Far east in Andromedae."

"Okay. You're set for the next shot. I'll move on as soon as the exposure is done."

Jillian cleared 61 Cygni and started to enter Andromedae's data. "How long?"

"Shit, let's bump it up to fifty-six minutes, straight out."

A full nine times their usual exposure, an hour for one star. They both had to look at the number to be sure: 3,360 seconds. Jillian grabbed at the knob that controlled the backrest. Of course long, lanky Kera let it slouch all the way back. "How do you sit like this?"

"We could call Tim, you know."

That was a slap, and Jillian knew it. Of course they could call Tim, who lived on the mountain. Tim, who was ready to step in at any time because this telescope, one of the most productive in the world, should never sit idle due to operator difficulties. Who knew, maybe Dan had already called him. Kera, Dan, Tim, they were probably all tired of putting up with Jillian's prickliness.

"I'm fine. It's just hard, isn't it? To stop and recalibrate."

The telescope's motor began to rumble below them. The exposure was done, and Dan was moving east.

"Don't you ever feel like we're a little off in our timing?"

Kera allowed one eyebrow to stray toward her. "A little?"

"I don't mean this," Jillian put her hands on each side of her belly. "I mean this." She spread her arms out wide, spanning the racks and shaking her hands toward all the wires hanging from the underside of the Shane's bowl. "When we first graduated, they were just starting to use computers in the engineering labs. What was that, about eighty-four? Everyone was making a big deal out of two-dimensional drawing tools."

"Atari, remember? Up-down, side-to-side." Kera nudged Jillian to hand over the star-finding charts. "Yeah, we were high tech."

How did people cope with this weather?

"People won't have to learn the night sky. They'll punch in numbers from a star chart and the telescope will guide itself. Can you imagine? No one will know how to locate objects or why. Why bother?" She was winding up and Kera was too busy to stop her. Which was driving Jillian crazy.

The imager's *Beep* sounded off and they stared, for a few seconds, at the final image of 61 Cygni. They were definitely going to have to recalibrate.

"Damn it." Kera's head fell, briefly. "Fire up the lamps again."

Jillian set the lamps for a longer exposure and they waited. "I know computers have done a lot for us, I know." But the tentacles hanging from the bottom of the Shane were really bugging her, and for some reason, she thought of Einstein, the man who'd been shrieking at her, nightly, in her dreams. Einstein had distrusted something about quantum theory, something too restless and intuitive to explain. "Sometimes all these boxes and wires really get to me. Really."

"Jilli. We are not at a disadvantage when it comes to technology."

No, they weren't at a disadvantage exactly, but Jillian could see what was going to happen. People, even astronomers, were going to stop listening to the stars. "You heard what Tim said. Even astronomers aren't really looking at the stars anymore. Even us."

But they would be. That was the idea. They would be.

Kera blushed, so slightly, that no one but Jillian would have recognized the quick pinking around her eyes, and instantly Jillian felt guilty. She had quoted from a passionate conversation between Kera and Tim, early on, before Kera's crush on him and their little driving metaphors had burned out. Which was probably due to Jillian too. If Kera had been able to stay, to sleep in researcher's quarters, to wake and gather 'round the commons table with the others, they might have started something. They might have hiked to the springs and slept in the sun as Tim said he did on warm days to keep up his color. But no, Jillian-the-pregnant had to stay down in their attic apartment, close to the hospital, just in case. And that meant her driver had to, too.

It was Tim's rocking that had gotten him uninvited. He had sat on the table behind them with his skinny legs crossed, rocking. And no one needed to turn up the tension now that Jillian was eight months pregnant. She was going to apologize for breaking the spirit of this incredible place, for keeping Kera from what might have been a much more immersive experience, for keeping Kera, perhaps, from finding what she had found with Jack. Which was what, really? A painful, long-distance pregnancy? But then Dan walked in.

"Ladies. I think you're going to want to take a look." He circled around the back of their chairs and turned on the monitor that hung from the far end of the rack. "Clouds are busting up and the wind is down."

Jillian and Kera rolled their chairs toward the screen. All night they'd been watching their stars spill over the slit—big, airy, baseball-sized stars drizzling and wiggling all over—and Dan had struggled to get each star centered as best he could. Now, upsilon Andromedae appeared, tightened down so that almost all of the star was focused over the slit. They were back in business.

"I'll bet you can get back down to ten minutes."

"Holy Shit. To the charts!" Energized, Kera leaned full over to get a quick start as she rolled back to the desk, pulling Jillian's chair with her. "Geez! You're heavy!"

Dan started toward the door. "I think I can get it even tighter. What's your next target?"

They both looked to Jillian and she realized her error: Andromedae and one of the numbered stars in Cassiopeia were the last two stars on her list, but they were already there. She looked up into Kera's wide grin and over at Dan, standing at the door ready to dash off, both of them reenergized, but she was too tired to make the leap. "I don't know." Kera reached for the short list and Jillian pulled it back. "I don't know."

"Well come on. We can get four more, maybe six."

When good images were coming fast, they found that six minutes was not a very long time at all to plan the next shot. They had standards: no binary stars if they could help it, sun-like compositions if they could find them, and they had to make sure whatever data they collected was in multiples. There was no sense in having a one-night observation of any star. But now dawn was slinking up in the east, and she'd spread their latest list evenly across the sky. They were learning a lot on-the-fly.

"I spread them all out, to maximize time at meridian. I don't have any collections. I didn't think about concentrating up high or moving back west. I spread them all out."

Kera looked alarmed, but kept to the task at hand. "It's okay, Jilli. You've been leading the charge all night. I can do it."

"Happens all the time," Dan tried to sound easy. Dan, who had been telling her just the other night, how tired his wife was at the end of her second pregnancy. She was the school teacher on the mountain, and she'd come home after school and put her feet up and fall asleep. "We'll go to the program, don't sweat it." And to Kera he nodded, "Grab the big list?"

Out in the dome, Dan and Kera pointed and nodded over the charts and the Shane began to move. Kera came bounding back in to show her. They might still get a shot at zeta Cass, then they'd go for the numbered stars near Perseus, Aurigae, and Gemini. They stopped for upsilon Andromedae's insistent *Beep!* and Jillian tried to smile with Kera as they watched bright lines form down the length of the screen. Dan came in to check, one more time, letting them know he'd stay out for the rest of the moves.

"Nobody does their best thinking at four a.m.," he said. "It's one thing to have patience in one or two-arcsecond seeing, but in these conditions? Six good images in three-arcsecond seeing? You made your limit."

She'd hit her limit, all right. Man, she'd hit some limit. Maybe that's why Tim rocked. The only way he could manage all that nervous energy was to let it manifest itself physically. She closed her eyes and tried it.

"Jilli, let it go. We're exhausted. Especially you." Kera's long-fingered hand squeezed her shoulder. "Baby thoughts, huh?" Kera's voice softened. "We should talk about it more."

Sure Jillian could talk baby: she could tell Kera how she'd decided to breastfeed for twelve weeks to make sure the baby got all the antibodies it needed for a good start. That was important to Jack and to her. She could tell Kera how much she was missing Jack now: his doting and his hands. Late at night, back at the apartment, she rubbed her own belly and tried to remember Jack's touch. But then, she loved this place and she never wanted to leave. She didn't want to be pregnant and fragmented by her lack of time to prepare. Soon, soon, there was going to be a baby who would expect her to think of nothing but it.

"This is my part, you know?" She motioned to her belly. The baby needed to know she didn't blame it. "Later, it'll be Jack's turn."

Kera gently rolled Jillian's chair aside and started entering zeta Cass's coordinates. "How do you know how you're going to feel?"

"Me?" Jillian felt as if she'd been struck with something as wide as her whole body. She wouldn't let Jack or this baby keep her from this place. She'd be back. They both would.

"What's going to happen if Jack can't take care of the baby? He's a resident, Jilli. Do you really think he's going to be flexible?"

"He'll have to be." *Beep!* Jillian felt her breath quickening, but forced herself to watch the image. Clean. Upsilon Andromedae had been written to disk, quick and clean. "His emergency duty is almost over, then he'll have daytime hours, pretty much." Jack had said he wanted to keep the baby with him. Kera knew that. "He wants to."

Kera paused. "I know. We'll do what we have to, right?" She pulled Jillian's chair back under the Data Taker. "We've got to stop this rolling. Look, you've got me rolling." She placed the ruler under zeta Cass and nodded to Jillian to set up the exposure.

"Holy shit! What are we going to do with a baby up here?"

Jillian wanted to hug Kera and apologize, but it was time to get back to work. Lately, her baby thoughts and Jack thoughts and concerns about the lack of an eyepiece had a way of pouring out with way too much passion. "I'm rolling because it takes way too much time for me to get up and down. I don't know what your excuse is."

Kera hadn't tied her hair back. It fell into her face as she sat before the image control screen, talking herself down the new star list. Jillian found a rubber band and got up and tied Kera's hair in a pony tail.

"Jack's not even going to see you toward the end."

Something in Jack's voice always tried to sound sincere. "Maybe he'll find a way."

"They'll never let him go, you know. You're stuck with me."

She smoothed Kera's pony tail, giving it a tug. "Who's stuck with who, huh?"

Kera patted her hand and motioned toward the vacant gold chair. "We're on the move."

Heaven was the word they used to refer to any extra minutes they were able to save, near morning, to scour the observable universe. They would position the telescope according to presets for distant galaxies or clusters other researchers had saved, and simply gaze at the imaging screen. On the fourth night (the atmosphere had cleared significantly and they were getting twenty stars again) Kera announced a change in plans.

"Heaven first tonight." She tugged Jillian toward the stairway, saying Tim wanted to see them up on the top level.

"Shouldn't we set up an exposure first?" They were leaving the control room?

They plodded up the second and then the third floor stairs, and when they stepped out onto the circular balcony that rimmed the sloped ceiling of the dome, Jillian saw Tim standing alongside the upper portion of the telescope barrel. Standing in one of the maintenance cages. At first, as Kera led her across the narrow catwalk, Jillian thought they'd done something wrong. Messed up a mirror or burnt out the motor.

But Tim smiled. "Look down."

Jillian held her shirt against her belly and bent forward. Below, directly below, the Pleiades lay pooled in the bowl of the Shane's remarkably shallow ten-foot mirror. "I didn't know you could see like this." See the mirror, the entire mirror, holding a piece of the universe.

Floating in silvery, liquid-looking clouds of purple and magenta and periwinkle, the young, beautifully blue-white stars of the Pleiades lay perfectly still, as if waiting. Not just Electra and Maia and the brightest seven, but so many unnamed sisters, so close that Jillian felt as if she could scoop them into her hands. But how wrong that would be. Isolated from the rest of the universe, the seven sisters were not so bold and mighty. They were young and periwinkle-blue and destined for so many changes. They peered up at her—up, not down—and they seemed to be asking questions, quiet, fragile questions. The stars, pooled below her, were not giving answers.

Kera and Tim pressed close and the three of them leaned their bodies into the open barrel, letting the light from the Pleiades pass through them. Dan called up from below, "Awesome, isn't it?"

In Jillian's dream, which recurred almost daily, she and Kera entered a huge lecture hall of students. Paula, the graduate student who had helped Jillian through particle physics, was there, as was Clay, the old boyfriend (briefly!) who had painted their names on the dredger. Vera Rubin sat off to the side in the first row. And Dr. Faber (as her nametag read) sat tucked into the center, doing something with her arms and hands. But most of the students and teachers were men.

Kera split off down an aisle and Jillian continued on toward Sandy, curious to see what she was doing. With every step, Jillian became more and more pregnant, her belly shaking and rumbling and attracting more and more attention. Purple with embarrassment, she ducked into an empty row.

Distinguished astronomers and physicists had gathered to have their PhD theses reviewed by Albert Einstein and a panel of his scientific pals: Gödel the mathematician and a plump woman Jillian figured must have been Else, Einstein's German wife, more a protector than a lover. There were several presentations: one on the study of elliptical galaxies and why their orbital velocities pointed to the existence of black holes; another on radio imaging and cosmic background radiation. Jillian found their hypotheses fascinating, and she became frightened. Their masking project was so unspectacular. Still, she rose from her seat, deciding to ignore the stares of those around her. Even Kera was behaving strangely, watching the panel and glancing at Jillian as she lumbered toward the lectern.

Jillian gathered their slides and approached the stage, but there were no stairs, so she approached the climb in her new, pregnant-bellied way. She turned her back to the stage and hoisted herself up to a sitting position on the edge, then scooted away from the edge of the stage.

Einstein became visibly irritated. "What is this? What nonsense is this?" His shrill voice attacked the crowd.

Jillian rolled up on all fours, prepared to rise the proper way: hand to knee and then pushing up slowly. She found Sandy's face in the audience, smiling encouragement between her own obvious bouts of concentration. What was she *doing*?

"Sandy, please." Jillian couldn't stand up for herself. It took all her effort simply to stand. "You know my work."

Sandra Moore Faber rocked up from her chair with some effort. She made her way around the others in her aisle and Jillian saw that she was juggling three round objects in the air.

"Please, Dr. Faber, share with the panel what you know of my dedication."

But as soon as Jillian asked for her help, a fourth object appeared. Sandy stopped for a moment, adjusting to the fourth object, and slowly, carefully, continued her approach. But walking and juggling and speaking were too much. Each time she tried to speak on Jillian's behalf, she dropped one of her objects and the crowd bellowed "Boo!"

"I have read Dr. Greer's work on high contrast—oops!" One of her objects soared too high in the air. A man in the audience caught it and threw it back. Sandy reorganized and tried to go on. "Her work here could lead us to—" The fourth object fell, vibrating the floor, and the crowd hollered, "Boo!"

And Dr. Sandra Moore Faber, esteemed astrophysicist, tried to explain. "I've been working on a future optics lab—oops!—and my teenage—oh, oh! there, got it. My daughter, she's moving to—ah! Oh! Hang on." She chased the rolling object and tried to get all four cycling again. "She had to be moved to a new college, and—oh! Oh, Jillian!" she cried, tossing the fourth ball to Jillian and Jillian just barely caught it. She'd just gotten to her feet! "I'm sorry!" she cried out. "Three I can handle, four is too much. Too much!" and Sandy juggled away.

Einstein stood, shouting. "This is a disgrace to serious study! Enough!"

Vera Rubin tried to plead Jillian's case, but there was some hostility between her and the crowd, and their jeers distracted her. "I wasn't even allowed in the Observatories on the east coast!"

The crowd of men began to look alike, their faces plump and red, their mouths open and hollering. Finally, Gödel and Else yanked Jillian offstage. Jillian noticed that Else's hands were large and bony, flat-knuckled like a man's. Kera tried to stop them, but Einstein simply shook his head and lowered his eyes as Jillian was hauled away. "Enough!"

From backstage, Jillian heard Kera pick up the presentation.

Everytime she had the dream, Jillian woke and could not get back to sleep. So it was the day after their night in heaven. She shuffled quietly out of her room and sat at the table in the center of the darkened apartment. It was eleven o'clock, several hours before Kera's alarm would go off.

When the landlady had first shown them the apartment, she'd told them the building was full of UC Medical students. "Quiet bunch, hardly ever around." And Jillian had huffed out loud. She knew exactly what hardly ever around looked like from the inside of one of those apartments. It had bothered her, at first, being surrounded by their comings and goings: the lab coats and especially the tall one who carried his backpack a certain way. But lately, her mind was full of images and lines and new, pressing worries.

She spread quick-print images across the table and sat back, holding a cup of hot decaf (yuck!), letting the white lines and dark blocks of absorption lines soak into her brain without analytical interference. She could do this. Back home, it would be her job to write the program that would analyze the spectra. First, to find the pattern, the overall shift toward red or blue that represented the gross motion of the star itself, and then she would write a program to subtract that motion. Finally, after months and months of line-by-line analysis, she'd try to ferret out any additional or unexpected shifts, shifts that might indicate the presence of an object orbiting the star. Without a baby, that kind of analysis could take a year.

Have faith, she told herself from somewhere deep behind tired eyes. In time, a solution would appear.

23

More Pictures

THE PREGNANCY BOOKS SHE HAD been reading before she left for Santa Cruz—she had left them home for Jack—made mention of a homing or nesting instinct that often appeared the week or so before birth. That's what Jillian attributed her Einstein dream to: her mind was preparing her for the baby's birth. Instead of fixing up the house and wallpapering the nursery, she was gathering and interpreting data day and night.

She was outside when it first happened, writing in her journal. Jack had asked her to record how she was feeling, what she noticed each day, so he didn't have to keep pestering her on the phone. Tonight, she and Kera would finish phase two. With just enough cool blue light to write under, she recounted the frenzy of their first two nights; how on the third and fourth nights the atmosphere had cleared and they'd gotten back up to twenty stars. She heard the creak and groan of the dome opening, the ripple as the ceiling panels parted. She smiled thinking of Kera, head tipped back in awe, watching as the barrel and the dome began their synchronized glide across the sky.

Please. She eyed the first few stars. *Just a little more time.* She rolled on her side to push up on all fours. Jerking up was dangerous, her inguinal ligaments—Jack said that's what those sudden zaps of electricity were—were likely to fire off in protest. A stream of wetness trickled down her leg, itching her skin. She pressed her hand along its path and hurried inside. She felt the trickle again as she stepped into the Control Room.

"All set?" Kera smiled. The sky was dark, the seeing great, tension was low.

Jillian settled into her seat, smiling back. "All set."

"All right. Let's get rho."

Rho Coronae, one of their sun-like stars a few degrees east of Arcturus, Manford's summer star. An image of her father, that red V creased permanently into his cheek came to her, and after that, a quick slice of her dream. Every night Sandy collapsed trying to juggle four balls and got angry with Jillian. *How can I help you when I'm barely managing myself?*

"Hey." Kera tapped her arm. "Are you all right?"

She wasn't having the heavy cramps or rolling pains the books claimed she'd have. She was leaking little by little, that was all. "Just Arcturus, I guess. Wondering how my Dad's doing."

Kera started a four-minute exposure. "Great seeing tonight. And I bet he's doing fine."

They made it through several four to six minute exposures, then moved on to some longer shots, lower magnitude stars they wanted to catch straight up. Water filled Jillian's eyes as Kera entered 51 Pegasi's coordinates and she watched the first lines of one of the numbered stars near Draco come down the screen.

Kera, checking the image, touched Jillian's arm. "You're not all right, are you?"

"Water or urine keeps trickling out." Could her water have broken? Everyone told her it would be a gush, a flood. Her bladder was getting squeezed, that was all.

"What do you mean, trickling?"

"I don't know. It feels like I keep wetting my pants."

Kera ran up the metal stairway making all sorts of noise and reported the situation to Jillian's doctor. Running back down the stairs, hollering over the ringing of metal, she barked out, "He wants to see you, now! It's probably the water."

Jillian sat in front of the imager, shaking her head.

"What do you mean?" Kera shook her head back.

"I just saved gamma Cepheus." Kera's eyes flared, but Jillian rolled to the Data Taker, refusing to stop. They wouldn't get out to Cancer, but they could get the numbered stars near Perseus. "Two more. We can get two more in twenty or thirty minutes. Please. Help me."

Kera entered the coordinates Jillian had highlighted, her eyes bright with fear. "I understand. I do. But don't you dare make me regret this."

Walking across the parking lot, Jillian stopped with a sudden sharp breath. "Calibrations." Without end-of-science calibrations her analysis wouldn't be solid.

Kera stood next to her with her arms awkwardly raised. "Dan called Tim. They'll handle it."

"Will you stop?" Jillian laughed. "It's a false alarm."

But halfway down the observatory road, as Kera guided the Jeep left and then right and then left, slaloming Mount Hamilton's notorious switchbacks, the first labor pain hit. And it was no cramp. Jillian's head and legs shook and she was forced to curl into it. Kera put her arm out in front of Jillian and tried to push her back against the seat. "What's happening?"

"Whoa. That was strong."

Kera stepped on the gas. "You want me to time them?"

There was no time between them! Another surge rolled around from her back, pushing up to her lungs and down to her groin. Whoa. Whoa! Nothing like the books said!

Between hanging on through the switchbacks and listening to Kera's "We're okay. We're making it." and trying to comprehend her own disbelief, Jillian felt as if they arrived under the Emergency canopy minutes—not the hour it must have been—later.

"We have to get to a phone," Jillian whispered, hoping not to rouse another pain. They had to call Jack.

The orderly gave Kera a clipboard. "You fill in the information on the ride."

He smiled a calming smile and guided Jillian into the wheelchair, but when she gripped the arms to lift up with her next contraction, his stride hustled to a jog and he pounded the elevator buttons.

In the labor room, Kera talked to Jack while the nurse helped Jillian into a gown and situated her on the bed, pointing out the purpose of each piece of monitoring equipment. She'd be checked each hour until she reached a stage of dilation that would warrant moving to a delivery room.

"Birthing room." She wanted one of the quiet, wallpapered, dimly-lit rooms.

Kera was talking on the phone, answering questions. "Yes. Well, she hasn't said. She was concentrating pretty hard. Whoa."

Jillian reached for the phone. "Hey."

"This is it, huh? How's it going?"

"They're coming on strong, there's not much space in between—" Instinctively, she blew breaths in short spurts.

Jack's voice cracked. "Slow it down babe."

"Can you make it?" She knew he wouldn't be able to catch a plane in time, but she had to hear him say no.

"If I can't, we'll stay on the phone when you get to the birthing room, okay? Put Kera on. I'll tell her exactly what to do."

She stretched the phone out to Kera and tears streamed down her face, tears she couldn't wipe away because she was too busy holding herself up off the mattress as the next contraction wrapped around from her back.

Jack was going to rub her back with the tennis balls. They were going to face each other and rock, and when she was tired of rocking, he was going to rub her neck and her feet and tell her nonsense stories. Kera was doing her best, but she kept expecting Jillian to talk.

"Positions" was as verbal as Jillian could get. Concentrating on making language was too distracting. She lost track of the wave in her uterus and was taken by surprise when it heaved its force and shook her legs.

"Birth positions?" Kera asked. But before Jillian could answer, the next contraction radiated from her back and all she could do was rock.

Breathe, she said to her lungs. Her body shivered but she was burning hot. *In-in-in, out-out-out.* You can do it. *In-in-in, out-out-out.* She decided to add a clump each time her uterus bore down. She'd give it a sound, like a bell for her mind. *Clump—in-in-in. Clump—out-out-out.*

She began to block things out. She gave Kera her eyes when she asked for them, but she was no longer seeing. She withdrew to a position of management, attending alongside her pain, treating the muscle of her uterus as something other than herself.

The nurse, when Kera rushed her in, took one look at Jillian and said to both of them, "Oh, no. You're not going to move anywhere. That baby's coming."

She took Jillian's hand. "Soon." She wrapped ice in a rag and talked to Kera as she wiped Jillian's forehead. "If she'll let you, give her a cold rag." To Jillian she said, "Try lying on your side, go with the pain. Sitting up like that, you're going to put more pressure on the cervix."

Jillian obeyed. That's all she could do.

Kera giggled as she wiped Jillian's face. "If she'll let you. You're not going to bite, are you?" Jillian thought she smiled. She meant to. Kera could still laugh. Jack would have become a wreck at that point. She was glad for Kera's joking.

They went through the next hour or so, Kera mopping her forehead while Jillian rocked on her side. The nurse was right. The pain rolled through her more easily, but it also took control. She could do nothing except shake when the end of one wave crashed into the start of the next. And then suddenly, she snapped into a state of alertness, sitting up when she felt something—the baby?—drop violently. She felt a slushy pop and the contractions stopped.

"Get the nurse. Now." Jillian barely recognized her own voice. Kera ran.

"The head's crowning!" the nurse exclaimed. "Time to go, ladies. Time to go!" She wheeled Jillian's bed out of the cramped room and into a huge, sterile, brightly-lit delivery room—stainless steel everywhere.

"Dim. Make it dim." She wanted the twin bed and the end table and the soothing colors. "Phone."

"It's a surgical phone," the nurse said. "We can't get an outside line."

Kera sounded angry. "Can't we at least dim the lights? And what about music? Don't you have something soothing?"

On the hill, they had taken to listening to classical music during observations. After phase two's tense start, Jillian had played Pachelbel's *Canon in D*, proclaiming it her new favorite. On the surface, it was simple and sad, but in the depth of its silences Jillian heard the same quality she loved in the sky. The opening notes of *Canon in D* floating up from the dome, surrounded by silence.

The nurse patted her shoulder. "The birthing rooms are full. We'll turn down the lights, okay?"

The doctor came in and Kera questioned him. "Are you a practicing OB or a resident? We don't want any residents, no rounds. Get that in her chart."

Jillian could hear, in Kera's voice, Jack's coaching.

"I have to push." Her stomach had suddenly turned into a heave of downward pressure. Frightened by the force of this new feeling, powerful and burning and demanding, she sat up and said again, "I have to push!"

The nurse scurried to her side and put her arms behind Jillian for support. The doctor stood and gave his instructions.

"Stay with me. I'm going to be watching the baby. We don't want him coming too fast, okay? When you feel that urge, you go ahead, but try to keep listening. We might have to slow things down a bit."

Slow things down? Was anyone listening?

She felt powerful, and even though she felt a burning, searing heat, she bore down. Her mouth and her neck and her teeth, even her eyeballs contracted.

"Again?" Kera asked. The nurse had shown Kera how to support Jillian's back.

Jillian nodded.

"You're doing great," the doctor said. "Just one or two more. Give it everything you've got."

"You're so strong, Jilli. You can do it. Ready?" Kera opened her eyes wide to signal a start, drew in a deep breath, then pressed her cheek to Jillian's and led her in a growl.

Propped forward, Jillian saw the baby's face—a slimy head with a large, flattened nose.

"One more now. Just one more."

Kera leaned in to take a look. "One more. Okay, one more." Red and sweating, she pressed Jillian into a more upright position and they growled again.

The baby seemed to slide out with an audible pop. "I heard it," Jillian whispered. "I heard it."

Kera stared at the baby the doctor was holding. Jillian tried to stare, but her eyes kept going in and out of focus. She relied on Kera. "Is it healthy?"

Kera nodded and addressed the doctor as he scraped a pasty slime from the baby's mouth and nostrils. "He's breathing, isn't he?"

Just then, the baby took its first deep breath, pausing with its mouth wide open before crying out a high, shaky cry.

"Oh, yes." The doctor stood and laid the baby across Jillian's stomach. "Jillian, meet your son. A nine pounder, I'd guess."

Jillian placed her hands over the red and white-slimed body lying on her chest. A boy, she had seen his swollen testicles just before the doctor stretched him over her chest.

The nurse bent close. "You can nurse, if he starts rooting."

Nurse? She needed a minute to believe!—his shoulders, his tiny butt, his long legs and arms. "Jack," she said. She meant to say, "You look like Jack."

The baby, propped on his elbows, strained to lift his head. She could feel the tiny muscles in his back tightening and shaking. He was trying to look at her.

She stroked his back and cooed to cheer him on. "Hey, baby. Hey," she kept repeating.

With a sweep, he lifted his head and looked directly into her eyes. Dark, very dark, and his eyebrows were blonde, the skin around them wrinkling as he pressed upward. His eyes knew immediately who she was.

"You did it. You did it."

His neck buckled momentarily under the weight of his head, but he lifted it again. He cranked his tiny eyebrows back and stared right at her. And she thought of Izar, the triple star in Taurus, blue and white and that orangey-gold. Flickering Izar.

"I love you." She smiled at the expression of wonder in his dark, dark eyes and his crinkled brows. "I love you, baby."

His tiny neck tired and his head plopped, face down, onto her chest. Jillian turned his head, gently, situating his cheek against her chest, her mouth moving on his warm, damp skull. "Love you."

She said "I love you" to Kera. She needed to say *I love you* to someone! They giggled.

"I love you too," Kera replied, and she snuggled noses with Jillian's tiny, slimy baby. "And you too."

Kera did her part to be Jack-in-absentia. "Was there any tearing of the episiotomy?" "What local are you using?"

Jillian spoke a steady stream of *I love yous* to the baby squirming in her arms. Was anyone watching? She felt so weak, she might drop him.

"Was the placenta inspected?"

Once Kera got her answer to that question she seemed relieved, and came over to coo at the baby. "His fingers are so long, and look, he's got nails just like yours, all rounded."

The nurse asked if she should bathe him or if Kera wanted to do it.

"You do it," Kera whispered. "But be careful." Kera turned to Jillian and kissed her on the cheek. "I'll take pictures for Jack."

Kera came in just after dawn saying she had overnighted the Polaroids to Jack. Tim had run final calibrations and saved good spectra on three more of their stars. Jillian thumbed through the pictures, wincing at her swollen face, red with burst capillaries.

Kera plopped in the bedside chair. "God, what a night. I'm still all wired."

Jillian stopped on a picture of Kera holding the baby, freshly wrapped on the bath table. "Jack must be so disappointed." She pictured Jack standing alone in their apartment, touching the photo, trying to be with them from two thousand miles away.

"Call him. We have to get this kid named. I'm sick of saying *the baby*."

Holding onto Jillian's bed as they wheeled toward the delivery room, Kera had shouted: *Too bad we don't have the video camera!* (What a gadget geek.) But Jillian was glad. The last thing Jack needed was a record of all he had missed. To see the birth going on without him as if he were not needed or wanted at all.

Especially the way she and Kera had pushed together.

24

In Tens

WHEN SHE WAS YOUNG, JILLIAN used to think her ideas, sudden flashes of insight, came from the stars. But now, lying on the roof with her family shut tightly inside, she wasn't sure if inspiration came from the stars, literally, or simply from the time and space created in solitude.

She was tired. Soggy with night moisture and tired of trying to maintain her balance on the peak, and the stars were all in hiding. Even the brightest—Aldebaran and Capella and Procyon, even bold blue Rigel and huge red Betelgeuse—were hiding behind slow, low-lying clouds. As hard as she searched, she couldn't find as much as a dim halo of light. Why so silent?

She'd been out on the roof for an hour and several more had passed since her fateful handshake with Evelyn Young. She'd done her best to clear her mind, restarting her breathing—in for three, out for three, in for three, out for three—so many times, but nothing but the past had come. Yes, she'd had it in her. She most certainly had. But that was no longer the question, was it?

She remembered Manny's hands over Peia's ears. Peia chanting, *Make them stop. Make them stop.* The stars were angry, and their message to her now: Figure out how to live without us.

Her left foot slipped on the damp shingles and she was about to roll right and crab walk back to the dormer when she saw three points of light, clearly. Well, not clearly, but distinctly—the shadow of a huge triangle off to the west, three quarters of the Great Square of Pegasus—and three tens emerged.

Three tens. Pure and simple.

Quietly, so as not to disturb her thoughts, she snuck the graph pad up to her chest and pulled the pen from behind her ear. Three tens and a triangle of muffled light. Okay. *Thank you.*

She sketched the triangle as she saw it: pointed downward and westward. Go west? She'd already done that. She'd gone west and left the NIRV and the VLC studies behind. The past was not what she needed. She needed a way to go forward.

In tens.

Ten years of marriage. Later that year, she and Jack would celebrate their tenth anniversary. She pictured his stupefied face as she had shut the dormer window. Celebrate was probably not the right word.

In a little over ten months, she would turn forty. And that part of her life, the make it part, the getting into NASA part, would be over. Truly. Ten was not about making it, anymore. Ten, in months, was about putting it all away.

The third ten was a mystery.

Two of the three stars were covered, the remaining star trailing through the moisture. The universe had offered her a glimpse, that was all. She wasn't bound to recreate the sky exactly, with its upside-down triangle. She didn't like the idea of her future funneling down-ward to some tiny point, so she turned the triangle point-side-up and began to draw, guided by her first, lightly penciled attempt.

She started with the leftmost point, which she labeled: *Ten Years of Marriage.*

She darkened the point with her pencil and from there, used the straight edge hanging around her neck to extend a line segment. It wouldn't be a ray because it had a definite beginning and for now, an end—*Ten Years.* Maybe it was easier to accept the "It just happens" model of marriage and motherhood, to overindulge your children, to fatten them up with "You can do anythings" because you couldn't do everything yourself. But she'd never been one to do things the easy way. She'd gone to a male-dominated college in the middle of rugged nowhere. Dropped a kid into the fight-for-your-life's-work years between her PhD and those first few post-doctoral studies. Searched for extrasolar planets in the most difficult wavelength. And still—still!—she was trying. Keeping these possibilities in the air with two children, a house on a hill, and a stubborn-blind husband who refused to recall at these key junctures in their marital life that he'd married a woman who would never accept self-sacrifice as her motherly model.

Though she'd done it, in increments, for the past ten years. For the good of her children. But that was over. Just like her shot at NASA. Over.

Exactly ten centimeters from the first point (*Ten Years of Marriage*) she placed a second point and labeled it *Ten Months of Planning*. Planning, because that's what she did on the roof. That, and begging the stars for guidance. But this wasn't one of those nights. The stars had appeared, inspired, and disappeared. The next move was hers, all hers, and she needed a plan.

She looked at point *Marriage* and drew the first side of her triangle as a continuous ray, running upward at forty-five degrees. She and Jack had joked, early on, that they could each keep one kid. She'd have to take Manny; he'd be more likely to adjust to a new school. But she couldn't leave Peia behind. What message would that send?

She shrugged and drew *Planning* a ray, careful to keep this second angle identical to the first. Where ray *10 Years of Marriage* and ray *10 Months of Planning* crossed, at the apex of her triangle, she penciled a third point. Then quickly erased it.

Another point didn't look right, not at all.

She was not planning an end. This was not one of those crises of integrity that would have her question every decision she had ever made only to decide she'd already birthed her future away. She hadn't. And she was tired of half-agreeing to see things that way.

She went back to the line segment between *Marriage* and *Planning*. From an all-inclusive, societal perspective, these last ten years might be termed "Stability." But this was math, and mathematical operations were done in exclusive steps. With her life—hers alone—as the only quantified value, the baseline *Marriage—Planning* represented steady personal decline.

Or did it?

She was a mother, yes, but that did not make her less. She was more: wiser, tested in ways she could not have imagined, and vehemently focused. Science should be glad to have a mother on its side.

Theoretically, from any given point (even *Marriage* and *Planning*) there were rays shooting out in all directions. If she considered her course independent, she could veer off on an unlimited array of paths. In reality, of course, she was toting around a bag of variables the size of a galaxy. Motherhood was heavy.

But Mother was strong, like the triangle.

Her isosceles, widest at the base, could support great weight and endure incredible pressure. In two dimensions, the triangle was the perfect building block. The architect's, the mathematician's, the engineer's favorite. And in three dimensions, the pyramid was nothing less than powerful, mythological, astrological in its compass. Reaching for the heavens.

Inverted, of course, it pointed straight to Hell. Fire and brimstone for the mother who put herself first.

But *Ten Years*! Wasn't ten years a good enough base? She didn't want to be first. She didn't want to leave, forever. She just didn't want to be last anymore. Last, automatically. Last, because "It just happens" that way. She wouldn't recognize herself in another ten years.

She tried simple addition: 10 + 10 + 10, but she couldn't find a single reference in summation. Thirty, yes. She had been thirty with a world of research before her. But that was in the past. Forward, now. Forward.

She tried multiplication: 10 x 10 x 10, but she wasn't aiming for a thousand anythings. Just one life. She persisted.

What she had was an unknown area. Simple geometry. Ten years by ten months by ten whats? She tried the formula for an isosceles triangle, one half times base times height, which she knew wouldn't work. Still, great lessons came from the exercise, great accidents and incidents of fate. If Bessel, way back in 1830-something, used nothing but his particular location on the earthly sphere and his triangles to determine the distances to all the visible stars, why couldn't she triangulate this distance to herself?

Why? Because marriage, as an event, was inherently skewed in scale. Marriage was ongoing, systematic, churning like a galaxy, continually disturbing the space around it, yet its pull was inward, always inward, toward the infinitely finite realm of function.

"Look for the edges, baby," her mother used to say. Forearms submerged in a pool of swirling paints, Gayle would dip papers into the pigment and drift back, waiting for the shape that would drive her next painting. "Endings and beginnings, baby. That's where life's at."

She held her triangle at a distance and let her eyes drift out of focus, so that its edges were blurred. The smudge left from her misguided point began to grow in her vision until it appeared as an area of its own. An area to move into.

Base Ten—place value, position—that was what she needed. Base Ten illustrated, so clearly, what math was all about. Change! In Base

Ten mathematics, the number ten, in and of itself, did not exist. Ten was never a fixed position. Theoretically, the numbers zero through nine were steps toward change and once ten was achieved, it was time to move into a new position, a new place or unit of value.

She drew a line, a sure, steady ray moving upward and away from the triangle's apex, and she named the ray *Back to Self*.

She liked it. What was math, really, if not a way to illustrate change? All of her tens were on the move, and they all seemed to be moving toward convergence.

The dark hard base of *Ten Years of Marriage* might be unchangeable, but it was not invincible. Big numbers, vast distances, the most powerful forces sometimes needed to be reduced to be studied and understood. In powers of ten, *Ten Years of Marriage* could be expressed as 3.652×10^3—as three thousand, six hundred, forty-five days.

Perhaps Pegasus had been right to give her the upside-down view. She needed to move back, back to that all important, pinpoint unit of one.

Ten Days. Her mystery ten was the day. There was nothing clean about the math, but this was life. And in terms of disproportion, it worked.

Ten Years.

Ten Months.

Ten Days. *Back to Self*.

There wasn't a muffled echo of light in the sky.

Scanning the horizon west to east, from blue-gray to gray-black, it was her father's voice that offered her the assurance she needed. She remembered being surprised at his sharpness, apparent even through that awful cough. "Don't let anyone tell you how to get by."

She held her triangle up to the sky as she would a star map, knowing all along that it was silly to be out on the roof with clipboards and triangles—a warm front in January!—but she aimed her new ray toward the place where The Pleiades should be anyway.

She would find her way to get by.

In the absence of their light, she thought of Electra and Maia, and her scientific sisters Mileva and Sandy and Vera and Kera—Kera whom she would have to release, so Kera could do more than get by.

And from thoughts of Kera and the value of place, came thoughts of Manistee.

25

Day Seven—His Body

JILLIAN WOKE ON THE BEACH and sat up, wiping sweat from her neck and chest, feeling in her groin that familiar mix of ache and anxiousness, ridges of muscles inside her warm and gooey and wanting to clamp down. She had dreamed of Jack's body, his arms spread wide as he held himself above her, his face hanging close. She had felt the back of his arms, followed the snake-like curl of his triceps with her fingertips. Men had such beautiful triceps.

She wiped drool from the corners of her mouth, looking south toward nothing but parched sand, and north where the dunes beyond the campground rose as steep slides of striated black and tan and green. Even if she had moaned out loud, there was no one to hear, no one for miles. Only the water.

The breeze fingered the sweat-lined edges of her bathing suit top and she blushed. It was the wind's touch that had made her pelvis start to curl. Even now, as the fabric blew and settled, she felt the strongest urge to lie back and let the wind touch her.

She untied her top and lay back, the weight of her breasts pulling out to the sides and she stretched her arms out wide, letting the sand cake on her slimy shoulders and sweat-soaked hair. The wind gusted and ceased, teasing her with lulls of full, hot sunlight. Heat so strong it opened every pore and made her beg for more wind, and when the wind blew, it felt like touch.

She missed Jack's body, the feel of corded sheaths under his skin, his thick, knobby bones. The wind pressed against the warm, wet fabric of her suit bottom and she dropped her knees out wide, letting the sun and the air closer.

Waves of an orgasm rolled through her, sloshing in her head like the water's rhythm in the sand, and the heat of her wetness began to feel like an oily presence inside her. She wanted to rip off her bottoms, let the wind in—in—in, but it was too late. Her buttocks tightened, rolling her pelvis to the sun. She cupped sand and rubbed it over her breasts and stomach, digging for deeper, cooler grains.

She let out a cry, a chopped cry, and it was over.

No Jack to look away from, no Jack to touch and soothe. Though she felt, immediately, that ache. Sometimes, she kept her eyes shut long after their lovemaking, imagining his blue-white eyes looking warm and lost, carried away as they used to be. She kept her eyes shut tight because she knew his eyes would match his smile: broad and wary and looking for untempered warmth in hers.

She found her straps and tied them behind her back. As much as the wind was gusting, the water was surprisingly calm and silvered by the sun. The heat! August heat. Her skin was covered in sweat—sand, now, too. She thought about dragging herself closer to the water, to feel its cooling spray, but she sat in the hot sun, instead.

Let the sun burn the ache away.

It had been so long since she had opened herself, truly opened herself to Jack. When they made love, she felt her body's anger. She wanted to take, and even when she got it, when her body arched and she let out a cry, her back was stiff and her hands slapped. Orgasms came upon her not in waves but in peaks that surprised and hurt her, jabbing away at some wall between her pelvis and her heart. And Jack's tenderness, afterward, when he touched her and tried to look at her with his tired but bluer eyes, folded into her chest, where it swelled and cramped her breathing.

Something had happened when they settled into the house and started to behave like a married couple—clipping shrubbery, making elaborate calculations for educational trust funds. Jack started to make love to her like a man who had everything. He said things to her body, smiling at it as she undressed before him, loving her body because it was in its place in his world. And she, unable to connect to this adoring and suffocating love, drifted away. She started to watch him as he made love to her. And it disgusted her sometimes, watching him have his everything.

He was so happy, at first, so relieved to have her and Manny home, for good, the three of them living together as a family. He trembled. He sat her down at the table and made weekly meal plans. He made grocery lists and shopped, alone, because she slowed him down with her wandering in the aisles and her lovepats when no one was look-

ing. She was enjoying, too, being a part of his daily life, his simple
sustenance. He talked to himself as he cooked, looked expectantly
into her eyes, "How's the orange roughy?" "And how about that
special sauce, bud?" He was constantly ruffling and kissing Manny's
fine blonde hair. There were so many rewards for letting him make
their lives everything he thought they should be. So much love, so
many smiles, so many sweet discussions.

Even Peia. If it weren't for Jack—Jack, not just any man—she
never would have had a second child. With another man, someone
she could watch the stars with, someone she could care for deeply
but not ache for as she ached for Jack, she wouldn't have felt com-
pelled to let his love be all that she knew it could be.

The memory of that sweetness was an ache, all the time, between
them.

Their lovemaking had turned into sex—more physical than it had
ever been. Sure, they had different bodies now, a little heavier, a little
more slouchy and tired, but there was also a different pressure. They
used to love being hot and slimy and pressed together. But now that
kind of heat brought them dangerously close to something that could
explode.

She had stopped enjoying the urgent pressure of his body. Now he
was careful not to let his body weight down upon her. He had learned
to hold himself back, muscles stiffened to stabilize his long, heavy
frame above or alongside her. And it was Jack who watched. Sometimes, she imagined his view of her face wincing, arms clutching, her
eyelids pressed tight and her heels digging into him so she could rise
up and thrust.

Once, she opened her eyes and saw sadness, maybe even longing,
as he waited for her to cry out, his mouth crooked and long and his
eyes soft-blue. The ache was there, always, and they both knew just
how far to go without opening it up.

She shivered, tempted to wrap her arms over her chest and roll up
in her blanket. The wind was still embarrassing her. How easily the
sun, the wind, the sound of the water could take her to such a place.
Such a swept away, pelvis-gulping state.

But no. She was not going to let her own body's ability to achieve
an orgasm be a credit to Jack. She would miss his body, terribly.
Probably more, here, under the sun and the stars, where she always

longed to be touched. To be loved without pressure.

She stood, shading her eyes from the sun, and headed for the water. Cold water would shrivel the ache and her engorged vulva.

The warmth, all of it, had to go.

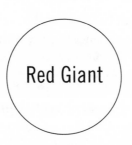

Red Giant

THE MORE MASSIVE STARS IN THE COSMOS DO NOT DWARF. They fuse and fuse, consuming all available resources until the speed and power of their consumption brings them to an explosive end.

In a star as massive as the Red Giant, nuclear fission never stops. At its core, hydrogen protons fuse into helium, and this pure helium center creates heat that expands into the envelope and ignites a shell of hydrogen. With temperature and density rising, helium in the core fuses to carbon, and the Red Giant expands again, this time igniting a second shell of helium. The star begins to fuse heavier and heavier elements in successive layers, burning through elements at faster and faster rates. Once the core runs out of carbon, it ignites a carbon shell. With temperatures reaching one and two billion degrees Kelvin, an innermost core burns newly formed oxygen, neon, and magnesium, while shells surrounding the core burn carbon, helium, and hydrogen. Finally, with up to nine elements burning in successive layers of hydrogen, helium, carbon, neon, oxygen, silicon, and sulfur, silicon in the core fuses to form the heaviest fusible element—iron. Hydrogen fusion lasts for millions of years; the supply of oxygen lasts for months; but once the star fuses silicon, fusion lasts but a day.

With the formation of iron, the Red Giant is doomed.

The fusion of iron does not release energy. Iron removes, extracts, absorbs energy, and the Red Giant's seemingly gluttonous growth is reversed. Gas pressure plummets and there is a massive rush inward. Gravity at the core initiates a complete collapse, sucking the once expanding core into a tiny ball of iron. The outer layers, still burning and fusing, suddenly find themselves with no internal support, and the mighty giant implodes.

With iron's extraction complete, the stellar core is reduced to a super-hard ball of neutrons. And into that super-hard ball come crashing the burning outer layers. The neutron, so tiny and so dense, bounces in space as if jolted, and the neutron bounce sends a shockwave so disruptive that the infall of the star's outer layers is suddenly, catastrophically reversed. Thousands of miles of burning outer layers are instantaneously bounced and blown away, ejected in a spectacular Supernova of radiation and light, of colors that burn so brightly in the sky that Supernova have been seen with the naked eye.

The Red Giant's visible and audible expulsion, a showering of elements that pelts everything in its path, rushes outward as a racing, screaming wind that sends a shockwave of debris hurling through space.

26

Namesake

KERA MERGED ONTO INTERSTATE 80, putting Des Moines behind them, and Jillian prayed to the universe, to any and all gods and goddesses who might be listening: *Please let us make it to the farm without another stop.* This trip they were repeating in reverse, a little over twelve weeks after their initial ride to California, was nothing like the first. For three days they had pulled off the highway to change the baby, feed the baby, wipe spit-up off the baby; to take him out of the carseat and hold him, burp him, bounce him so he would stop crying. They took turns going to the bathroom, one holding the baby while the other spent precious seconds alone in the stall. It had been hell— no driving through Bear Tooth Pass at four o'clock in the morning, no oohing and ahhing over the arid nights, the stars, not even a sunset—and without such wonders to sustain them, they were exhausted.

Kera's eyes, in the rearview mirror, fixed on Manny. "Oh. Now he sleeps."

His tiny body was slumped to one side, his chin crumpled into his chest. Jillian wondered if the buckle on the harness was digging in. But—they'd been given these moments to think, to think in peace, listen to the tires whine, watch faded corn stalks and rusty soybean clumps whiz by. She dared not disturb the carseat or his precious sleep.

Manny. The mystery of what to name him had resolved itself.

"It's a boy, Mom," Jillian had said, calling home the morning after he was born.

"A boy? Oh, baby." She listened to Gayle's tears stream along with her words. "Oh, I have to wake your father."

"Wait!" Manny—not Manford, not a duplicate—but Manny, short and distinct, came to her. "Tell him there's another Manny in the world."

"That's wonderful, baby. That's so wonderful." Gayle put the phone down, and Jillian listened to her feet scamper away. "Man! Man! It's Jillian. We've got a grandson."

And in the background, Jillian heard her father cough. Faintly, distantly, she heard him ask, "How is she?"

There were more hurried footsteps. "I'm sorry, baby. I forgot to ask how you were. You're okay? It was the name, sweetie, it threw me. I'll get your Dad and you can tell him yourself. Don't hang up."

Her father's wheezing had dominated the conversation. Each time he spoke, he drew in a big whiff of oxygen, removed his mask to talk—she could tell by the change in his voice—then he wheezed from under the mask again.

And Jillian's tears had streamed like her mother's. "His name is Manny, Dad. Manny."

Leaving the hospital, her biggest concerns had been the healing of her episiotomy (The doctor said the stitches should dissolve within two weeks and she'd be able to sit comfortably) and how to keep the noise of their observatory work from waking the baby. Manny had been sleeping, then. Her first week in the apartment wasn't too bad, though everything seemed foreign, especially breastfeeding. Manny seemed to suck for a long time, and to eat quite often, but the *ABCs of Breastfeeding* recommended frequent feedings. Baby's suckling would build up milk supply. She hadn't thought of a baby carrier or a stroller, and surviving on grant dollars didn't give her an extra cent to play with. She and Manny lived off the diaper bag her mother had packed for the first few days; then Jillian carried him to a neighborhood store to buy diapers and wipes.

Whenever Manny slept—less and less as that first week drew to a close—Jillian reviewed star lists and tried to compile a list of must-gets for phase three. More than once she fell asleep and woke to Kera pulling notebooks and pencils out from under her face.

By the end of the second week, Manny was fidgeting and whimpering half an hour after every feeding. When Jillian tried to stave him off—frequent feedings were advised, but mothers were cautioned not to feed more than every two hours—Manny worked himself into fits of hungry rage. The lactation specialist, the pediatrician, Jack, they all figured it was colic. The screaming might last for weeks. She breastfed him, burped him, bounced him tummy-down, and prepared to go up the hill regardless.

Near the end of their third night of observations, with Jillian jumping in and out of her seat at the imaging station, rocking Manny's baby seat with her toes, trying to check and save spectra one-handed while holding him—which didn't quite work because his head was so unpredictable—she broke down, and so did Kera.

"We can't keep this up." Kera hollered over Manny's cries.

Jillian stood, bouncing Manny. "Put on some music. Softer this time."

"I can set up and run exposures on my own. It's not your fault, Jilli, but there's too much down time."

Jillian pulled her ear back from the onslaught of Manny's screams. "What do you know about babies? He'll get better."

After a few more nights, Kera called Jack and made Jillian take the phone.

"Babe, listen." His voice was soothing. "You need to take a break. Neither you nor the baby are going to be able to relax and get a good feeding."

A good feeding? What about sleep? And their stars! "I can't get anything done. I sit and make things all cozy, and breastfeed him for forty-five minutes, and another forty-five minutes later, I try to lay him down, and he's up again, screaming like he's hungry."

"You have to go back to the pediatrician. Something's wrong."

Their phone conversations got worse. No, Jack couldn't come and help, he was on the last two weeks of a cardiac rotation. But his parents offered to fly out and get the baby. His mother could stay at Jack's apartment while he was at the hospital. Grandma could move in until Jillian came home.

Home? "No!" Jillian imagined Jack's mother constantly holding Manny, stroking him, pulling him to her to the point of limiting his movement. "No!"

During one of their last late-night telephone calls, Kera bounced between D-Take and the Image station while Jillian walked circles around the telescope, hoping Manny's cries would drift up and away through the slit in the dome. But Manny never stopped screaming.

"Does he always scream like that?" Jack asked.

"Yes! And it's getting worse. I have to go!"

But Kera had scooped up the phone. "Jack, we have to do something."

"Stop it!" Jillian had sobbed. "I'm doing okay!" She'd been holding herself together by chanting, in her head, *Sandra and Vera had days like this. Sandra and Vera had days like this.*

In the end it was Sandy Faber who convinced Jillian to go home and take care of herself and the baby. Jillian was sitting in front of the imaging monitor with Manny lying across her lap—pacified by the slow ellipses she was tracing with her knees—when Sandy entered the control room. Kera lifted Manny off Jillian's knees but wouldn't look her in the eye. Sandy, holding Jillian's hands, eyed her directly. "I know what you must be up against, in your own head. But you've already collected some great spectra, and you've got a very capable partner. Let Kera handle this for now and take care of yourself." She had added, "Remember, I want both of you back here."

Twelve weeks before, Kera had backed out of the driveway while Jillian watched Jack and Gayle and Manford shrink, and she had felt a vague sense of dread. Now, as they rolled toward the house, she felt weak with relief.

Her mother took the baby seat, with Manny in it, out of her hands, and Jillian stood, staring. Without a word, Gayle covered Manny's face with his receiving blanket and walked into the house, and Jillian and Kera simply followed. In the kitchen, with tears streaming down her face, Gayle placed the baby seat on the counter and drew Jillian, then Kera, into her arms.

"Go ahead," Gayle whispered, as the two of them sighed and whimpered and then giggled. "You made it."

For weeks, Jillian had been permeated by anger: Jack's when she refused to come home until the third phase was complete; Kera's when she refused to leave until their third phase was complete; Manny's, when her breasts did not produce the milk he needed to thrive. For weeks she sat rocking and feeding, the nerves in her back and neck lit up with tension, watching Manny's round, wide-eyed face crimp into *V*s of anger. *V* for *vengeance*, *V* for *vindication*, *V* for *victory!* Jillian sang all sorts of *V* words when his face contorted. Babies responded to tone, not words. She let the *V* words fly while keeping her voice soft and pleasant.

Finally, Jillian pulled back and nodded. "We made it."

Kera let out a huge sigh. "If we had pulled off the road one more time, I would have gone insane."

Gayle unclasped the carseat's harness, scooped Manny's curled body out, and hoisted him onto the cloth diaper she had angled across one shoulder, all without waking him. "You know what you should do, baby? Grab a cold beer, sit out on the swing, and relax. One cold beer, it's the best thing you can do for the let-down reflex. And for you." She looked from Jillian to Kera's faces. "Both of you, you look like hell."

"What about Dad?"

"Sleeping." Gayle spoke away from Manny's face. "He's staying in bed now."

Kera uncapped a beer and instructed Jillian to open her hand. She did, and noticing how wonderfully cold and moist the bottle felt, she began to salivate.

Standing outside the door to her father's room, she could hear the timed hiss of the oxygen tank.

"Go ahead," Gayle said. "It'll be all right."

But it wasn't. Seeing him lying in her parent's bed, looking too long, as if lying there had caused his skeleton to fall loose and his skin to droop, Jillian didn't feel okay. She stood over him, listening to the click-push, watching the mask separate from his skin, wondering for a tiny second if he was actually alive.

Gayle sat on her side of the bed, stretching her legs alongside his. "Hey, Man. Guess who brought a baby home?"

The darkness of his irises seemed to leak into the whites of his eyes. They looked smoky and dry.

"Dad, it's me." She crawled onto the bed, not sure if she should hug him.

He pointed to the beer in her hand. "For me?"

Without thinking, she extended it toward him. He smiled and turned his head toward Gayle. "Hey, hey," he whispered, looking at Manny. Jillian watched Manford make slow, purposeful eye contact with her mother, the same eye contact that used to make Jillian's stomach queasy when she was a teenager and she realized her parents were communicating their passion.

She pictured Jack in the car, on his way to her and Manny. Her chest filled with an ache that suspended her heartbeat, watching her mother slide her father's mask aside to give him a kiss. Jack had never seen, or touched, or smelled his son. He had heard him cry, though. Boy! Had he heard him cry.

Her father's hand on her arm felt dry.

"Hey, hot mama." His voice too, was drying out. Does it hurt? she wanted to ask. "You okay?" he asked.

She kept her smile as her mother placed Manny on his chest, fighting off a wince when she noticed the hardening of his skin. "So, what do you think?"

"He's a big boy, isn't he. Going to be tall."

"Kera!" Gayle called. "Get in here. It's a bed party!"

Kera sat cross legged on the end of the bed and she and Jillian told Manford all about the computers and the imaging equipment at Lick, about the room-sized spectrograph and their plans for a future coronagraph.

"Drink that before I do," he told them, so they did.

Jillian tapped him. "It was weird watching the stars being focused over the slit, so tiny on the good nights. And the noise! Even when you don't pay attention to it anymore, there's this low-level presence of clicks and creaks and moans."

At one point, Manford's chest started to shake with a silent spasm. Gayle grabbed the baby from his chest and barked, quickly but quietly, "Everybody up. Up." She placed her shoulder behind Manford's, worked him up to sit, and he coughed up something brown and dry.

Jillian stood watching, unaware that she was crying until Manny started to worm against her neck and his face touched the wetness of hers. Before Manford looked up and patted the bed for her to sit back down, she used Manny's burp rag to wipe her tears away. They were all dry and sour: her, Manny, and her father. And dry and sour was not what Jillian wanted to remember.

She wanted to remember the fork she and her father had electrified, how it glowed orange on the table until the finish started to bubble; the door buzzer they nailed into the crease of her bedroom door, which drove her mother crazy; the time they were sanding a telescope mount and a wood sliver burrowed under her thumbnail. Her father, holding her hand down so the doctor could work on her thumb, told her in a big, wet voice, "Go ahead, holler shit, damn, holler whatever the hell you want." And when the hot-orange tip of the cauterizer sank through her nail and trapped blood spurted out, she had yelled, "Shit! Damn! Shit!"

Manny started to whimper. Kera jumped up to find the pacifier, Gayle patted Manny's rounded back, Manford patted his own chest, calling for the baby, and Jillian smiled. In the presence of all those arms she was able, for the first time in weeks, to think beyond the immediacy of Manny's needs. She stretched out next to her father and fell asleep to the gassy click-hiss of his oxygen pump.

Kera and Jillian were swinging on the porch, having their second beer, when Jack arrived. In the yard, he threw his arms around Jillian and dug his face into her hair and cried. Gayle brought Manny to them, stroked Jack's wet face and kissed him on both cheeks, then Kera and Gayle retreated into the house.

Up and down the driveway they went, Jack cooing at Manny and Jillian, Manny squirming on Jack's forearm, his eyebrows arching and crimping in curiosity, and Jillian leaned into Jack, narrating every part of their baby's body.

27

Day Seven—A Theory of Dreams

JILLIAN LAY BACK IN HER day beach chair, a third chair she had sculpted near the water, trying to feel the pressure of light. She could certainly feel the sun's heat! Her shins and her belly were on fire and her
chest and neck were covered in an oily sweat, but what she wanted
was pressure.

She'd read, long ago, that the pressure of light on a human body at
rest was equal in mass to the weight of an ant's thorax, and she believed
it. Light, not just wind, had a touch: the bombardment of particles as
they struck and passed through her, and she wanted to feel it.

She ran her fingers over her stretch marks, silvery, ribbon-like welts
that fanned from her pubic hair out toward her hips. How maddening.
She worked hard to keep her body in shape, to be prepared mentally
and physically. But Jack refused to see scars. The worst was when she
lay naked on the bed and Jack traced her stretch marks with his fingertips. Sometimes he kissed them.

She sat up, which felt like punishment, propping herself up so the
mid-afternoon sun could beat even more fiercely upon her chest and
face. Why was she punishing herself? Parching herself in this world of
heat and sweat and sand?

Because she had to purge Jack's touch from Day Seven. Because
pressure had become Day Seven's unifying theme. The pressure of
Jack's body (his whole life, really) hanging over hers, and this sun and
the water and the sand and the heat—this unbearably windless afternoon, was all part of it. She sat gazing at the water, admiring its uni-
formity and today, its silent silver grace.

She'd been thinking of the night she left, that awful phone call to
her mother. In the middle of the night—four in the morning of Day
One, just hours before she packed Jack a lunch and drove away—
she'd called her mother. Poor Gayle, sitting alone in that huge farmhouse kitchen, wondering what she had done to make her daughter
so angry. Jillian had barked at her. "Why did you cut your hair?"

She'd meant when her father was sick, and Jillian knew the answer. Gayle had cut her long, thick, graying-blonde hair, the most striking thing about her identity, because she didn't have time to take care of herself. No time for hair while caring for her dying husband.

When Jillian dreamed about the call, the meanness in her voice gave her the shivers. Her voice came down in blows around her mother's face.

"Why did you do it Mom?"

"Was I wanted? Was I planned?"

"Why did you get married?

"Did you have to? Did you want to?"

And in her dreams, Jillian knew all the answers. She witnessed the interrogation and she enjoyed it. Gayle was to blame. She'd filled her daughter with the want of a marriage that never really was, a happy union of two people who respected each other's differences and drives. But Gayle had given in long before Manford's death. Of course she had.

In the real phone call, Jillian had practically begged Gayle for help.

"I'm no good at it Mom."

"No good at what? You've never been bad at anything, baby."

"I can't do it anymore. I watch myself being a mother, and Jack and the kids, they think that's actually me, but it's not. You were always there for us, for me and Dad. I was trying to remember a crisis or a weekend, one single time when you weren't there, and I couldn't. How could you do it? How could you give up all of your own things?"

Her mother had tried to argue, "I've never regretted having you." But Jillian also knew the truth of what was not said. Little by little, her mother had stopped painting because it was too painful to do in spurts. Jillian had wanted to say so much more: how unfair marriage was! Jack didn't worry about the future and clean water and clean air! But how fair would that have been? To condemn marriage when Gayle was sitting in that huge farmhouse kitchen, in the middle of the night, still playing mother—alone.

For years Gayle had plodded along after her daughter, dying to be up to her elbows in her tubs, and Jillian wanted to know, now that Gayle was alone in that huge Iowa farmhouse kitchen, how did she feel about those years of waiting?

Jillian got up and walked south, toward the low, parched dunes and the scrubbiest brush, thinking about love and guilt and science's new fascination with choice. Some of the wackier physicists claimed that the behavior of photons provided proof of the possibility of other dimensions, parallel universes in existence all around us. But the basis was too far removed, too abstract for a world so sensory— especially the stars. She could feel them, always, and space. Light and sand and water and wind were the universe's fingers, its points of contact, and the Multiverse was simply too egocentric. How could we claim to assemble and disassemble nature based on our flimsy human choices?

In the tiniest of experimental universes, photons passed through a special, one-at-a-time screen and produced a pattern that was not radiant and wave-like as light should be. Single photons passed through slits in a screen and seemed to duplicate themselves. They came out on the other side radiating in all directions, which could happen, theorists supposed, if photons existed in two, or three, or even ten different places simultaneously. Or—if light had an invisible companion, a whole group of companions, traveling in parallel worlds. Where there was double the light (so the theory went) there could be double or triple or unlimited dimensions.

The dimensions she understood, but the rest was candy-store physics, a choice-filled fantasy come true, where the universe was a service counter for every individual desire. And what really bothered her was this: If there were other universes, other versions of us occupying and developing any number of alternate life paths, only our decisions would determine which life—which universe—we walked in. What a heavy responsibility!

Trying to imagine more than one Lake Michigan, more than one lolling, silver-topped, thousand-foot-deep glacial gully in the sand, was draining. Let alone the necessary space for so many lakes and Jacks and the kids. Would the kids be held accountable for every choice?

She was tired of blaming herself, her and Jack both, always, blaming her body for their children's busy lives, for the interruptions in her work, for the trouble between them. Yes, she'd made choices, but so had Jack. Manny was as much his choice as hers. And Peia, Peia and Jack adored each other. But Jillian was their mother, their beginning. How could she blame herself for being their mother?

She'd known all along that having Manny and Peia would make hers and Jack's lives busier, that they would lose the simple freedom to decide, hour by hour, where and what they wanted to do. But she'd never expected that the bulk of restrictions would pile up on her side, and so quickly. Because of her choice, one could say. Because Jack could always think—and even say: *You chose.* That's how men, even good men, got away with it. Pregnancy might not have been her choice, not the first time, but deciding to remain pregnant was. And what was always implied but never honestly spoken was: *Nobody forced you to bring these children into the world.*

She saw it on Jack's face, sometimes, warm blue guilt.

She could still remember her wedding day, a day almost perfect except for her father's absence. She had stood near the grassy bank of the Iowa River thinking the sky couldn't have given her a better color, a pure azure so bold it made the wedding tent and the floral sculptures, even the bushes and trees, look as if they had been painted into place. Her mother had come to her and taken her hand, silently, and the two of them had stood watching as Jack and Manny had their father-son picture taken under the wedding trellis. She had waited that long to get married, waited until after she and Kera had completed their second study, the NIRV II. Jillian had smiled, watching Jack and Manny in their identical shirts and ties, knowing both would have their tongues curled into the back of their teeth, folds of tongue showing in the pictures later. And she'd felt the strangest feeling for a moment, a sense of loss. She and her mother, hands clasped, were trying to hold onto something Jillian was losing. They both wanted Jillian's marriage to be different—wonderful, equal—but they knew, watching Jack and Manny, that Jillian would be under constant pressure. She would love them too much to leave.

Jack had noticed her and mouthed *I love you.* Manny had turned his red-cheeked face, and then Jack had blown Gayle a kiss. Her mother had shooed Jack off from a distance and the two of them, mother and daughter, had walked along the riverbank together. "He's here with us, baby. I can feel him."

Jillian had felt her father's presence, but every time she looked to the bend in the river where tangled thicket lined the banks, she could not see the image anymore, she and Manford sitting on the station wagon tailgate with fireflies snapping in the dark. But she hadn't been able to tell her mother. "Me too," she'd said. "I feel him too."

There was no Multiverse. There was only one Jack and one Manny and one Peia and her mother's pale yellow dress and that calm, calm hand, and she couldn't go back and make different decisions. The candy store was a nice idea, but she'd probably regroove the same path anyhow.

Personally, Jillian wanted to believe in Strings' Theory. Strings promised some hope, some offspring of possibility in each interaction. In a world so entwined, interaction counted. She loved the idea of clusters of molecular energy tying us to our thoughts and interactions, of our lives buoyant upon a web of strings. Like a kiss, a more grounded scientist had said, we exchange elemental structure with the world around us.

She blew a kiss over the big lake and blushed, and in the puckering of her embarrassment, a grain of sand pulled loose. After days of living in the sand her toes, her underwear, her hair, even her mouth had some degree of granularity. The single grain dislodged itself from a pocket in the back of her mouth and it crunched like a boulder as she walked on.

Some distance down the beach she came upon a triangle of dunes, a smooth dip of sand between three pyramids, each tufted with a shoot of dune grass and waving her in. The lake-universe couldn't have offered her a better think-tank, so she took it.

She had only three more days and the past was becoming much too weighty, reminding her, like an extra water bottle or an unnecessary tarp in her backpack, that these days were not meant for carrying extra burdens. The past was having its heavy, uncomfortable way with her, making its way around her body as a stiffness in her neck, the cramp in her lower back, and most recently, as that long, slow ache in her left hip as she plodded along on sloped, hard-packed sand. And she knew what was coming next: the pounding down upon tired ankles. She knew, now, not to pack extra burdens, not to carry them from one day to the next. The past was no place to live.

Sitting in that still but welcoming triangle, she rubbed hot sand over her legs and let a theory of her own take shape. A theory she'd been formulating in doses all day. She didn't have a lifetime to devote to monuments of thought, like Einstein and his successors who grappled for that single strand that would unite the chaos of the tiniest particles (the boulder-grain still breaking down inside her mouth) with the framework of the entire universe, with everything and beyond. No. Hers was not a grand, Unifying Theory, not a Theory of Everything. Hers was a TOD—she smiled at the acronym, irony alive in its sound—hers was a Theory of Dreams.

Elegantly simple, her theory had but one assertion: Most people live only three or four decisions away from their dreams.

Her own theoretical proof was fulfilled in three steps.

One: Her decision to join bodies with Jack.

At the time, the attraction between them may have seemed unavoidable, as if the night air around them and his hands rubbing her shoulders had made love happen. But when he leaned over her drawings, firing questions at her about the stars and their masks and where they were going next, she had made a decision. She rode out those last few seconds of doubt and followed him to his bed.

Two: Her second pregnancy.

Her first pregnancy, theoretically, did not count. As an accident, it was directly linked to the first decision (joining bodies). Manny was an associated consequence, a tertiary result. But Peia's existence was primary. She and Jack had talked about having a second child. She had discontinued her birth control pills, realizing, of course, after she'd already gotten pregnant, that she did not want to be. But decisions had consequences. Peia's conception, however mal-timed, was a consequence of decision.

Three: Breastfeeding.

That's where things became complicated. Overly simple, completely natural, and yet incredibly, inextricably complicated. Her eventual demise was linked, one associated decision after another, to her very own breasts.

"You're so maternal," Jack would say, watching her cup Peia's head to one breast and tuck her squirmy legs under her other arm, the football hold. They'd spent those first few weeks caring for Peia and Manny together. Of course this time Jillian was more relaxed. She wasn't trying to make the best use of a multi-million-dollar telescope while breastfeeding a colicky infant. But that's when it started. Jack saw her mothering and her cooing. He felt those deep, intertwined hugs the four of them would have, lying on a blanket on the floor together, Mama and baby and brubber and Daddy, and he started to think of her mothering as the love that made them all happy, the love they all needed and deserved.

After Jack's five-week parental leave ended, she found herself at home alone with two kids to take care of and her own body desperate for reconditioning. She tried to create those blanket moments, those special hugs, but there never seemed to be time for anything but breastfeeding.

Later, when her twelve-week maternity leave was up, she changed her work hours to maximize Peia's feedings. Her milk was flowing white and rich, and after not being able to supply Manny with milk, it seemed wasteful, disrespectful to her body, to let such a plentiful supply dry up. For months, she carefully maintained Peia's morning and night feedings. Because she was home later in the mornings, Jack was able to leave earlier and earlier. He was setting up a new laboratory class, and after taking five weeks off to help care for Manny and the new baby, he had to get the class rolling. She tried to understand, that was just the way things were, but what about her work life?

That's when things took a turn. Slowly, silently, she agreed to stay, and quickly, on the sure feet of one seemingly entitled, Jack slipped away. She felt deeply duped, and her own body had given him the excuse to desert her.

There were constant stand-offs: she with her arms crossed over her breasts so she didn't feel so vulnerable and Jack standing, defensive, with his arms crossed over his heart. But Jack could hold out longer than she could. Jack kept hold of himself even when the kids were in danger of losing. Why? Because of her Theory of Dreams (TOD):

TOD-1: She decided to love him.

TOD-2: She decided to have Peia.

TOD-3: She kept breastfeeding.

She walked away from her think-tank of hot sand, brushing grains from her suit bottom, this time heading for the dark-duned north. She'd been moving this way and that all day: south and north, up and back, from dark cliffs to parched sand, in and out of the water.

She had always thought the toughest part of child rearing was the physical dependence, but time and her marriage had proven her wrong. As her children grew, they left the visceral spaces surrounding her abdominal organs and invaded the viscera of her mind. They seemed to prefer dwelling in cortical, white matter, filling her mind with their friendships, their difficult situations, their lessons to learn, overpowering her thinking spaces. Her heart continued to beat. Her nervous system continued to respond to external stimuli. Her internal organs filtered proteins and excreted waste. She functioned, but that was all.

Usually, the successful test of a new theory brought satisfaction. With the impulse to prove spent, she would settle into a quiet peace between body and mind. But her TOD had not brought peace. How could Jack know her, love her, and watch her decline?

One: Marriage.

Two: Kids.

Three: Decline of the Self.

Four? Stagnation with Acute Awareness.

There was no Multiverse. There were no do-overs or alternate choices, and she didn't want to un-decide Jack and the kids anyhow. What she wanted was to be able to move forward, to some degree, unhampered. She wanted to be at peace. To hell with candy-store physics! The universe she knew could be kind.

She ran. She ran halfway up the dune and stopped. Damn it! She knew better! *That's* why she had called her mother. They were both supposed to know better!

Would it feel better to believe some Multiversing copy of her was getting to do all the things she wanted to do in life?

No. No! She would not mother some Multiversing, second-chance self! She ran again, hollering like a mad woman, and jumped into the water.

But even as she ran she understood that Jack could not have taken more than she had given. Some part of her was maternal and loving and wanted to give. If only Jack could love her for that, for *wanting* to give, but respect her enough to know that some things—her heat, her pressure, the stars that were essential to her being—he could not expect her to forsake.

Lake Michigan, the one and only Lake Michigan, wrapped its cold currents around her and she gladly received every universal but unique molecule.

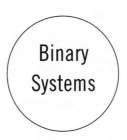

Binary
Systems

OVER HALF THE STARS IN THE UNIVERSE EXIST IN PAIRS. SOME pairings are rather loose: two stars of equal or near-equal mass orbit a common center of gravity, a center of balance that keeps them orbiting each other but does not burden one or the other with excessive restraint. Others orbit in much tighter arrangements and are not so evenly suited. Differences in mass and rates of development can affect close pairings in peculiar and even violent ways.

A low-mass star orbiting in close contact with a higher mass star can become misshapen, elongated by the pull of its primary companion. And—if one of the stars in a close-knit system experiences rapid growth, its burgeoning mass may be syphoned off, transferred through the pair's mutual gravitational center to benefit and enhance the other. Sometimes such syphoning and redistributing of mass goes back and forth between two nearly equally massed and distanced stars.

At its worst, mass transfer between binary stars can have devastating results. An expanding star, one that, left to grow and develop on its own, may have been capable of achieving the size and luminosity of a giant, can suffer great loss due to the gravitational tug of its companion. A closely orbiting star can begin to loosen and strip away a growing companion, unraveling its gaseous outer layers and winding these layers around itself as it spins through its orbit. The reduced star is left in a state of severe imbalance, and fusion, deep in its core, may come to a halt. This once promising star, its mass peeled away to feed the growth of its companion, dwarfs. But size cannot predict volatility.

When a Giant collapses, its core is usually empty, out of fuel. But the Dwarf's core is filled with unspent potential. After years of being showered with the hot, heavy byproducts of its companion's constant growth and expansion, the dwarfed star ignites. Hydrogen and carbon and oxygen instantaneously detonate and both Dwarf and Giant explode in a Supernova so bright and so complete that nothing, perhaps not even a black hole, is left behind.

Still—in a universe sprinkled with potential, supportive pairings are not only possible, but probable.

At their best, loosely bound binary stars evolve independently, with seemingly little effect on the potential or development of their companions. To the eye these pairings may appear as one, a single star that twinkles in two colors, but under close study, their individual sizes, colors, and positions on the stellar life cycle remain independent, unchanged. Each star retains its own mass, its own patterns, its own growth. Whether alone in orbit or layered in our sight lines as a color-blending pair, each star shines the light of its own compositional identity.

28

Day Eight—The Waters of Hamlin

SHE WOKE THAT MORNING FEELING as if she were stuck in the biggest limbo of her life; directionless after pacing the beach on Day Seven, sweating thoughts about heat and light and Jack's body and dreams. She couldn't bring herself to chant: *Day Eight. Eight. Eight.* How was she going to make peace with only one or two days to go? She'd driven to Hamlin Lake with a purpose: to search for the Lost Lakes.

Hamlin was a man-made lake, formed when loggers walled off a narrow strip of Lake Michigan by damming a natural bay with the lake's own sand, creating a long, deep cavern with a river-like current. Loggers thought they'd use the current like a spillway, rolling logs down the heaped dunes and floating them out to harbor. But their own barren stretch of dunes got the best of them. Lumberjacks buckled under the intense heat of the sun, horses pulling supplies and saws died in the sand, and eventually, the logging operation was abandoned. Now, high in the dune walls between Hamlin Lake and Lake Michigan, two tiny lakes were said to appear and disappear depending on weather and drought, and Jillian set out to find them.

She rented a beat-up canoe and sat, first, in the middle of Hamlin's shallow, golden-green lagoon, taking in the smell of freshly-sawed wood. Park rangers had built a new boardwalk that rimmed the round lagoon and arched over the water as a bridge to the lagoon's spongy round island. The stillness and the sunshine were thick with hot wood, and she thought of the old man, who had said the lagoon was always warm and good for swimming. Did the old man know about the boardwalk? He stood in her memory with his teary eyes and his hands wrapped around hers, grateful for the star charts she said she would leave. But she hadn't gone back to pin them to the board. She was afraid she'd run into him. The old man lived too much in the past.

She managed the canoe quite well once she mastered the lone paddler's side-to-side stroke. She glided over tangles of yellow-green vines, watching a cloud of gold flecks flutter behind her. Goldfish, huge meaty ones, followed her drifting canoe, flickering. What could she do, now that she'd decided Jack might never love her as she needed to be loved? She had always known what she was working toward: fighting for space and time in her marriage, fighting Jack's unstated expectation that her life would fold in with his, fighting the meanness of Houghton's winters and the maleness and the sheer force of the place. And all along, she supposed, gliding over vines she'd already disturbed, she'd been fighting love. A family required a tremendous amount of supervision and communication. And Jack and Manny and Peia could always take more.

She sat for a long time with her arms wrapped around one of the island's bridge supports, holding her canoe back from Hamlin's angrier waters, gathering sounds and smells from the campground and trying to work up her nerve. Paddling against the navy blue current of Hamlin's deeper, darker water was not going to be easy. But, as she'd told herself earlier in her journey, it was going to be. So, with the smoke of early morning fires hanging over the water, she paddled away from the sheltered lagoon. She didn't need shelter, she needed shock. Cold, mean, unbiased shock to jar her from this drifting.

She was unprepared on her first attempt. A strong, steady wind refused to let her pass through the current and so she sat, drifting backward from Hamlin's long, deep, navy blue water. The second time, she tightened her grip on her oar, tucked her chin to her chest, and faced Hamlin's angry, opaque waters head-on.

Feet set wide apart, she dug into the wind with her back and legs, plunging her back and her shoulders and her arms, side to side. She leaned and stroked and blew hard breaths across a mile and a half of Hamlin's stubborn current. The current, the wind, the desperate dig-dig-dig rhythm was just what she needed, and she smiled between forceful grunts and exhales. With a surge of strength—*Give me one more, one more!*—she drove her canoe into Hamlin's western wall of unnaturally steep sand, and jumped out to beach her canoe. Tired and proud and exhausted, she fell into the sand, letting her arms and legs rest out wide.

She tried to make a sand angel, which must be impossible, and a deep sense of wanting surged through her. Desperately, she wanted to make that angel in the sand. She wanted to see the Suitcase through to the orbital station she knew it must become—it would become—

with or without her. She wanted a future filled with new work: back on the Shane, at the University of California's new Keck twin telescopes, maybe even the binocular telescope on Kitt Peak. A binocular telescope! And she would always, always, want to float in space.

Scaling the final fifty feet of Hamlin's nearly-vertical sand, she dug into the dune, working her way up and sliding back on all fours. People overheated trying to stay upright on the dunes. The secret was in the angle: decrease the resistance, lessen the slip. Up-up-up, and if she was lucky, only one slide-back.

At the top, the wind slammed her with gusts of moisture, and she smiled even before she was able to focus her sun-bleached eyes on two bowls of shimmering aqua-white in the sand below. The Lost Lakes, this year, were not lost.

And that's when it came to her: neither was she. Why, every time she decided that people could not give her what she needed, did she blame herself? She had to stop punishing and parching herself. She'd come to rest, reclaim, recover—to face whatever the future held for her head-on. And these three R's led to some choice F words as she tipped her head back and chugged hot water: Fuck the old maternal model! And the new one too for that matter! She was sick of being ashamed of herself for being maternal—and—for being trapped into thinking her own happiness had to wait so her family could have theirs. One should not be dependent on the other! Let them make their own happiness as she would make hers, alongside.

Of course, that only worked now because her children were older. They were capable of "making" for themselves. For Ten Years she had "made" for them.

After a long, windless time of sitting in the shallow hot water of the Lost Lakes, she packed her daypack and slung it loosely over one shoulder. The warm, shallow pools were more golden up close, miniature versions of Hamlin's lagoon, with tiny plants and vines growing near the edges and rings of greenish sediment that marked years of higher water levels. Plodding along, keeping her feet flat so as not to sink too much, her R words returned, reeking of action and power. Recreate. Revolt. Reform. Because she could not Return, Relinquish, Resume. The passion of these words made her blush, which, oddly enough, made her shiver when the heat tingled to the surface of her skin. For a brief moment, she sympathized with the loggers, dragging their horse teams and saws and cut trunks across the sand, getting nowhere, seemingly, step by step, as the promise of water wiggled over the hot sand. If she were to watch another year of possibilities pass her by, she would *R*age and *R*oast and *R*oil her own mind.

Roil—really!

Her trudge back across Hamlin's wall of dunes was not without humor. The rental boy—young man? he might have been twenty— had said something as he lowered her canoe into the water, but she'd missed his words, watching the muscles in his back. She'd handed him the twenty and run away, pushing her canoe across the lagoon, knowing he must have been watching, thinking *What's she going to do? Push it around the lake?*

She let that image of herself pushing the canoe around the lagoon, her feet continually slipping along the mucky bottom, lift her spirits. Sometimes, a little restlessness, a little slip and recover, went a long, long way.

29

Day Eight—Telescope of Trees

SHE HAD FOUND THE OLD man on the deck at sunset. She owed him something, something she knew, deeply, that he would appreciate: a night of stars. Now, he lay on one of the new boardwalk benches next to hers, squinting into the night sky with her constellation map stretched above him. There had been an uncomfortable moment in her car, when they both realized they were too close. She had pushed her knees together and gripped the steering wheel, he had shifted in the passenger seat. What did she know about this man, really? He liked to drag his toes through the bubbles of receding waves, he had striking silver hair, and his wife, Ada, was gone.

Of course, Jillian was no astronaut.

"You know all these names, huh? And the constellations?"

Towering oaks leaned into the clearing over the lagoon, forming a great rim, just as she had imagined. A telescope of trees, and with the light of the horizon blocked by the woods, its edging of leaves made the dome especially deep. "Oh, yeah. It's such great seeing here, through the dark phase."

He lowered the map and looked toward her, confused.

"Dark phases of the moon cycle, when there's not as much moon-light."

"Never thought of that. That's why they're so bright. No moon-light."

Jillian pointed. "Just a slice." Waxing, just barely a crescent, four days after the new moon. Night Four on South Manitou Island would have been spectacular.

"I suppose there's other names besides crescent and thumbnail."

"Crescent works. Crescent works just fine."

The old man lifted the map again, straining his eyes. Jillian had highlighted the ones and twos and threes, the bright lumen stars, but with so many stars shining, unobstructed, the light was overwhelm-ing. She moved and focused her eyes every few seconds, remembering those first few views through the rectangle, the convex, and the cat-eye mask. The super-slat had produced erratic results, as expected, though she still suspected that shaving away or scattering the light would work.

"Ada and I, we didn't know all these names, just the big dipper, and the little dipper, but we loved to look." He let the map rest on his chest. "The Milky Way on a night like this, that's what I remember most."

"The road of the gods, that's what the Greeks used to call it." Though the Babylonians were probably the first to name it.

"Road of the gods," the old man repeated. "It is, isn't it."

It occurred to Jillian that she and Jack should talk under the stars, once she knew what she was going to say. It had been so long since the two of them had shared such darkness, let alone stayed up past ten or eleven o'clock. Jack was an early riser.

"See the planets?" She pointed them out. "Three of them, in the west, just northwest. Planets don't make light, they reflect it. So they don't twinkle." Stars didn't twinkle either. Shifts in starlight as light traveled around planets, stars, galaxies, made the stars appear to jiggle.

"The blue one, that's Venus right?" The old man turned to look at her.

If they kept that up, craning to make eye contact, they'd strain their necks. One visual contact was the rule. He'd figure it out. "Right. That's Jupiter, just below. You can barely see the faint red of Mars, above."

"And the Big Dipper." Which was not a constellation, but an asterism, a common name for a stick-figure of stars. "Straight up. That's Ursa Major, the bear."

"The bear. Why the bear?"

She traced the bear's head and neck, its large front paws, and its boxy "Big Dipper" hind quarters and tail. "Those stars have been the bear since the Ice Age. They've found it in cave paintings. The other really bright star, straight up from the center of Big Dipper's handle, that's the tail of the Little Dipper, Ursa Minor."

"The little bear." The old man made a click with his mouth. "You don't say."

Jillian took a rest, not wanting to teach too much, and she thought of Kera, of the two of them lying head to head in the Porcupine Mountains, on the boulder at Mount LeConte, on the rocky bald of Charlie's Bunion. Who wouldn't miss that life?

"It's a sight, isn't it?" the old man said.

Yes. Yes, the lagoon's sparkling night sky was a sight, one of the most dense and beautiful she had seen in years, but the sad truth was, she could no longer look into the night sky with pure joy. She had burdened the sky with promises she had made long before she knew how difficult those promises were going to be to keep.

"Course, you're probably used to it. Maybe they seem plain to you."

"Never," she said, looking straight up at Albireo, the Head of the Swan, at blue Gayle and orangey-yellow Manford in the sky. "Never. There's nothing like the Milky Way in August. We're seeing it at its brightest." Hundreds of thousands of stars rotating and swirling, although all the human eye could see were the solar systems and clusters nearest to Earth, those only a few hundred light years away.

"There!" she said, excited. "If you look over the trees, above the beach house, you can see a fuzzy swirl. That's Andromeda, the closest galaxy."

"Another galaxy?" The old man sounded surprised. Most people mentally substituted solar system when they heard the word galaxy.

"The Andromeda Galaxy is a spiral too. We see it on a tilt, so it appears as an ellipse."

"From home, we'd see the Milky Way, vague like that. Ada used to call it a blanket of stardust."

"I love that idea, of the stars blanketing us." In the undeveloped countryside, the Greeks' road of the gods would have filled the entire sky. They may have seen beyond the Milky Way's arms and into the heart of the galaxy. She knew that world, where night was bright and blanketing.

"They're doing a study right now," she said, "mapping how much light we're throwing into the night sky. Polluting, really, they're calling it light pollution. There's an entire generation of kids growing up without the Milky Way."

"It's all the cities and the highways," the old man said. "You can see the orange haze for miles."

Jillian knew the haze he spoke of—the low glow from Toledo to

Detroit to Pontiac. In her lifetime she had studied a thousand stars. The next generation might see only twenty or thirty of the brightest. She let her eyes relax, allowing the lights and darks to paint a wider picture in her mind.

"Chiaroscuro. That's what my mother would say is missing. Artificial light is drowning out all the contrast."

"She a scientist, too?"

She'd never thought of Gayle as a scientist, but of course she was, a scientist of light and shape and color. "She's an artist, a painter. Chiaroscuro is a Renaissance term for the way lights and darks highlight and define each other."

"An artist, huh? Anyone I've heard of?"

Jillian pictured her mother leaning over the huge, rectangular pools she used to build. How she'd squirt inks and dyes into the water, layer swirls of oil paint and acrylics on the surface, then press her papers into the tub. Press them, over and over, waiting for the paint to tell her what it wanted.

"She's retired now, but she taught for years." She'd spent years drawing and sculpting and carrying out right and left brain research in her studio classes. Jillian had tried some of the exercises but they made her head hurt, literally. She never could turn off the critic. "She has an amazing eye, really. When she was young, she had exhibits of her work."

She was going to tell the old man about her mother's early shows in Chicago, but they were her mother's private almosts. Before leaving, Jillian had phoned her mother and bullied her, to admit her own regrets. It was all part of the same pattern: blame yourself, blame your mother, and eventually, throw all of your faith onto your daughter.

"See the really bright star, off to the west?" She pointed at His Brightness, Alpha Sirius. "That's Sirius." Lumen number one.

"Sirius. I've heard of that one," the old man said.

"The brightest star in the sky." Jillian swallowed, trying to relax her eyes, and as she focused on her target, the rest of the sky grew thick and gray. "See how he shimmers blue to white?"

"He does, doesn't he."

"That's because Sirius is a binary star, a twosome. There's a smaller white-hot star, a white dwarf, shining behind the blue one. That's why Sirius seems blue sometimes and at other times white. The two stars orbit each other."

"White Dwarf, what a name." The old man made his clicking noise.

"Yeah. It's a star that's imploded. It overheats and shuts down, from within." What a mystery, really, that the White Dwarf does not explode, that the star's own nucleus calls on the principal of exclusion to put up its stiff, inner fight, but it doesn't strike out. Did women somehow learn this from the universe? Were we learning it from each other?

"I have two children."

The old man spoke quietly. "They must love having you around."

A great huff escaped from Jillian's mouth, a spasm of frustration.

"Because you're such a good teacher, I mean." The old man hummed. "I bet your kids are proud."

"My son, he used to travel with me. He's been on site for some of the research I've done. But my daughter, I don't think she knows."

Manny and Peia and Jack, they all got fidgety, lying in the grass or pulled off to the side of the road. Her stars were old stories. Old, exaggerated stories that made everyone uncomfortable. But here Manny and Peia would look. Look! she'd say, and they'd be dazzled by this Milky Way. She'd told Manny about letting his eyes go slightly out of focus. But had she told Peia? Had she ever shown Peia how to relax her eyes and wait for broader patterns of light and dark, like artists do when they're seeing and feeling and painting all at once?

"I'm surprised," the old man said.

"Surprised?"

"It's hard to believe, with kids, you managed to become an astronaut. Ada would have loved talking to you."

"Yeah."

Surprised. What an odd word to stick to an accomplishment. A woman with children could be *almost* anything—but an astronaut? For a minute she felt her anger flashing. Would Jack, as an astronaut with two kids, be a surprise to the old man? Would Jillian, as an astronaut's wife, be a surprise?

The old man was straining toward her, she could feel it. Then he lay still, silent.

If there was one thing central to her survival, it was honesty, and she felt like letting the old man have it. Like she always said to Jack, he never had to guess whether or not she was happy. But why, really? This old man owed her nothing. Nothing. And he didn't mean anything by it. This was not the time to do anything she'd be sorry for later. It was time to let go.

"I'm an astrophysicist. But I'm not going up on the ISS. Ever."

"No?"

"No. I work for a private company, programming software and making graphic models, mostly."

"Well, that's a big job too, isn't it. Huge job."

Hot, salty water filled her eyes but she held it. "Sure. Big job."

"My Ada. This is my first summer without her."

"I'm sorry."

She found the Pleiades, all seven sisters: Electra, Maia, Taygete, Alcyone, Merope, Celaeno, and Sterope. One of the tightest clusters known. All seven stars—and tens of less brighter stars—in true, physical proximity to each other. Most of the stars humans drew together as constellations were hundreds, even thousands of light years apart, in terms of their distance from Earth. But the Seven Sisters were extremely close. Born from the same cloud.

"I'd like to stay out here, if that's all right by you," the old man said.

"Sure."

There was a long silence.

"Got any more names you want to share?"

Jillian ached to be head to head with Kera as she was with this old man. But then, Peia's face came to her. Peia's round, wide-set eyes and her thin red lips, Jack's lips, open and smiling. No black go-go boots. No stomping. And Jillian longed to be head to head with Peia.

She pointed out five stars in the northeast, stars that looked like a *W*.

"Got 'em," the old man said.

"Cassiopeia. That's what I named my daughter, after the queen of Egypt who refused to be treated according to the notions of her time, and, I guess, after a star." Eta Cassiopeia, one of their earliest stars of promise.

"You don't say."

"She insulted some of the most beautiful goddesses, the sea nymphs, and disobeyed her husband, Cepheus the King. So Cepheus and some of the Greeks had her banished to the sky, upside down. Her head, that topmost star, circulates the celestial north pole, forever."

When Peia was younger and asked Jillian to tell the story, Jillian told her the Nereids, the sea nymphs, didn't like the fact that Cassiopeia claimed she was more beautiful than them. *But what if she was?* Peia would ask. *Exactly!* Jillian would agree. Maybe she wasn't as vain as the legend suggested. Perhaps Cassiopeia was powerful and honest and the gods were afraid. She had certainly proven to be quite a handful for Cepheus. It was Cassiopeia, after all, not the King, who had challenged the gods.

Whenever Jillian pointed to the upside down chair, the zig-zag formed by Caph, Schedar, Navi, Rudhbah and Zet Cas, she would tell Peia, *Look, the queen got the best of them all. She's high in the sky with her daughter, Andromeda, close by forever.* And she would add: Orion, the hunter who was forever after Andromeda (and the Seven Sisters, Orion was relentless!) didn't stand a chance with the Queen of the East standing guard.

What stubborn pride, flaring up and up and up, even when she knew she was handing Peia a load of crap. Pumping Peia full of her own unused mother's potential, continually passed down and down and down.

She didn't mention, to Peia or to the old man, that it was Cassiopeia's boasting that had gotten Andromeda, the Chained Lady, chained to a boulder in the first place. The Greeks were forever sacrificing some mortal's daughter.

"Ever hear of Atlas?" She pushed tears out of her eyes.

"The man who carried the world on his shoulders?"

"That's the one," Jillian settled in to her bench. "Actually, he carried the celestial sphere, charged forever with holding up the sky. If you look straight up and a little over to the west, you'll see his daughters."

She told him the story of Atlas's seven beautiful daughters. So beautiful in fact, that Orion was constantly on the chase. The sisters—not a single one of them wanted Orion—stayed close and fought him off together. But eventually, with their father stuck on the western horizon holding up the sky, Zeus took pity on the young maidens and made them stars in the sky. The Pleiades she and Kera shared.

Kera was the only one smart enough to have named one of the Pleiades her very own star. With all the choices in the sky, little Kera had picked Electra as her own. Which they often joked about. One of the married ones. Electra, mother of the Trojan Race, the original "go out and grab what you want" folks. It must have come from the stars.

"Well," the old man scoffed, "sounds to me like Zeus should have banished Orion. Put him up there."

Jillian laughed. It was good to laugh. "Oh, Orion made his way up there, eventually. He landed right between Andromeda and the Seven Sisters, where he could hunt beautiful maidens for eternity, but never catch them."

Perhaps Zeus had a sense of humor after all. Justice.

"If you want to get some rest," the old man said, "I'll keep watch."

Jillian allowed her eyes to close and stay closed, her ears to open and relax. "I wouldn't mind an hour or so." She yawned, already preparing for sleep. "We could take turns."

"You go ahead." He clicked and sat up. "Ranger said the fishing's great here. I'm going to go take a listen."

Jillian wanted to tell him about the goldfish, about the huge, sharp-finned fish she saw in Hamlin's deeper water. Had the rental boy called them Pike? But she was exhausted, and once she gave herself permission to relax, sleep moved in fast. Like her loosened, chiaroscuro-seeking eyes, her ears opened and let the full spectrum of sounds build a wider world around her, a dense, blanket-world of frogs and crickets and tiny splashes. She heard the old man rise and tip-toe away. She knew she shouldn't trust a stranger—that's what he was, after all—but she did. She trusted him.

Finally, the close of Day Eight, after all of Day Seven's shifting, sweaty thoughts. Her walks, and—Whoa!—rubbing sand over her breasts. That jarred her awake for a moment. She remembered running down the dune, hollering about the Multiverse, sitting in the Lost Lakes with the wind moaning around her. All that uncomfortable nervousness had brought her here to fulfill a promise, first to the old man and then to Kera. And finally—finally—to herself.

Goodbye almost.

She woke in the dark. Mosquitoes were working to crack her lips open, spiders working to wind her up. She wiped the mosquitoes away from her face and brushed at the dampness that had settled over her arms.

The old man sat on the boardwalk, dangling his feet in the water. He always had his feet in the water. She should ask if he was a swimmer.

The sky was warm and cold and moody. Red-pinks were just beginning to rise, while cold blues spread down from the black, and Jillian felt a deep sadness as well as silly, irrational hope. She had always thought of her own father as an Atlas of sorts. He had held out the world, there for her taking. *You can do anything you set your mind to.* But what encouragement had Manford given his wife, her mother the painter? She didn't have to ask to know what had happened. Her mother had stopped painting over time, because she couldn't stand the pain of doing it halfway. Passion, like particles of light, knew no almost.

Jillian pulled strands of webbing from her neck, watching the sky warm to rose.

The old man noticed it too. He looked up at her, swinging his toes in the water, and smiled.

Manford had died believing that Jack was the man who would keep his daughter on track. Jack had proven to her and to Manford too, that he could maintain his research and support hers too. They took turns keeping Manny, and it had worked for a while.

"He's a good man," her father had said. She hated the way her memories of him included the rasp and the sucking of his air hunger.

Jack had won both their hearts. Not at first, but over time.

At first, Jillian had held back, just in case Jack wouldn't turn out to be the man she thought he could be. But when he proved himself to her, when she was *almost* certain he wouldn't take more than he needed, she gave more. And when her father died and she missed him with all her heart, she gave Jack everything, because love should not be wasted. She allowed herself to love him and she let him love her, without restraint. And she would never, ever, understand how that could be so wrong.

Time—good old linear time—had beaten her in some ways. But she could take a long, hard look at the rest of her life and stop the

Almighty Almost from sucking up any more of her future. There had to be a better way than she and Jack and science and society had worked out so far. There had to be more than blaming her body for the interruptions of pregnancy and child-rearing. There had to be something beyond the guilt and resentment she felt when Jack and her colleagues and those of the great schools of thought pretended not to notice. *Rage, Roast,* and *Roil!* Hah!

The old man seemed to sense the purpose in her eyes. "Time to go, huh?" He jumped up. "You got some sleep."

"More than I intended to."

"Well, that's good. Good."

She felt a little foolish. Exposed. They had spent the night together. And just like any one-night stand, it pointed to some weakness, some vulnerability.

In the car, she traced streaks of pink across the sky and they chatted about the Northern Lights. The old man had seen them once. Jillian told him how she had watched huge ripples, like flags, waving purple and cobalt and mint green over Lake Superior, sometimes all the way up to the dome. And with the sky half alight, you could see the gases striking the atmosphere as if Zeus himself were throwing light-dust down upon the earth.

In the campground parking lot, she took his hands. "It's too bad you didn't have any daughters."

"Ada and I always thought so, too."

"Get one of those sons to come next year."

"Sure. Sure. How about you?"

"Well. I'm going to take one last hike, you know?" Of course he knew. "Then, if all goes right, I'm going to pack up and head out."

They shook hands and she bounded into the trees, this time feeling the bounce of a clean break. Day Nine, and she could feel the beginning of weightlessness. Early in the hours of Day Ten, with the sky at its lonely but hopeful best, she would head back to South Manitou Island. Manitou and Kera. The last of her almosts.

30

Day Nine—Late Night Radio Call

JILLIAN OPENED THE BOX AND wiped off the damp palm unit. Panning the sky, she pointed the antenna to the southeast, down the lake and angled up over the dunes, careful not to extend it too far. If she could make it over the trees, pick up a satellite, she'd get through.

It took two rewires to fire up the battery cell before the numbers on the receiver lit up. She'd already crank-charged the auxiliary battery. "Yes!" she whispered out loud. She had a connection.

She heard faint words and tuned in to the frequency.

"Jilli? Jilli, is that you?"

"It's me." She felt a huge smile.

"What am I saying? Who else would it be?"

Loud crackles spit in her ear as if Kera had sent them. Jillian eyed the receiver's rusty metal case, its archaic knobs and dials. She couldn't have known, when she wrote Kera that hand-written letter and mailed it, how symbolic the old radio would be. She was reaching out to Kera with their ingenuity, their spirit, still alive in the old box.

"I just wanted this to be us, all us." For a few more minutes. Whether Kera liked it or not, Jillian had called to set her free. And to get some help, Kera's help.

She heard Kera moving about, waves being distorted as Kera walked or sat or wrapped herself in something warm. Kera never wore appropriate outerwear, she was probably wrapped in nothing more than a sheet.

"Jilli. Where the hell are you?"

"Manistee."

Kera slapped her forehead, Jillian heard each *whap*. "Damn it! I was going to fly up, but I was sure my parents would call if you showed up. Where, exactly?"

Jillian took a wide, sweeping look at the sky, at the dune ridge, at the shadow-shrubs and grasses around her. "On a two-hundred-twenty-seven foot dune about four miles south of the Manistee campground." She inhaled the lake mist. "Right this minute, actually, I'm sitting at the edge of the water."

"You're kidding."

Jillian shook her head, grinning. "Nope." And if it weren't for the electrical device in her hand, she'd be floating on the great silver-black with what little starlight this evening offered piercing through her.

"Holy shit. Shit. Okay. What can you see?"

Meaning, what stars or constellations could she see; what could they look at together. The entire sky, gray and black and puffy, seemed to be moving eastward. "The Pleiades, barely." A pale ring of light came and went over the dunes behind her.

"What the hell are you doing all the way out there?"

"Being alone." What a different word *alone* was for Kera. Except for the occasional sleepover—Kera's words, not hers—Kera was always alone.

"It's a little overcast down here, but I can just see Electra and Maia, and must be Alcyone, about . . . " Jillian waited, knowing Kera was holding up her fingers, measuring degrees. Jillian estimated by sight. "Forty to forty-five degrees northeast."

And she drew, with an imaginary beam of light, a triangle from her to the Pleiades to Kera, aiming her beam over the wall of dunes and forest behind her and then sending it off, far off to the southwest. Kera had never really settled into life in Houston. "Got it."

"Holy shit, Jilli. How do you do these things?"

"I don't know." Jillian started to laugh, to snort even, and so did Kera. She imagined Kera's triangle coming down out of the sky, lighting up the lake and the sand. How she missed lying in the dark, talking under the stars with someone who loved the sky as much as she did.

She turned sideways to the water, keeping her eyes on their hazy diamond of periwinkle. "I've only got one more day. What am I going to do?"

Kera took a deep breath—it waved into Jillian's ear. "Well, we've got all night, right?"

Jillian lay back in the sand. "As long as this battery lasts."

"Crank it up all night if you have to."

"I have to call Jack."

Jillian heard the clicks and snaps of a fold-out chair. "Yeah. He's called every day. I can't believe you didn't call me."

"You got my letter, though, didn't you?"

"Wednesday, which helped a whole hell of a lot." Kera's sigh was accompanied by a final creak-plunk.

Jillian pictured Jack with his pen tapping on a notebook, the phone cord dangling. "I was afraid I wouldn't go if I heard myself talk about it."

"God, I can't believe you're out on the dunes. You are so fricking brave."

Wrapped in Kera's unfailing belief in her, Jillian felt her body relax. A good night's sleep, what a treat that would be. Kera would stay on the line. "You know, about the only thing, besides the kids of course, that I truly miss is that pre-sleep feeling, when you're falling into the subconscious abyss and you welcome it."

"He's worried, Jilli."

"Well. He should be."

"No. I mean really worried, that you're not going to come back."

"Yeah, well, for the perfect man—"

"Don't you dare. I never said he was perfect. I said he was about the best out there."

"Well, it's not good enough."

"I know."

A rush of angry heat, and of wanting, made Jillian's skin shiver. Jack used to be her best man out there. Why couldn't they do that for each other anymore: listen and problem-solve and send each other back out with a renewed sense of purpose? *Go kick some U-Cal ass.*

"I told him we hadn't talked, but he didn't believe me. It was pretty comical. He kept saying: Okay. We'll do it this way. I'll tell you what I want Jillian to know, and . . . " Kera paused and Jillian thought she heard a whisper, a fuzzy radio whisper. "You got a call." But the connection wavered. Kera was moving about. "Jack really want—to be—to tell—this."

"Hold still! You're wavering."

"Arnie wants you to teach for the Consortium."

"What? Teach what?"

"I shouldn't be telling you this right now, did you hear me? Jack wanted to be the one to tell you."

The conversation wasn't at all what Jillian had expected. She wanted Kera, not Jack. She should have known Jack would get into the mix. Kera was always sticking up for him. But Kera loved men. In her own way, she adored Jack. But, like she always said, she didn't have to play doctor's wife. "Kera. Tell me what?"

"Arnie wants to start a project with the Space Consortium, for his doctoral candidates, maybe some graduate researchers. Oh, what the hell. To put together a new coronagraph, literally, now. The optics, orbital plans, whatever we need. He wants in."

"You're kidding." Jillian tried to remember how long ago she had sent the proposal to the consortium. Three or four years, at least, since she and Jim had decided to go forward with specifications for a future orbital station.

Kera was pacing, her voice warping as she turned back and forth on her apartment balcony. Jillian imagined her eyes tied to the ocean. "Hey, did you hear all the hype about light pollution? Even CNN's carrying articles on Harvard's study. Santa Cruz, too. They've paired readings from Lick and Keck and now everybody's in an uproar."

As they should be. Jillian found Sirius. She'd decided to give the old man Sirius, and to try to like the star. "I was just talking to someone about that last night."

"Last night? Who?"

And here, she tilted her head and let her mouth fall open in her best Kera impression. "Oh, some old man I slept with."

"Old what? Why in the hell would you go all the way to the Manistee National Forest to take care of another man?"

How well she knew Kera! Playing Kera as she'd walked along the lake with the old man, she'd used those words verbatim.

Obviously, Kera knew her equally well. She didn't even pause to consider Jillian's potential infidelity. "I guess we'll cover that one later. But listen. I talked to Hal about it. All I could think of is we might get a chance to work together after all. Hal wants you and Arnie to come down and pitch the idea to anyone who has anything to do with whatever's coming up beyond Hubble."

"Kera." Conversations with Kera were rarely peaceful and they had so little time now. "I haven't even talked to Arnie yet."

"I know, I know. Sorry." Kera pounded her forehead with her fist. Jillian heard it. "Now's not the time."

The pounding stopped and in the silence, Jillian felt selfish. Kera was working so hard for her, too hard. Carrying Jillian on her back along with every chance Jillian might have left—just the way they'd always joked about men. *Too damned heavy to pack!* "It's okay. Of course it is. I'm just surprised."

"It's all the effort you've been putting out. It's coming back to you, finally, that's all. Finally. Shit."

"Kera? When you're training underwater, remember how you told me how you're all tethered together? Do they ever tell you what to do if someone gets cut loose? Like climbers. When they're tied together, if one of them falls and they know their weight will pull everyone down, they'll cut themselves free. If there's no other way, they'll do that."

She had learned this much from the climber at the outdoor store: to tie her tent to the youngest trees because they were supple; to leave the tent flap open during her hikes so the wind and sun would dry the night mist on the nylon. There'd be bugs, yes, but she'd be dry. It was amazing, what you could learn from one well-placed conversation.

"Jilli. Come on."

"Seriously. What do they tell you?"

"No one's ever said. It's understood, I guess. That's where the jetpacks come in. If someone gets loose, there'd still be a chance to steer their way back."

"All right then. That's what I'm doing now. I'm cutting my weight loose from you."

"What?"

"You've done it, Kera. Everything we set out to do. Nothing left to prove."

"Believe me, I don't feel like I'm pulling my weight here."

Jillian shot a look of utter disbelief up to the stars. "Kera. This is your someday."

Kera's voice sounded low and weighty. "Every night I come home alone. I look at the stars, alone. And you know what keeps me going? You. And I know they're not mine, but Manny, he'll always be special to me. And Peia. God, don't you realize how special Peia is to me?"

Of course: Kera and Peia out in the yard, sticking dandelions in their hair and clapping their hands. Giggling and talking and clapping their hands.

"She's my hope, Jilli. I look at her and I see infinite possibilities."

"I know. I know, but what about me?"

That night on the roof, with Jack yelling at her through the dormer windows, she'd imagined that Mileva Maric and Sandra and Vera and even Kera were all trying to help her draw her way out of her predicament. But she'd also known that it was over. She had to set Kera free and find her own way.

"I don't know what you're after here, Jilli."

Jillian had always wanted a life more rugged, more adventurous and far-reaching, like Kera's. But she was different. She would never choose to live alone, not now. But she could if she had to. If things between her and Jack didn't work out, she could live without him (and he without her). But neither would want to live without the kids. They'd put too much into their lives to pull out now.

"What do you see when you look at me, now? And don't you dare lie in the presence of our heavenly sisters."

"I see infinite possibilities."

"Bullshit."

"Damn it, Jilli. I see infinite possibilities, different maybe, but still infinite. And . . . lying under a lead blanket."

An old joke, as if, as women, they were always being weighted down. Jillian laughed outright and Kera laughed too. The palm unit in Jillian's hand vibrated until it stung with their laughter. Everything was going to be all right.

"Jilli?"

"Yeah?"

"If there was any way we could go up together—any way—I'd do it. I'd do whatever it took. I'm still trying to figure out what it will take."

"I know."

The water lapped over her outstretched legs and she scooted back. "Everytime I imagine what it would be like, I see us standing in front of one of those huge space station windows. That's the only way I can see it. I feel like we've been unfairly split up."

"That's exactly how it feels."

"Kera. Do you ever think of Chris?"

"Once in a while, I guess. Sure."

"I mean, really. Really wonder." What if Chris were the man the universe had meant for Kera? It would only have made sense, that she and Kera would have received their men as a pair.

Kera's voice was soft and low. "He wasn't the one."

"Oh."

"No."

"No." Of course not. Kera wouldn't have let him go if he was, and she would have managed to stay on track, regardless.

"But. It would have been great, wouldn't it?"

Yes, it could have been great. But Chris had married an elementary school teacher. He'd stayed in Buffalo after his residency and married a teacher. Jillian could still remember watching Chris and Kera together, the best woman and best man at her wedding, the two of them sitting on the park's playground swings, facing each other as they talked and twirled, Kera with her dyed-to-match shoes kicked off and her bare feet pushing off in the dirt.

"Yeah. If we could put our two lives together, we'd really have something, wouldn't we?"

"I'm going up, in August, Jilli. Next August. One year."

Jillian's arms and legs shook with a cold jolt. "You are? You are!?"

"It's been so hard to figure out how to tell you." Jillian could hear Kera's wide mouth shaking.

"No, no! This is wonderful! Damn it, Kera. This is it!"

"I know. I know, but I've got to tell you something. You won't believe it. I wanted to train on Evelyn Young's team. But everytime I pushed to get assigned with her, I hit a brick wall. Even with Hal. I couldn't figure it out."

"You know what it was? Too many women." Kera's voice was mad now, low and steady and mad. "Guess what they tried first? Two rookies on one mission, can't do it."

"Sure they could," Jillian said, feeling their togetherness. "Apollo 13. Two rookies and one old pro." They weren't apart. They were right tight together on this one.

"I tried that. And then it was, we can't have both lab specialists on the same flight. Which was complete and total bullshit. Then it was, we need you on Stan's team, no one else knows optics as well. Bullshit, all of it."

"Evelyn has Patty, doesn't she. Two women already on board." Jillian remembered something Evelyn Young had said. She and Pat Hall, they always went up as a team. And she felt Kera's loneliness.

An entirely different consequence of cutting Kera loose appeared: Who, if not Jillian, would squeeze Kera's hand and be the one to share everything that happened up there, forever?

Kera's voice came across the radio in strong belts. "Do you realize there's never been more than two women on a mission? Never more women than men. Never. Evelyn, Patty, and me, on a six-person crew. We'd be three and three."

Jillian recalled being at the Space Center, looking at photographs of all the shuttle teams. "You're right. It's always five and one, maybe six and two."

"You know, I can take some of the excuses. Women haven't been involved in flight that long, and there's all those male pilots waiting. But there's never more than one or two pilots on board now. We could put together two or three female crews. Ground crew and mission control too."

"And they know it." Jillian's skin rippled with goosebumps.

"What are they afraid of? We're perfectly capable of managing the adventure."

She heard Kera settle back into her chair, and Jillian found the Pleiades. Their struggle *was* ancient. "Remember being young and holding hands with your girlfriends? Somehow, intuitively, we knew what we were doing. Holding hands and going out together, two and three against the world."

"We have to stick together, Jilli, no matter what. And if there's any way I can pull it off, I'll get assigned to the future coronagraph installation and take our work up there with me."

Hah! Kera was going to drag her up after all. "That's all I've ever really wanted, you know, from Jack. For us to be able to hold hands and beef each other up."

"I think he's figuring that out now."

"Only because I'm gone."

"Maybe so."

Kera knew so. Jillian could hear something left out. "What aren't you saying?"

"I'm just wondering. Jack really is worried."

"Well. Good." She pushed her chin higher. "Good."

"I know."

Jillian drooped. "It's not all him though, is it. It is and it isn't."

"I'll never live with a man," Kera sighed. "It's way too much work to keep yourself intact."

Jillian had warned Kera, over and over: *Don't give in! Wait until after!* After, like Evelyn Young. "I should apologize, I guess. Us married women, we of the diminished sort, we tend to want to save the rest of you."

"Forget it. And don't call yourself diminished. Redirected. Redirecting, maybe."

"Right." Jillian looked up toward her tent on the ridge. *Recreate. Revolt. Reform.* "I'm redirecting, all right."

"Are you, Jilli? Are you going home?"

What were her return words? *Return. Relinquish. Resume.* "Ten days, and look where it's gotten me." She felt herself drifting back into limbo-land, prickly, irritating, limbo-land. She'd never meant to leave forever, only to figure out how to stay and survive. "I went to the Depot. But I stood across the street. The train cars look so different." How old and peeling the caboose had looked, so sunburned and worn.

"I was there, you know, earlier this summer. We could have done this together."

Their lives were bound to grow further and further apart—in action, not in intent. Never in talk—they had to keep talking. But with Kera assigned to a mission, a real, scheduled, *STS-One-hundred-something* mission, she would be training more specifically and intensely than ever before. Jillian settled back into the sand and watched for a satellite. "Kera. You're going up. That's what we concentrate on. You're going up." She picked up a satellite speeding through a low, northern orbit, and called for the game to begin. "Someday. You ready? Fifteen degrees north, northeast."

Jillian had always wanted to be a person who didn't need anyone. And she didn't. She had never felt as if she truly needed someone— no one except Kera. Because talking to Kera, even over a crude, old radio, was affirmation. Instant and continuous affirmation.

Kera's voice hummed with her line of sight. "Got it. If we're going to stay up all night, we should get out the cell phones."

"Someday," Jillian began, "an all-female shuttle crew will launch and complete a mission. And people will begin to see women as scientists, once and for all."

"Hear-hear, once and for all."

Jillian imagined herself aboard the speck of light, and the thought punched a hole in her chest. With what was left, she mustered a tone of conviction. "Tough and kind and even pregnant women and mothers, scientists that they are. You do one, then we'll call back on the phones."

"Hard south," Kera said. "Up about thirty degrees." Her voice cracked and split low. "Someday. You got it?"

"Got it."

"Damn it, Jilli. Someday you and me and Peia are going to be sitting right where you are, drinking Salt City Sluggers and laughing about this." Except Kera wasn't laughing. Her voice was high with emotion. "Holy shit, Jilli. How do you do these things?"

In the most oddly backward way, motherhood had made her strong—nearly fearless. For there was nothing more frightful than losing yourself. Looking in the mirror and watching some part of you begging to be let back, but having to say, *Not yet. Later,* for the good of all.

The first night, she'd been scared to sit so close, surrounded by the water's sounds. But she'd gotten used to the lake's voice, its rumbling and those long slow moans in the night. And she knew where she was headed. Into the richest, darkest night of all. Why fear?

"All right." Kera was coming in strong again. "Crank up that battery or let's go to cell phones. We've got a lot more work to do."

31

Day Ten—Back to South Manitou

THERE WAS COMFORT IN RELIVING her first trip. She took her time through the clearings where young cedar and pine saplings grew, intertwined for support. She watched the trail for those wormy red blossoms and the tiny, dirt-colored frogs. And as she climbed higher, passing under the giant white cedars, she slowed and stepped softly, feeling reverent. Then she bounded up the trail, stopping briefly to see the shipwrecked freighter, swinging from tree to tree where open air invaded the cliffside, wondering what her footprints would look like now, in that creamy plunge of sand. But she soon discovered that she had, as island regulations dictated, left no trace.

Bleached, wind-worn pebbles lay on the surface of the sand, sprinkled about as if undisturbed, all the way down the incline, but her tracks in the Perched Dunes were gone. Gone.

She let her backpack slide from her arms and she sank to the sand with it. Of course. Of course! What had made her think her shallow depressions could withstand forces that buried boats and trees? Whole trees, dead and as white as anything in nature, lined the shore. Others poked from the sand, only their tops exposed, as if they were growing from the dune.

The ferry captain, watching clouds roll from a hard line between lake and sky, had warned her, "There's a front moving in. They say it's going to stay up around the Straits, but I don't know. Smells like a rough one to me."

The air did smell of change. Not just cooler, but thicker, more saturated. If smells had a color, the wind would have been grayish-brown, a mix of mist and dirt.

After a few moments of rest she stood, looking down on swells of purple-blue that separated near shore into hard fast slaps of white. "Be kind," she whispered. This was her fresh start, what she'd been trying to accomplish for days, and she was staying all night no matter what the lake threw at her.

She turned toward the center of the island and went off trail, feeling that to obey the "Leave No Trace" rule was futile now. With the wind gusting and rain on the way her tracks would be gone by morning. She might snap a few saplings, crush a few withering ferns, but didn't all pioneers? The first one to blaze any trail, in the process of making that path followable, had to bend a few sprouts.

Several times, as she descended the steep, wooded interior of the Perched Dunes, she had to throw her arms around a tall oak to stop herself from skidding. Once, she went down on her butt, caught her hiking boot on a root and went tumbling. But it felt good. It felt good to be slightly out of control, to triumph over chaos and regain.

On level ground she sprayed antiseptic on her scraped knees and palms, poking the bruises on the fleshy pads under her thumbs. If women were left to develop on their own, this is what they would look like—scraped, dirty, but grinning with the energy of risk. She wished she had a mirror.

On Day Four, she had fled from the chance to see the stars over nothing but water. Tonight, she was going to make the most of it. Tonight, she would experience ultimate solitude—she and the Lake of Glass and the stars. If those clouds stayed north. The captain knew these islands. He had smelled rain, and so did she.

The Lake of Glass was surrounded by black pines and cedars and evergreen brush so thick she had to crouch under interwoven branches, and she was misted by pine sap each time she pushed the prickly limbs out of her way. Eventually the darkness gave way to a band of gold sand between water and forest. Here, in a circle of trees as dense as any brick wall, the air was calm. And the lake, aqua-gold where it was most shallow, lay perfectly still.

This time, she had packed every conceivable item, doubling on some, her three-way lantern as well as a second, smaller one. She had several Ziplocks stuffed with treated kindling and, as a last resort, lighter-fluid-soaked charcoal. She insulated the tent with two tarps: one under, the other stretched above. The cell phone was practically worthless. Even if she could get a call through, help was hours away. Still, she was glad to have it. The flare gun felt even better.

She dug a fire pit, deep enough so the wind wouldn't disturb it, rectangular so her fold-out cooking grates could be propped over it. Last came the chair. She unsnapped its tiny frame, pinned the locking legs in place, and pressed together the Velcro corners of its seat. She walked around the tent, prodding stakes, testing tarp ropes. Satisfied that everything was secure, she sat down and relaxed.

She calmed her breathing and listened for the ferry's four o'clock whistle.

At one point, she heard something far off—the wind, she supposed, working on some pliable trees—but it sounded more like a rumble. Again, she heard the captain's warning. "In a big storm, the islands will shift a foot or two."

She peeled off her shirt and walked into the water in her shorts and sports bra. The lake bottom was grainy, with just a few ferns and weeds, and the water was bath-water warm after days of full sun. Guppies whirled around her legs. Each time she lifted and lowered a foot, sometimes with a playful stomp, they scattered, scales glittering. She had to wade quite far to get chest deep, too far from shore to take off her clothes and toss them onto the beach. She settled for taking off the sports bra, tucking it into her shorts.

The clouds weren't staying north. As she dipped underwater, she noted their fast-moving reflections gliding across the surface of the lake.

She swam in this direction and that, watching her ring of guppy companions flutter at a distance. She came up, wiping water from her face, at the south end of the lake, the sandy beach where she and Manny and Peia and Jack had rested years ago. She pictured Manny sitting in the water with his legs outstretched and Peia squatting next to him. She remembered the tenderness in Manny's voice and the love in Peia's pats. She might have let her head rest against Jack's chest. Would they have been happy? After chasing Peia through patches of poison ivy, after digging a hole for Manny to go to the bathroom, they would have enjoyed that moment when neither of their children needed them. But happy wasn't the right word. At that time, with Peia two years old and Manny in school, her life had taken several of those sapling turns. She might have been relieved. Jack's face might have softened. Perhaps they allowed themselves to feel contented.

Her feet sank, just a little, where the sand pressed into her soles. She sensed a vibration, a pulse below, and she felt naked. Far-off thunder, it must have been, put her body on the defensive. She dipped underwater and put on her bra.

After a meal of vacuum-packed tuna and cheddar cheese stuffed in hard rolls and roasted over the cooking rack, she washed the tiny aluminum pan which also served as her mixing bowl. Cleaning her outdoor cookware was part of her regimen of self-care. It was soothing, scrubbing the pan clean and readying it for use the next day. Day Eleven. Hah! Without meaning to, she had taken an extra day.

The wind blew so suddenly that it seemed a powerful voice had passed through her and on to circle the lake, sprinkling the trees' needles. She rinsed the pan and filled it with water, setting it over the fire to boil.

Her campsite was littered with dried pine needles. She scooped them into a garbage bag. Just a handful would make the fire re-flare to bright white, but the effect was short-lived. With the thickening clouds and the dense trees, darkness would come early. She needed kindling. A lot of it. She grabbed her flashlight, made sure her knife was attached to her belt, and crouching a bit, walked into the trees.

She hunted for over an hour for bigger branches and returned to camp with her tote full of twigs, and dragging a large fallen oak branch too thick to bend and snap. She peeled away its smaller branches and left the rest whole.

As she threw handfuls of needles into the fire, a whoosh of heat spread over her. She smiled and pulled out her tiny ax, digging into the dead oak. By the time her wood pile was sufficiently stacked, the lake and the trees were melding into a vaporous gray-black.

She sat with a cup of hot chocolate, watching the light from her fire paint orange and blue highlights on the dark wall of trees. The water rippled with gusts of wind and she tossed more needles. She wanted to keep the water boiling—for heat, for drinks, for protection. The sizzle of boiling water thrown into dry leaves was enough to scare most pests away.

No bear, the park ranger had said. *Not enough foraging room. But the squirrels and the chipmunks, they'll make you think there's a bear around.* That first night on the dunes, she had reached a point when she had taken a club and a knife and her light down to the middle of the dune to get away from the crackling and snickering of those pesky red squirrels.

She wrapped both hands around her cup, thinking about the ferry ride back to Leland on Day Four. The little boy who gave her a bottled water had stood next to her, watching as she drank. She had looked down at him and said, "Thanks," thinking he would go back to his family. When Jillian finished the water, he reached for the bottle. "I'll take it." He walked over to his mother and handed the empty bottle to her. Jillian had waved, embarrassed, thinking the boy's mother probably thought Jillian had asked him to take care of the bottle. But the boy came back. He stepped onto the ledge over the ferry's endgate, leaning over it just as she was and said, "Why didn't the mother bear turn around?"

"Mishe-Mokwa?"

The boy had nodded. "Why didn't she turn around?"

On the boat that day, she had answered the boy with a shrug. "I don't know."

And the boy had pressed. "But, how come?"

"I'm sorry," Jillian had told him. "The story doesn't say."

She had tried to find out. She'd walked from store to store, asking booksellers, but no one in Leland seemed to know. Most tales were clear in making their point about behavior or responsibility or customs. The bear's name must mean something. And she wondered, whose story was it? That could make all the difference in the meaning. Was it Mother Bear's call to mothers everywhere to save themselves? Or was it Manitou's story, the Great Spirit who knew, even as Mother Bear saved herself, that she'd be buried by her own grief and guilt.

A shadowy form and silver-green eyes flashed with a snap and she stared into the trees. Raccoons didn't like to be caught eye-to-eye. Jillian watched its humped form fade back into the woods. It would keep its distance from her fire.

She threw more handfuls of needles on the dwindling flames and rose to get another log. Eight logs left—plenty to keep the fire going. She pushed the log under the grate, filled the pan with more water, and sat back in her chair. The clouds were picking up speed, their pressure heightened by firelight. Through short breaks she saw the sky, black as the trees, and faint lights began to appear. Stars! Perhaps the rain would miss her.

She looked across the lake, to the south beach, and now her attempt to recall the earlier vision of her family brought gray, ghost-like shapes. She pictured stick-versions of them all, white and bare like the ghost trees. She saw Peia, her face close to Manny's, and she felt Jack behind her, his arms around her waist and his hands folded over hers. He used to rest his face against hers, taking long, slow breaths of her hair. Now, they rarely held a long embrace.

Anger made things seem so simple. Eight months before, she had driven away from Evelyn Young's presentation feeling like space junk, and she had foreseen her future with great clarity. She had to stop consoling herself: they had good kids, Jack was a good man, she didn't *need* whatever it was she was pining for.

She loved Jack and Manny and Peia, but the love that they relied on was not all she was. She considered them, always, but loving them had not made her forget the Jillian Greer who had grown and developed long before them. That Jillian was her core.

She was meant to leave a trace on the world, a trace of her work, not only offspring. Yes, having a family offered her an "out." She saw working mothers crumpled by the "call it quits" out, the "of course with a family you're doing less" out. Not because *they* couldn't hack it; because their families couldn't. Because men and children were weak team-players. They expected a god-head, a Mother to rule their inner universe. And working for them (not with them) was exhausting. She wanted Jack to protect her, not from the world, but from being consumed by her own family.

How come none of them seemed to know how to love her?

The wind surged, scattering her pile of needles. She chased after them, but they were gone. The tarp over her tent shook, the plastic snapping as if someone were shaking out a rug. She caught the raccoon's marble eyes and he didn't turn away.

"You think my fire's going out?" She untied the double-bagged pine needles and threw fistfuls on the fire. White-hot flames jumped and she stared down the raccoon as it shrank one tree deeper into the woods. She was getting used to being eyed by the raccoons. In a way, they were company. She threw another handful of needles on the fire, smiling in the bright white rush. If nothing else, the logs under her pan would be shielded from the rain. She'd toss needles all night if she had to.

She arranged her bed roll in the tent and put on her rainpants and poncho, the inside linings feeling moist and fleshy. Red squirrels— she recognized the sudden swish and crack of branches—rustled the trees, showering her tent with needles. Outside, the wind was sticky with sap, musky with the scent of cedar. She added a log to the fire, tucking it under her water pot.

If she pulled an Einstein and never came back, could Jack love Manny and Peia as they needed to be loved? Probably not. Without realizing it, Jack didn't celebrate them as individuals. He hardly celebrated at all! When he cared for them, it was always with a subtle expectation that they would conform to his life. He could pick up the functions of parenthood. He might make some sloppy sandwiches and send the kids to school in wrinkled clothes. But he'd be overwhelmed by the constant need to illustrate, to take advantage of those teachable moments, to help the kids *become*. Become, she supposed, more than Jack and Jillian. Because nurturing two human souls was no small task.

Ground level gusts stretched the flames of her fire into threads that fought to maintain a connection from log to log. She looked up, her face spattered with hard drops, and she thought of Kera on the ISS, orbiting without her. She remembered the two of them standing on a doorstep, prepared for their first day of classes at Michigan Tech, parking the Jeep at the bay of Santa Cruz and greeting the Pacific Ocean, holding hands. Why couldn't she have that with Jack?

Every day she left the house, alone. She brushed off the remnants of her family's needs and went out into the world slightly shaken. Not broken, not dispirited, but stripped and vulnerable. Did Jack leave the house feeling skinned?

The wind gusted—hard.

Only when she wanted him to.

She lifted her face to the sky. It was too late for many things: to feel what it would feel like to step onto the ISS, to walk through its pod-connected-to-pod chambers, to perform tests while standing alongside a window of pure, fused silica glass that exposed her image, backlit, to deep space. Kera's success, Kera on the ISS, would never be enough. Not exactly. But she would be a part of all that made it happen. And damn it, if she could toughen herself up enough to spend Eleven Days in the woods, she could toughen up enough to stop thinking of her family first. She was not going to give up. She would never give up. She could *make* something happen.

"Someday," she whispered, trying to call back that sisterly feeling.

A rustle, close, sounded in response. She looked to the spot where she knew the raccoon was waiting. "Not tonight, pal. Tonight, I'm toughing it out."

Rain gusted into her face and she lowered her head, pulling her hood tighter. She threw handfuls of dried needles under the fire grate, but they soaked up the moisture and would not burn. Someday, like Kera said, there would be all sorts of planet-finding systems in space: small, simple scout telescopes and more complex interferometers and coronagraphs designed to do the same thing they had done, to scout out stars of promise and then zoom in for a good, close look.

What an end to her journey. Instead of clear skies and the new moon, both the sky and her fire pit were hissing and spitting at her.

The ranger had warned her he might be leaving for the night since he hadn't registered any other overnight campers. He couldn't force her to leave, he'd said, but he had advised her to stay inland, near permanent structures. Well! This wall of trees and this Lake of Glass were certainly permanent. More permanent than her or her family or this rain. But not the stars. Could she live without the stars?

Squinting against the rain, all she could see was low, fast, silvery movement.

What a fitting end.

No richest darkness and brightest stars. No triumphant, final show-down between her and what—Fate? Like life and science and love: Just when you thought you'd worked your way to an answer, all you found were complications.

Of course, no end. No end at all.

No climax. No resolution. Just survival.

32

Day Ten—What Mishe-Mokwa Knows

HER FIRE WAS FLARING, RISING in red licks even with the rain, and the lake, lying vertical before her, split the world in two. *She must be dreaming.* To her left, pines lay on their sides, poking into night. To her right was a shimmering moon of dark water, which made her smile. Drawn to the water—thick and black like space—she stood.

The lake-skin rose to meet her and the Great Mother Bear, huge and wet and round, lumbered toward her, stopping where the water met the land. Leaning back on her haunches, she shook her coat dry and muddy droplets spattered Jillian's rain poncho. "Why do you come to Manitou, what do you want from me?"

In Mishe-Mokwa's eyes, black and close, Jillian saw herself and the Bear surrounded by the lake. A question came forward and Jillian blurted it out. "Why did you leave them?"

"Why did you toss them away?"

Mishe-Mokwa's question was not hurtful. The Great Bear was sparring, and Jillian felt both swaddled and swatted, guided by something great and grandmotherly. This was a fight she would learn from.

"We are mothers," Mishe-Mokwa waved her on with a huge paw. "We will make of it what we can."

Jillian could smell the Great Bear's musky scent. The spikes of her fur were golden with firelight.

"Mishe-Mokwa? Do you fear?"

"Of course I do."

"What do you fear?"

Mishe-Mokwa gazed out over the water. "I fear the end of the river."

"You do? Really?" Jillian stepped closer, excited. This was a mother's fear.

The Great Mother inched toward Jillian. "You have been to the end of your river?"

"Almost."

"And did you fear?"

"Oh, yes!"

"No fish?" Mishe-Mokwa's eyes were concerned.

"I was starving."

"That is what I fear."

Of course. No fish, no stars, no pursuit. And when it came right down to it, another stop and start, another half-attempt, was more than Jillian could take. She either had to go for it, or put space and Kera and the Suitcase away—forever. There were certain things that could not be reopened and shut indefinitely. "What am I supposed to do? Leave?"

The Great Mother's gaze drifted out over the water, her snout raised and gently sniffing. Seeking.

"Mishe-Mokwa? Why didn't you turn around?" The Bear's lips trembled, but Jillian pressed on. "How could you keep swimming?"

Mishe-Mokwa's head dropped with a sigh and Jillian nodded, quiet.

"If my children were to make it, they must make it by following their mother's strong lead. These two cubs were daughters."

Of course. What did Peia know, after all, but the angry mother who stormed the house, picking up socks and giving lectures. The agitated wife who sometimes hopped up and down, whisper-scream-ing at her husband, suffocating herself with exasperation when he refused to understand. Peia should know her mother's stars and her great sense of wonder and the questions that plagued her mind. Peia should know: First, we must imagine. Then, we fight. Fight like hell.

Mishe-Mokwa looked into her eyes, intent. "Your gift is not self-sacrifice. There is no gift in drowning."

The ground rumbled as Mishe-Mokwa backed into the lake, her round backside spreading flat under the darkness of the water.

"Wait. Please. I'll try harder. I'll try harder!" But even as Jillian begged, she knew: how much harder could she try? Mishe-Mokwa's eyes grew small and Jillian watched the fire die out of them. "Please. Please don't leave."

People were always leaving, as if she were invincible, unhurtable, completely without needs. Her father, and now the Great Mother Bear, sliding away as if Jillian didn't need help or guidance or care.

Jack and Manny and Peia—it never occurred to them that she might need someone to prop her up and see her out the door.

The Great Mother's nostrils floated just above water, her tiny eyes fixed on Jillian's. "You are right, to find your new someday."

It broke Jillian's heart and refilled it again to hear Mishe-Mokwa's ancient, weary voice using her and Kera's magic word. And then she heard, as the Great Mother Bear disappeared beneath the silver-black water, *It is never easy to keep swimming.*

She awoke alone with the rain and the wind snapping branches. She tried to find one shining point of light to give her sadness a pathway in the universe, but there wasn't a single star. Not Jack's Antares, Manny's Izar, not one of Cassiopeia's, not even her own R Aurigae. So she hollered at the low streaming clouds and the rain and the branches that were snapping all around her.

"Manny will grow up sweet and loving and strong!"

"And Peia will grow up sweet and loving and strong!"

"I'll teach Peia to use her anger, because, damn it! She'll need it!"

And she would give Jack what he *said* he wanted. *Everything.* "Jack will have his everything! Do you hear me?" And now she was yelling at the low, fast sky and an occasional trail of starlight above. She was not invincible or unhurtable. She was not without need.

"I need! Do you hear me? I need!"

She needed a mother, a sister, a friend—always. She should not have to live so alone. Dreams could change. They could be modified. But they should not die. For Peia and for Manny and for Cecelia and Annie and Mileva and Vera and all the others whose spirits had climbed inside her, she hailed the stars.

"And you'll help! Do you hear me? You'll stop staring and you'll help."

"You will."

The universe did not support waste. Every atom, every particle, every wave and wind had its say. If her day was not today, then someday—"Someday soon" came out low and steady—her day was certainly coming.

"I can do anything, do you hear me?" She'd already done it. She and Kera had done it years before Princeton's lasers and cat-eye mask and cut mirrors. "I can do anything!"

And this last "anything!" she let hang in the air.

33

Day Eleven—Call Home

WHEN JILLIAN GOT OFF THE ferry, she went straight to the dockside gift shop and bought a faded denim hat with "South Manitou" embroidered on it. From there, she strode up the hill, entered the bookstore, and bought the most colorful hardcover rendition of *The Legend of the Sleeping Bear Dunes*. She had her own reasons for choosing the painful pinks and preachy purples.

But now, sitting on the hood of her car taking deep breaths of the air around the dock—part fish, part gas and oil, part sun-warmed breeze—she was wondering how to call home, how to put an end to Ten Days and at the same time, guarantee she would never again turn away from or put an end to the essence of being that her being alone had reconstituted. Standing, walking, sitting down low or high above the big lake with the day's hot wind or the lake's night breath roaming over the sand, she had known what she needed. But home would be her true test.

She walked around to the side mirror, adjusted her cap so the sun-yellow "South Manitou" emblem was centered, and dialed home. She would be bold, bold like Mishe-Mokwa's turquoise sky.

Jack answered. She hadn't thought about who would answer, until she heard his voice. "Jillian?" One of the kids could have picked up.

"It's me." She straightened her cap. She could do this.

"You're okay," he stated.

She filled her eyes with the lake and the ferry and the pleasure boaters from faraway cities who looked so obvious, dressed in their sailor-perfect gear. "Yes." She hoped they weren't taking over her dear, rugged Houghton too.

"It's been eleven days."

Stay—go. Win—lose. You said ten—it's been eleven. She and Jack had been coming to the table for years, prickling with defensiveness. Jack with his arms wrapped across his chest, knowing that if he unclenched those arms and let his heart breathe he might give something away. She with her reasons ready, knowing she had nothing but love to lose if he didn't loosen his elbows and lean forward, just once, to listen. God, she didn't want to console herself: *Well, it's been a good Ten Days.*

"Yup. It's been eleven, and I'm glad. I'm glad." Already they were digging into position.

"I didn't mean anything by it. I was worried."

After all her emphasis on tens, inadvertently, accidentally, she had accomplished what she wanted—reciprocity. Jack was waiting for her. *You take turns fishing.*

"I didn't mean anything by it either. Eleven just happened." But oh, was she glad it had.

The last time they had been together, she and Jack had worked around each other in the kitchen. "Let me pack you a lunch," she had said. Jack had grinned and touched her back, his fingers spread wide. "Really?" His eyes had looked especially blue next to his wet hair and shower-reddened skin. "Really?" She had made his favorite sandwich—turkey, ham, and cheese on nutty whole grain bread. She had added crackers, grapes she had washed and plucked from the vine, and her note. *Ten Days.* But eleven—Eleven didn't sound like an end. Eleven had forward propensity.

"So, this is it." Jack stated. "This is it, isn't it."

"The kids. How are they?"

"They're fine. They're still asleep. You're okay though."

She thought about Mishe-Mokwa's claws digging into the muck as her massive body slid backwards. "We have to be able to count on each other, Jack. For strength." Talking, finding meaningful words to express thought, was incredibly draining.

"I know." He spoke quietly. "I know."

Jack might never understand the numbers that had helped her get away. The ten years she had given to Manny and Peia, to him too, to some degree. Ten years was certainly a good enough base. She had drawn, scribbled, chanted those tens, knowing she could leave. And she had. She had! Now, she had to decide what to do with the knowledge that she could leave forever; that back at home, she may never truly be able to put herself first.

She tried to remember what date it was, what day in August. "Manny and Peia, they're okay? School start off okay?"

"Everything's fine."

She wanted to ask, what did he tell them? But she didn't want to know, not yet. The house had been so full of tension for months, for years, really. Manny would certainly be wondering. She smoothed her hand over the hard cover book in her lap, smiling at the tender pinks and oranges and golden highlights on Mishe-Mokwa's fur. The giant bear was tough, incredibly tough, but oh so maternal. It was a good combination. The best. Why did the world know that, but then, not let it be?

She stroked Mishe-Mokwa's humped back and the space behind her ears, opened and vulnerable because her gaze was turned out, over the water. "I'm going home."

"Going?"

"Coming, I mean. I am. Coming home. But we can't keep fighting."

She couldn't leave for months, not for a year again, but she could leave in little doses, as needed, to keep a project going. A memory of a baby song, a videotape Manny used to love when he was little—*Mama comes back, she always comes back, she always comes back to get me*—sang into her thoughts and made her smile. A daycare song that was meant to reassure toddlers that their mothers would pick them up at the end of the day, but for her and Manny, it had meant something different. And of course she felt angry when the videos never seemed to show Daddy picking up the kids. Why couldn't we model what we claimed to be true?

She was never going to have the marriage she wanted. With our society and our work-worlds crazed on productivity, the messy, ongoing demands of home continued to fall on the backs of women. Amidst, of course, silence—that dumbfounding silence and feigned ignorance. *What? The demands of home and work aren't being equally shared?*

"What are we going to do, Jack?"

"We'll figure it out, Jill, we will. Things won't be the same." Why was it that the minute she let go of her toughness, the minute she sounded troubled or confused, Jack sounded so soft?

"Arnie from Tech has been calling for you."

"He has?"

"A lot."

Nice addition of degree—a lot. Kera had left something special, just for Jack.

"It must be a pretty hot issue because he's called several times. I didn't want to tell him, you know, that I didn't know where you were."

Jack didn't like things out of place. But she had to resist his tendency to centralize. She tipped her head to the mirror to look at her hat. She liked this new number, Eleven, its propensity. Jack should understand. He'd always been good at moving forward.

"I've been in Manistee."

"Manistee. Really. Manistee." Jillian could hear his mind checking all his possible locations, trying to figure out how he had missed. "I guess I owe Kera an apology. But you're all right."

"I'm all right." She absolutely was. And she wasn't going to play anything but all right. She missed him, she missed the kids terribly now that she and Jack were talking, now that she was connected again to home. But—she had sought solitude, fought solitude at times, and come out of the woods entirely all right.

"I haven't slept much."

"You've never slept well in hotels."

Their conversation would get much too intense if she told him she'd been alone for ten days in the woods, on the dunes, to the island and back. Hah! She longed to tell him about her dune chairs, about the way she'd carried a club for the first few nights, about lying on the surface of the water with starlight streaming through her, unafraid. But these stories, they could wait.

"Jill?"

"Yes." Talking was so difficult! All she wanted was to listen, to listen and see.

"If you do less than you need to do . . . " He let out a moan.

So much energy was wasted in the stand-off, that's what she hated about marriage. The positioning, the competition, what had happened to their trust? She answered her own question, of course. Jack's leaving and her standing and yelling—that's what had happened.

"That's all I'm trying to say. You've got to do what you need to do."

In her lap, the Great Mother's face was turned away, but Jillian knew those serious black eyes. *Keep swimming*, Mishe-Mokwa had said. It was all right to seek the comfort of home, but she must keep swimming.

"Kera's going up next August. On the ISS."

"Oh." Jack didn't say *Babe*. So many times she had felt the finality in his *Oh, Babe*; the simple acceptance. The night of that awful fight, when she'd climbed out on the roof and drew those triangles, her first base ten notions, Jack had stood there, shaking. She hadn't seen him shake, but she had heard it. He had screamed when she refused to come inside. "Kids change everyone's lives!" Of course they did. That was exactly what she wanted him to understand and to live with, to put himself in that place he expected her to stand in for him. He'd shouted something else, too. "When are you going to learn to live with it?"

Even the way she'd been taught to view the stars, the very way the universe formed matter and prospered, was based on gravity, on mass, on the way smaller beings were incorporated into those that were larger, moved faster, spun harder. There were different ways of knowing, of that she was sure. She refused to believe that the universe was shaped by power and conquest.

"It's not the kids, Jack. Not directly. It's you and me, and I lose too often. I can't lose like that anymore."

He drew a quick breath. "I know."

"No, I have to say something and I can't worry about whether it hurts or not, or even who it hurts." She was going to learn to do what she needed even when there was discomfort, and her family would be better for it. Together *and* apart, they would learn to get by. "I can't be the one who gives in. Not always, and it's not automatic, it's not natural. It hurts, it would hurt anyone. You, me, the kids. You say you want to support my best work, but you've never made more than the slightest move to make that possible. Not since Manny was a baby. I can't wait for you anymore. I can't wait or bend or even consider anything else. This really is my last shot."

She hadn't meant to use the "last shot" words, but they were true. She was no longer trying to convince Jack or herself that she had a right to do what he did best—protect his time and his space. If she were going to clean up ten-plus years of research and get it ready to be heard at a national conference in a few months, there could be no delays.

He hesitated, breathing around some words he was going to say.

"I've made a few changes we need to talk about."

He'd made changes because she'd left.

During their months of apart-time, phone-time had always been tricky. Over the phone there was always a sense of agitation, of wanting so much more than words. But now, she found herself withdrawing, instead, from these changes he was making so late.

"I'm going to have graduates teach the lab, and I'm working on a new schedule. I've always blocked out lecture time so it didn't cut into lab time, but with graduates running lab classes, it will mean more paperwork, but that—"

"Stop." Listening to these changes—now—was unbearable. "Stop, really. Not now."

She knew, now, why adventurers always said they found their strength in solitude. She would tell Jack and the kids plenty: about her crazy run down the Perched Dunes, about the melted wheels on the Depot caboose, about the stars over the lake, late, late at night. But some she would not tell. Some would remain deep and centered. She'd found strength in solitude and it would be hers, all hers, to fall back on.

She'd always thought their lives would meld together, but not now. Now she knew that to manage love she needed to stay firm, encased, protected. Love should come with protection.

"I know we need to talk, we do, but not now. Literally, right now, I need to get this project going."

"I was angry at first. I kept thinking, I would never do that to you. I would never leave."

"Jack, please."

"But I have, even though I couldn't help it. I couldn't really, Jill. But I know, I know, that I left you with the kids, literally." He let out a long, slow breath. "I guess when it comes right down to it, I knew you'd be there if I wasn't."

She heard something in Jack's voice that she hadn't heard in a long, long time. Something raw and open, and she waited. She had found listening too, in solitude, and she was going to keep it.

"Am I too late?"

"I don't know." How long would this new awareness last?

"You've got to do this, Jill. Do whatever you can to get the Suit-case going, for all of us. The kids and I, we've got quite a plan."

She laughed out loud, imagining the three of them huddled around the table, pondering the question, What can we do? Peia would offer to pick up her things, if they would only remind her. Manny would make a list of all his activities and see if he could give one up. But really, give up what? Private music lessons, when music was his center?

She and Jack, with their equally strong desire to use their talents in the world, weren't the problem. And neither were the kids. A society that refused to recognize that people filled careers, that careers were not people, that was the culprit—a society that thought of itself as the universe.

And Jack—he was not going to be the half she needed without first destroying, then recreating the patterns of work and life that had become him. Just like she had—for the kids.

"No plans, not for now Jack."

"Except for Arnie. I told him you'd be calling today."

Leave it to Jack to make an appointment for her. "I'm afraid." She was making good on one promise: give him everything. "I'm afraid to come home."

She'd been in the woods for days, spent the night at the Lake of Glass with pine needles blasting her in the wind and rain. And yet the only real fear she felt, now, was going home. Feeling forced to give in, slowly, all over again.

He took a breath and another quick one that he tried to blow out, away from the phone. "Okay," he said, his *Okay, I'm listening.*

"I'm going to head up to Houghton." She opened the map book lying on the passenger seat. Quadrangle maps for the entire lakeshore, lower and upper peninsulas, she had folded in eighths, the way Kate Sullivan had taught her, and then she'd bound them in a scrapbook so each map would accordion out and fold back in place. "Arnie and I will get a lot more accomplished if we can sit together, face to face."

"We'll sit together too, when you get back."

Yes, there would be many sit-togethers. Hopefully with Jack's soothing voice, not the short, defensive one. And hers too, she need-ed to stay open.

"I signed us up as Two-Week Keepers."

"You did?"

She imagined the two of them out on the lighthouse deck, Jack leaning against the tower and her leaning against him. Perhaps they'd leave the kids downstairs, in the keeper's house. Peia was good at math, she could run the register.

"I remember talking about that, years ago."

Years ago—that was the frustrating thing about a turn-around. Looking back and thinking, why did I wait so long? The answer, honestly, was the same one she hated other people applying to her life: because she had kids. And honestly, because she couldn't turn away when the kids needed something and Jack could, because she would be *there*.

"The Milky Way, it's incredible here." Hopefully, it always would be.

"I miss those times."

"Me too." But not enough to do anything stupid.

She and Jack and Manny and Peia, they'd see the stars from the top of the lighthouse and from the crest of the Perched Dunes. But for now, she had to head north: to Houghton, to Arnie, to this chance.

"You've got an eight- or ten-hour drive up to Houghton, right? You better get going."

She wanted to tell Jack that she loved Manny and Peia for certain things that reminded her of him: Manny's tongued smile and Peia's milky-blue eyes. But they should all have separate lives. That's what they needed to fix.

"It's marriage I can't stand," she said, and she meant, *not you*. It was a system Jack knew how to use, but she'd always wanted him to be bigger than the system. "It's not natural." So much about the marriage system was dirty with lies and manipulations.

Jack's voice was hurried. "Okay. I want a call, as soon as you get settled. Call tonight. I love you." And he hung up.

At first, she thought he was simply trying to avoid another argument, but as she sat, holding the phone, she realized she'd heard Manny's voice. "Dad?" Manny's voice calling softly. Then, just as Jack hung up on her, she'd heard Peia. "Hey! What about me?"

Standing on the deck overlooking the Great Sleeping Bear Dune— alone, thankfully, alone one more time with the lake-universe—Jillian thought she saw the last of the Lake Michigan car ferries off in the distance. Years ago, four coal-burning ships ferried travelers, their cars, whole freight trains across the lake. Now only the Badger remained.

After Day Six, when her sixteen-mile trek in the sand hadn't produced decent sleep, she had considered taking a midnight cruise, renting one of the tiny state rooms. *Best views of the sunset, May through October.* She had even considered asking the old man. Watching now, she knew it must be a freighter, she was too far north to see the Badger. She smiled and her face did not heat with embarrassment. With fish and frogs stirring the water beneath the boardwalk, she had slept with the old man standing guard. Every journey had its stranger, didn't it?

Perhaps the old man was sleeping now, sunlight streaming in his trailer windows and the noise of bustling campers all around him. He probably liked hearing the kids. There were plenty of them: on bikes, slamming the bath house doors, drawing on paved fifth-wheel lots with colored chalk. She'd never asked. Did he have grandchildren?

Far across the water Mishe-Mokwa's cubs, black rounds tinged golden-white in the morning sun, seemed firmly anchored against the movement of the cold, purple water. The islands, this morning, seemed at peace.

She sat, paging through *The Legend of the Sleeping Bear Dunes*, taking in the purples and those awful pinks, the watery greens and blues that glazed the islands in regret. Just as Kera had once used the plain ink version to desensitize herself to the sadness, Jillian had purchased the pastels to confront it, head on. And to share it with Peia. She needed to prepare her daughter for the conflicting tides of emotion—the sadness that would spike up, always, alongside love. When Peia fell in love with an idea. When she fell in love with a man. When she fell in love with herself for what she was capable of, but couldn't help but doubt. A great sadness would chip away at her strength, at the very boundaries that defined her body and the openness that defined her soul. Always, unless Jillian could prepare her, give her Vera's armor and Kera's sword.

And what would Peia learn from her own mother? Hopefully, she would learn to accept her own great purple depth, to accept her gift for loving and keep swimming.

It is never easy to keep swimming.

Jillian gazed along the length of the Sleeping Bear Dune, wondering if Mishe-Mokwa's eyes, low in the sand where her snout turned toward the water, were open as she slept. The night before, lying at the edge of the Lake of Glass with her tent only half-covering her because it was continually blown half-off, she had thought: *So, this is survival.* And she'd asked herself, what couldn't she live without?

She'd come up with only two things, after food and water, just two things: her children and the stars. And she'd put them in that order, because that's what life did, continually asked you to prioritize and reorder. But neither one of them—not her children or the stars—should cancel each other out.

She was setting off for her most difficult, perhaps most meaningful test. She looked up into the yellow-hued sky, finding the spot where Ursa Major would appear at first darkness. The universe had sent one of its own.

In Mishe-Mokwa's world, birth names were not final. Each soul chose its own name to reflect a life-changing journey. Perhaps her father wouldn't mind, now, if she chose a new star.

Who can know this journey from birth?

Her father must have known, somehow, how alternating his daughter's life colors would be when he'd helped her select her star, her pulsating R Aurigae, a variable star. She loved its changing colors, its flashing red and sometimes blue or green, and she loved winters at the farmhouse, so she'd picked a fall and winter star.

If she gave herself one of the Pleiades, if she put herself up there forever beside Kera, which one would she be? They'd always figured she'd be Maia or Alcyone, one of the brightest that made up the central diamond. But Merope, seemed more fitting now—and true. And in honor of Mishe-Mokwa, she must be honest. For a time, according to the purveyors of proof and science, Merope had gone invisible.

Since the time of the Greeks, it had always been agreed that there were seven sisters. But only six were readily observable with the naked eye. The seventh, Merope, had earned the name "the lost one" because she was visible only to those with the keenest of sight. Whether she'd been wooed by Orion (unlikely) or had married a mortal, Merope had lost her place—supposedly. The Greeks might have lost track of her, but her sisters never had.

She couldn't fix a society that demanded so much sacrifice; that expected nothing short of hour-by-hour devotion yet continued to claim that whether man or woman each one of us could do anything we set our minds to. Because we were more than minds. We were hearts, too, and this same society pitted man against woman when children came along and there was work time and productivity to lose. This same system subtly and silently supported Jack when he folded his arms across his chest and waited for her to do what was best for all of them while he held full claim to himself; yet this same unreliable system left her alone and without support when she tried to do the same. (How could she, with the children?)

No. She couldn't fix what marriage wasn't—not yet. She had a feeling that would take a lot more women and time and eventually, men. Someday she'd be able to trust Jack as she trusted Kera, but for now, for the next few hurried, harried months, she had to get back to her sisters.

She said a long, slow goodbye to Mishe-Mokwa and headed for the car. It was amazing how fast these people—her immediate and her scientific family—came pouring back in, once invited. First Jack, with her phone call, and then her mother. Her mother's "Edges baby, edges." She'd better call her mother and apologize for that early morning call, days ago. She hadn't understood, until now, what Gayle's edges really meant. Sometimes one hard line butting up against another, or the way one color bled under and seeped away, was all that was needed to spur some action. To know something had to be done. And of course the kids. Manny and Peia poured in, breaking her heart and refilling it, instantly, as they'd called out for Jack. For their father. They were all right. Of course they were all right. They would all be all right.

She had much to do. So much to do so differently.

But Jack had said drive. He was giving her the time and the space she'd been asking for for years. He was giving, and she had to honor that.

She had to drive.

Shutting the car door and rolling down the window, Jillian opened the mapbook to Petosky. She'd grab a warm—Oh, cooked!—lunch and take a coffee out to the bay. Dip her toes in the bay of Petosky in honor of the old man. She hoped he was resting now, with this cooler breeze and kinder sun shining in his windows.

Driving with the islands at her elbow and the wind whipping her hair, she asked herself, all right then, if anywhere, where?

It wouldn't take much money to get the NIRV or the VLC studies updated—again!—but it would take a fast, seasoned team. And they were going to need credibility. With the boys at Princeton playing around with the same ideas, they were bound to raise some eyebrows. And the ethics of showing up at the same conference claiming to have investigated the concept with similar but unpublished research a decade before—Holy Shit!—they were going to cause a ruckus. Who would be willing to take all that flack?

Herself and Kera and maybe Evelyn, of course, Evelyn Young. And Evelyn's mission-mate, Patty Hall. They'd be a great help in discussing the feasibility of an orbital station, what the team could realistically expect to do in two or three years.

Sandy. Could she get Sandy and Vera involved? Sandra Moore Faber was no stranger to pressure, she'd certainly put herself under intense scrutiny when she and her team came in to fix Hubble. And Sandy knew, intimately, of their studies. She had read and approved Jillian and Kera's first proposal. She had helped steer them toward the coronagraph and the future of adaptive optics. She had understood, from the beginning, what they were working toward. And Vera. What a dream that would be to work with the Mistress of the Dark; the woman who'd hung in there, for so many years, fighting for them all. Fighting for new particles and energies, new ways of knowing that the scientists of her time had not wanted to see.

Arnie wanted one of his PhD candidates to work with them, a "sharp thinker" (Arnie's biggest compliment) named Sravani. Arnie would remain as the team's organizer and the university would fund whatever equipment and peripherals they needed, but Sravani would represent Michigan Tech on the team. Jillian would bring her up to speed. Sravani was desperately interested and already combing through their old research, Arnie had said, they shouldn't need more than a few days. Then Jillian and Kera would take the lead.

Hah! Seven Sisters. She counted names on her fingers. Hah! With Sravani on board, they'd be a pleiad of female scientists. It wasn't the shuttle mission she and Kera always dreamed of, but it was a start.

And if the Suitcase went up—rather, if a coronagraph or a system of four masked mirrors went up—it only made sense that Kera should be involved. In the most important sense, they'd be up there, together.

First we must imagine. Then, of course, we model. And if there was one thing Jillian knew, she knew how to make a damned good model.

Could she do it? Could she round up all seven women in time to deliver a ground-based and an orbital solution at NASA's Planet Finder conference?

Really. What seven women *couldn't* she round up?

She drove on, curving in and out of tiny sunlit bays, smiling at the sun-sprinkled dunes, heading north, not south, not home just yet, making her list of women in seven.

GLOSSARY

The information included in this glossary is intended to enhance the reader's understanding of scientific terms and techniques introduced throughout the story. Readers wishing to study the science behind these terms might consult a print or online encyclopedia of science, a beginning to intermediate college astronomy text, or specific, project-based websites such as The Catalogue of Extrasolar Planets (http://exoplanets.org) or NASA's highly educational Planet Quest site (www.planetquest.jpl.nasa.gov).

Light (Electromagnetic Radiation)
Because light is composed of oscillating electric and magnetic fields that travel together through space as waves, and because light spreads out or radiates from its original source, light is often referred to as electromagnetic radiation. Light can also be detected as a particle, called a photon.

Wavelength, Frequency, and Energy of Light
Lightwaves move up and down in crests and troughs as they move through space, much like waves of water. The measurement of distance from one crest to another is referred to as wavelength. Light is also characterized by its frequency, which, simply stated, is a measure of the number of wavelengths that pass by per second (rate). Higher frequency light moves with a shorter wavelength and greater energy (more frequent rate of oscillation), while lower frequency light has a longer wavelength and lower energy (lower rate).

The Spectrum of Electromagnetic Radiation
Not all forms of electromagnetic radiation (light) can be sensed or seen. The array of different wavelengths includes shorter wavelength, higher energy forms of light such as Gamma Ray, X-Ray, and Ultraviolet that travel at higher frequencies than visible light. The spectrum also includes longer wavelengths of light that move at lower frequencies or energy levels, such as Infrared, Microwave, and Radio. Astronomers use specialized telescopes and observational equipment to detect light in all of these forms.

Visible Light Spectrum

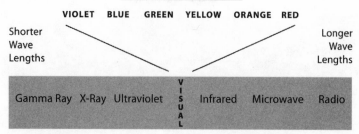

The Visible Light Spectrum

Visible light, the form of light our eyes and brain can perceive, makes up only a tiny portion of the entire electromagnetic spectrum. Different wavelengths within the visible light spectrum are interpreted as different colors, with red representing the longest wavelengths and violet representing the shortest wavelengths that we can see. Beyond the longest red wavelengths we see is the Infrared, which our skin senses as heat. On the shorter end, beyond Violet, is Ultraviolet, which affects skin pigment, producing a suntan (or in high doses, sunburn).

Adaptive Optics

Turbulence in Earth's atmosphere causes distortion in the light gathered by telescopes, similar to the shimmering of images you see when looking out over a hot asphalt parking lot. Stars appear to "twinkle" for the same reason, because light is passing through areas of fluctuation or disturbance in the atmosphere. Adaptive optics uses computers and other optical instruments to adjust telescope mirrors and optics to reduce the blurring effects of atmospheric distortion and to increase clarity in the final image.

Interferometry (Interferometer)

Interferometry is possible because of the wave nature of light (see also the next entry). In optical interferometry, the light of multiple telescopes is combined to synthesize the results of a much larger telescope. For example, the light from several small telescopes strategically positioned over a region measuring ten meters across, can be combined to produce an image with the resolution of a mirror that actually measures ten meters across.

Light Nulling or Nulling Interferometry

Constructive interference occurs when the waves from two or more light beams combine in such a way that the crests (peaks) of the lightwaves are in phase (troughs match troughs, crests match crests). Light nulling involves combining the waves of two or more light beams out of phase, so that the troughs (valleys) of one wave line up with the crests (peaks) of another, causing the combined lightwaves to cancel each other out. Light nulling interferometry thus involves the application of destructive interference.

Coronagraph

A coronagraph is a device attached to a telescope that blocks the light coming from a star in order to allow observers to search the area immediately surrounding a star; an area which is usually flooded with starlight. In its simplest form, a coronagraph includes an occulting disk placed in the focal plane of a telescope or out in front of the opening (aperture) of the telescope. The occulting disk functions to occlude or block out the light from the main body of the star. Additional techniques or tools may be used to suppress the halo of light still visible around the blocked body of the star. More complex coronagraphs utilize specially shaped apertures or pupil masks to suppress starlight in certain areas around the star, allowing observers to search for planets or other satellites in these "darkened" areas.

Extrasolar Planets

Extra-solar means beyond or outside of the (our) sun. Extrasolar planets, then, are those planets orbiting other suns; planets outside of our solar system.

Spectral Classification of Stars

Stars are classified according to their surface temperatures into seven spectral classes or types, called the spectral sequence. The spectral sequence is a temperature sequence: O, B, A, F, G, K, and M, in which O-class stars are the hottest and M-class stars are the coolest. Also of interest is the direct relationship of color to temperature: the hottest stars are pale blue while the coolest stars are pale red. Our sun belongs to the G type (yellow) spectral class of stars.

Spectrograph (Spectrum)

A spectrograph is an instrument attached to a telescope that uses either a prism or a diffraction grating to disperse incoming light into separate wavelengths or colors. Light entering a glass prism is "refracted" (bent) at different angles according to wavelength. Shorter wavelength light (e.g., blue light) bends at sharper angles as it passes through a prism than does longer wavelength light (e.g., red light). A diffraction grating is generally a mirror that has finely-spaced lines ruled into it. Light reflecting from the ruled mirror is "diffracted" in different directions, again ordered by wavelength, with longer wavelength light redirected at larger angles than shorter wavelengths. This separation of light into its different wavelengths or colors—the formation of a spectrum—helps astronomers identify the temperature and chemical composition of a star, as well as many other properties.

How Stars are Named

Proper (Historic) Names

Hundreds of the brightest stars in the sky have proper names which were given to them long ago, many of them derived from the Arabic language, which reflects Arab observers' early role in astronomy. Examples of proper names are Deneb, Vega, and Altair, the three bright stars that form the Summer Triangle (an asterism, or commonly recognized shape in the sky).

Location (Constellation) and Brightness (Greek alphabet)

In the 1600's, a German astronomer developed a system that numbered stars lying within the boundaries of what we now refer to as the 88 modern constellations, according to a star's brightness within each constellation. Lowercase Greek letters (symbols) such as alpha (α), beta (β), gamma (γ), and delta (δ) were assigned, with alpha stars being the brightest in a constellation. The bright star Vega, using this system, is referred to as alpha Lyrae or α Lyrae, because it is the brightest star in the constellation Lyra. (Note that the names of constellations appear in Latin.)

THE GREEK ALPHABET

A, α	alpha	N, ν	nu
B, β	beta	Ξ, ξ	xi
Γ, γ	gamma	O, o	omicron
Δ, δ	delta	Π, π	pi
E, ε	epsilon	P, ρ	rho
Z, ζ	zeta	Σ, σ	sigma
H, η	eta	T, τ	tau
Θ, θ	theta	Y, υ	upsilon
I, ι	iota	Φ, ϕ	phi
K, κ	kappa	X, χ	chi
Λ, λ	lambda	Ψ, ψ	psi
M, μ	mu	Ω, ω	omega

Sequentially Numbered within Constellations

Because there are only 24 letters in the Greek alphabet, as astronomers began to detect more and more stars within the area of each constellation, new stars were given sequential numbers, such as 61 Cygni, which refers to the 61st star within the constellation Cygnus.

Catalogue Numbers

With thousands of stars and celestial objects being discovered and classified, catalogues such as the Henry Draper Catalogue (e.g., HD 1879) and the Messier Object (e.g., M45) numbering systems were developed, usually named for the lead observers involved in each project. The International Astronomical Union (or IAU) is now recognized as the authority for naming astronomical bodies.

ACKNOWLEDGMENTS

I could not have completed this novel without the patience, knowledge, and support of many scientists, mentors, and friends.

I would like to thank Sandy Faber, Professor of Astronomy and Astrophysics at the University of California, Lick Observatory, for reading early chapters and for pointing out errors in my scientific goals while encouraging me to fix them—and for her graciousness in telling me that I had gotten her, as a character, right. Vera C. Rubin, Senior Fellow in the Department of Terrestrial Magnetism at the Carnegie Institution for Science, also gave me words of encouragement. Elinor Gates, Staff Astronomer at Lick Observatory, was absolutely essential to my completion of the final manuscript. I am especially grateful for the hours she spent educating me on the actual work of an astronomer, and for her draft-by-draft comments on the Lick Observatory chapters. I could not have written my characters' scientific goals and challenges clearly and credibly without her. N. Jeremy Kasdin, Professor of Mechanical and Aerospace Engineering at Princeton University, took time, even as he and a team of graduate students were completing a proposal for a new coronagraph, to introduce me to earlier studies and instruments. Kirk Korista, Professor of Astronomy at Western Michigan University, welcomed me to his Astronomy classes and spent precious summer hours answering questions and commenting on my earliest attempts at writing about the inner workings of the stars, about interferometry and light nulling, and about the life of a researcher in general. Physicist John C. Morrison generously shared his knowledge well before I knew exactly what I needed to know. Even earlier, a public presentation by NASA Space Shuttle Commander Eileen Collins provided an important spark. If any errors of fact or science persist, they are my own.

Several books remained on my desk as I researched. Some of the most helpful include Michael A. Seeds' *Horizons: Exploring the Universe*, the American Museum of Natural History's *Cosmic Horizons: Astronomy at the Cutting Edge*, edited by Steven Soter and Neil deGrasse Tyson, Donald Goldsmith's *The Runaway Universe*, Gary Mechler's

National Audubon Society First Field Guide: Night Sky, with sky maps by Wil Tirion, the Routledge Classics edition of Albert Einstein's *Relativity*, and Michele Zackheim's *Einstein's Daughter*. Though the Mishe-Mokwa story present in this novel relies on the traditional oral story, two books were especially helpful: Kathy-jo Wargin's *The Legend of Sleeping Bear*, and Gloria C. Sproul's *Mishe-Mokwa and The Legend of Sleeping Bear*.

As a student in the MFA Program at Spalding University, I had the great fortune to work with Julie Brickman, my first reader and mentor, who understood, instructed, and shared her passion for writing exactly as I needed, from the outset. Mary Clyde shared my sense of wonder and several occasions of frustration, and Kirby Gann was the first to view my manuscript with an editor's eye. My deepest gratitude goes to the Novel Goddesses, Charlotte Rains Dixon, Linda Busby Parker, Deidre Woollard, and to Katy Yocom (who read *every* draft), who shared their love of writing through a once-in-a-lifetime workshop at Spalding, and to Karen Mann who kept us all going. Heartfelt thanks goes to Sena Jeter Naslund for creating the program that brought us all together, and for her own insights and comments on a later manuscript. Arnie Johnston, a mentor and friend, provided the name I couldn't help using when I envisioned an important mentor for my characters.

Certain friends have been interested and involved throughout the writing of this story. Beth Kellogg and Deanna Ray accompanied me on many research trips. Karen Hunter artfully expressed her unfailing confidence. Heather Stevens and Bob Gillenwater read (braved) lengthy early drafts. The enthusiasm of David Cope and the Feminist Reading Group at Grand Rapids Community College has been a source of great support. No one but Aunt Erin could have taken my place all the times I was away. A special thanks goes to the DeWitt family for their hospitality.

Anjoli Roy, Michael Clark, and Jeanann Pannasch of The Feminist Press at The City University of New York were especially helpful; both kept me informed and excited about the publishing process. Florence Howe, my editor, was pure comfort to this first-time novelist. Her wisdom and experience are deeply appreciated.

Maryann Lesert

Afterword:
Balancing Lives for Women
(and Men) in Science

In *Base Ten*, the first question asked of a female astronaut who has been speaking to an audience of elementary school children and parents is, How did she do it? How did she balance the life of a wife and mother with the life of an astronaut? Times may have changed, in that women are today doing what only men used to do, but if one looks closely at women's lives, some things have not changed at all. Women may simply be adding on a work life to their responsibilities for households and children. Men's lives, in such cases, remain the same.

But what if a particular woman has in her the urgent vision of a research scientist who cherishes her scientific work as much as her children and husband? What if she has been forced by the culture in which she lives, and with which she colludes, to sacrifice one love for the other—and for ten years? What if she is at the breaking point and what if she is wise enough to spend ten months planning how to escape into the Northern Michigan wilderness for ten days in order to figure out what to do next? How can she bring balance back into her life? She has two children, a twelve-year-old son and an eight-year-old-daughter. But another clock is closing in on her work life: at thirty-nine, it's now too late for her to train to go up as an astronaut. What is she going to do?

Maryann Lesert has written a lively novel that attempts not only to answer those questions for a particular woman with a particular history and a particular family, but also to use as unique subject matter the life of an astrophysicist whose early "eureka" experience is significant enough to provide scientific work for two dissertations, her own and her friend, Kera's. But Jillian has not been able to continue the work she began, since it requires the accessibility of great telescopes. She has married a scientist who is also in medical school in Ann Arbor. Instead of her own research, Jillian has been doing sup-

306

port work for other scientists and living vicariously through her former colleague and best friend, Kera, who has not married, has not had children, and is in line to go up as an astronaut. The novel asks the question, Can a woman for whom significant intellectual work is essential carve out a life with a husband and children as well?

During ten critical days, therefore, Jillian searches for ways to reconceive her life. She leaves her family to tough it out alone along the shores of Lake Michigan among the unpopulated dunes and forests of Michigan's northern lower peninsula. She wants to save herself, her career, and ultimately her family. During these ten days, she relives scenes from her college and graduate school life in which she became a scientist, as well as the ten years in which she became a wife and mother. In doing so, Jillian engages with many of the tensions that empirical studies, in-depth interviews, biographies, and anecdotal stories have also revealed as central for women scientists.

Women Scientists: Numbers Tell a Story

One of the important effects of the women's movement, now more than forty years old, has been the sharp increase in the percentage of women entering higher education and earning advanced degrees. But the curve has moved more sharply upwards for fields outside the hard sciences. In 2004, for example, women earned 57.6 percent of the bachelor degrees awarded in the United States in all fields combined. As one might expect, however, men earned most of the degrees in the physical sciences (57.9 percent); in the earth, atmospheric, and ocean sciences (57.8 percent); in mathematics and statistics (54.1 percent); in computer science (74.9 percent) and in engineering (79.5 percent). (NSF, 2007)

Similarly, at the master's level, women earned the majority of degrees in 2004, even in agricultural sciences (53.5 percent); biological sciences (58.6 percent); and psychology (78.1 percent); but less than half in earth, atmospheric, and ocean sciences (44.6 percent); mathematics and statistics (45.4 percent); physical sciences (37.5 percent); computer sciences (31.2 percent); and engineering (21.1 percent). At the doctorate level, the statistics drop still further for women who earned 38 percent of the degrees in agricultural sciences; 46.3 percent of those in biological sciences; 20.5 percent in computer sciences; 33.9 percent in earth, atmospheric, and ocean sciences; 28.4

percent in mathematics and statistics; 25.9 percent in physical sciences, and 17.6 percent in engineering, while men earned most of the degrees in the physical sciences (57.9 percent); in the earth, atmospheric, and ocean sciences (57.8 percent); in mathematics and statistics (54.1 percent); in computer science (74.9 percent); and engineering (79.5 percent). (NSF, 2007)

In short, in many of the social sciences and the life sciences, women have reached parity in the percentage of degrees attained. In other areas, including the geosciences, mathematics, and physical sciences, the percentages have increased, though not to parity. Conversely, during the last decade the percentages of women earning degrees in engineering and computer sciences have either reached a plateau or have dropped. Unfortunately, these represent the fastest-growing areas in science, with the greatest demand for a burgeoning work force in an increasingly technological society.

The foregoing data mask the attrition of women at every phase of the educational and career ladders. Despite grades and other academic attainments equal to or surpassing those of the men who remain in science fields, more women than men leave science and engineering. The obvious result: very few women hold senior leadership positions in the science and engineering workforce. One place where this is immediately clear is academe. At four-year colleges in 2004, women in all science fields combined were 34.2 percent of assistant professors, 25.8 percent of associate professors, and 22.8 percent of full professors. At the top fifty PhD-granting institutions, women in science fields accounted for 21 percent of assistant professors, 22 percent of associate professors, and 10 percent of full professors. (Marasco, 2006)

The paucity of women in leadership positions means fewer role models, and as important, fewer female mentors and fewer senior women able to help younger women advance. Sue Rosser's multi-year study of some 400 women scientists asked specifically, "What are the most significant issues/challenges/opportunities facing women scientists today as they plan their careers?" Many of the responses focused on mentors and role models, some focused on the unwillingness still to grant that women's brains function as well as men's, but the most significant and numerous responses focused on the major theme of *Base Ten*: balancing work with family. Here are some excerpts from Rosser's study:

For me, the difficulty is balancing a "normal" family life with a "successful" career in science. I know that if I spent more hours on work-related activities...that I would be more productive. Instead I choose to work a normal work week of forty hours, and when I am at home...I am doing little else other than playing with my children, cleaning house and spending quality time with my husband.... (1999, respondent 12)

For me, the biggest issue was children—not just the physical act of bearing them, but the emotional act each day of raising them.... I had two children in graduate school and still finished in four years. Now I'm trudging along trying to get tenure, having become a single mother along the way.... I know that if I were a male with a wife at home raising the children, my work would be different. But the institutions have no way of dealing with this inequity. (1998, respondent 11)

On managing dual career families (particularly dual academic careers): Often women take the lesser position in such a situation. PhD women are often married to PhD men. Most PhD men are not married to PhD women. (2000, respondent 16)

On low numbers, isolation, lack of camaraderie and mentoring: Although possibly less now than before, women scientists still comprise a small proportion of professors in tenure-track positions. Thus, there are few models to emulate and few to get advice/mentoring from.... (2000 respondent 26)

On obtaining credibility and respectability: The biggest challenge that women face in planning a career in science is not being taken seriously. Often women have to go farther, work harder and accomplish more in order to be recognized. (2000, respondent 21)

I think women have to prove their competence, whereas men have to prove their incompetence. For example, I have often heard men question whether a particular woman scientist (say, one who is defending her thesis or is interviewing for a faculty position) actually contributed substantially to the work she presents, whereas I have never heard a man questioned on this. (1997, respondent 6)

Has Anything Changed?

In 1982, Vivian Gornick "set out to document discrimination against women in science." (2008, 5) She interviewed 100 women scientists, researchers both inside and outside academe, both younger and older. Twenty-five years later, she interviewed some of the same women and a few young newcomers, using as touchstone the 2008 report of a distinguished committee of eighteen university presidents and provosts, deans and chair heads, named professors, policy analysts and outstanding scientists and engineers led by Donna Shalala, called *Beyond Bias and Barriers*. Gornick judges as "most significant" the following sentence in the report: "Single women without children appear to be equally likely as all men to complete a science and engineering graduate degree." (11) The most damning sentence of the report concludes that, "The evidence demonstrates that anyone lacking the work-and-family support traditionally provided by a 'wife' is at a serious disadvantage in academe." Gornick adds:

> About 90 percent of the spouses of women in academic science hold full-time jobs; less than half of the spouses of male faculty work full-time. A majority of male scientists testify that their wives are responsible for 80 percent of the child-rearing and home-making that make their working lives possible. (11)

Towards the end of her volume *Women in Science: Then and Now*, Gornick asks whether the glass is half empty or half full and answers her own question optimistically. What she is reflecting are not the still dismal statistics rendering academic appointments, retention, and promotions, nor the still too few leadership positions held by women in science. Rather, she sees the young woman scientist as "of a different order altogether. It's the purity of her self-confidence that sets her apart. She sees that the struggle for parity among women in science is ongoing, but nothing in her experience thus far has compromised the belief in her that it is coming." (142) Gornick also notes the relatively new insistence of younger women scientists that they will not choose between having a family and having a career as a research scientist. They will choose how they want to live their lives.

Jillian's Attempt to Choose

As the novel opens, Jillian is heading north early in the morning of her first day away. It is clear from the start that two sets of thoughts are uppermost in her consciousness: one concerns her behavior as a mother and her guilt for leaving her children even for these ten days; the other concerns her work as a scientist. These thoughts continue to stretch in time from the present moment in which she drives out of Ann Arbor, to her destination, the location of her first "eureka" moment as an astrophysicist, on the staircase of a lighthouse in Northern Michigan. From its first pages to its last, the novel's structure reflects the tensions in Jillian's life, as her mind swings from time present amid the dunes, the forest, the water, and the islands to various points in the past, some of them in the same places, but with her family, or with Kera.

Essential to the portrait of Jillian as a woman who wants a career in science and a family is her decision, planned through the past nine months, that she will go alone into a challenging wilderness, and not to a hotel or resort, and not with a friend or her mother, but absolutely alone. She will also tell no one of her destination. There is something both in the planning and execution of this journey that insists upon the palpable in-body experience that she expects will give her life the direction it needs. And in the execution of this challenge to her body, she expects a challenge to her mind. The formula is classic, but rarely executed by a woman alone.

So the novel offers a classic rendition of a wilderness trek and camping conditions, as well as realistic fears both of animals and possibly a male predator. Her experiences include her beloved star-gazing, and her habit of thinking about the stars in relation to such people as her parents, her children, and herself. She remembers the scientific work she has done with Kera, how she met and fell in love with her husband Jack, and especially during the current year 2000, several key family moments.

Through Jillian's memory we learn about her supportive parents, her wondering whether her mother had to give up her focus on painting in order to be most supportive to her husband and daughter. Jillian's memories begin in the early 1980s at Michigan Technological University (MTU), where she and Kera are the only two women to major in physics and participate in a fledgling program in astronomy.

In a chapter early in the novel, Jillian remembers the "eureka" moment that most scientists treasure. While searching for a subject for their doctoral dissertation in astrophysics, as she and Kera are climbing the stairs to the top of a lighthouse, Jillian sees the stars through the slit of the lighthouse's trap door above her, and realizes that this cropped view of the stars is similar to a masking process she has used at a print shop, where she has worked summers. She explains to Kera that, in the print shop, she has used masks to screen out the bright glare of the lights from the camera, thus ridding the process of excess light in order to gain high contrast black and white images. She suggests to Kera that they try to do something similar as they view stars: that they mask the bright light coming directly from the star, in order to see the objects—possibly planets—orbiting around the star. This idea becomes central to their dissertations which they work on through the rest of the 1980s, in the Smoky Mountains and later at Lick Observatory, completing a study of twenty to thirty stars using the spectrograph. They want to find stars that may have objects, perhaps planets, orbiting them. They assume that eventually they will be using different kinds of masks or building a coronagraph to do this work.

Appropriately, in the center of the novel Maryann Lesert places two key groups of memories. In the nineteenth chapter, called "Evelyn Young," Lesert places the instigating experience in January 2000 that moves Jillian as a mother and failed scientist into the active mission of the novel. The three chapters that follow, called "Pictures," "Time in Heaven," and "More Pictures," portray Jillian as a scientist who becomes a mother. Set in 1987, Jillian remembers her first pregnancy and the excitement of preparing for and driving to California for work with Kera at the Lick Observatory. Sandra Faber, lead astronomer at Lick, is their mentor. She encourages them by recalling that she had three children while teaching and working in the Observatory. Lesert depicts vividly the daily work of an astrophysicist, the diligence, exactness, patience, and repetition required in order to experience the awe and excitement of sighting a potential planet orbiting a masked star.

"Evelyn Young" Marks the Instigating Moment

Eight months before the novel opens, Jillian goes to her twelve-year-old son Manny's school to prepare students for the appearance of a woman astronaut in Lansing, to which her son's class would go as a field trip. She takes the day off from work to accompany him, after giving his sixth grade class some background on the Hubble Space Telescope. In a large auditorium before an audience of students and parents, many of them mothers, Evelyn Young, looking "like a goddess," speaks and shows slides, presenting herself as not special, encouraging them: "*You can do it. You can.*"(171) She and Jillian know each other, but they get only a brief moment together, after the question period, when Evelyn says to Jillian, "I get asked about my family every time."(179) Evelyn has a four-year-old daughter, but it's clear that she went up in space first and had the daughter second. To women who want to have careers in science and children, she says: "Sure you can. As long as you do it in the right order." (181) At the same time, she urges Jillian: "*Don't give up.*"(175)

Jillian's reactions are complex:

> "All her life she'd been taught to work—to work hard. Never to give up. Hadn't she said it herself, a million times? To Peia, to Manny, to his class, just this morning? You can do it. But there, in the hush of wonder, she'd felt cold, heavy despair wrapping itself around her. Braiding itself, slowly, coolly; bonding like a helix to her hot, silly hope." (174)

Seeing her tears, two "elderly women behind her had patted her… as if they knew that Jillian had turned away from a woman too bold and too bright for her to look upon. So she'd turned back. *I am a mother, yes, but that does not make me less.*"(174)

When Jillian takes this afternoon's experiences home, when she shops for and prepares dinner for the four of them around the table that evening, she realizes that she can't go on as she has been going.

Something has to change. The dinner scene around the table, with the eight-year-old Peia's demands, the twelve-year-old Manny's wisdom, and husband Jack's good humor is memorably, even in part humorously rendered. Jillian recalls Evelyn's speaking of "neutrinos—particles that streamed from the stars and passed through everything.... And Jillian had loved her for it. Most people figured kids couldn't handle it: the invisible, the indefinable. But that was the point, wasn't it? First, we must imagine. . . ." (176)

At the same time, she remembers that "the particles assembling over the dinner table were quarks—not neutrinos." In part, this is her joke, since she sees these electric charges in colors reflecting the emotional confusion or clarity of the feelings beginning to overwhelm her. When Jack reaches for the rolls, she sees some of these "quarks" as "streaming like a nest of disturbed wasps," and then settling. As Jillian grows more tense, the quarks whiz and disappear, then race "around the table" and slow "to swirl around her and Jack." (177-178)

She asks herself, "Why didn't he see them? Why didn't he feel their tiny, busy pressure."(177) And then she has her most honest moment, though she does not speak it aloud:

> *I love you. I love you all. But I'm dying here.* (The quarks, in her vision, flattened themselves on the table and wobbled) *From the day I married you* (Quarks lined up in front of Jack and pelted him) *and then gave birth to you* (Quarks circled Manny's head, a few pulsed over his heart) *and even with you, sweetie* (Quarks danced around Peia's eyes) *I have been slowly dying inside.*
>
> The quarks hovered, scared, waiting.
>
> *I can't possibly exist without you, is that it? My mind has nothing but space for you?* (178)

After dinner and cleanup, Jillian continues to focus on that afternoon's experience, remembering that she and Evelyn and Kera had been e-mailing each other about a new NASA call for "planet-finding technologies," and that Kera had hoped that Jillian and Evelyn would have had some time together to plan a meeting. Jillian remembers the few seconds alone with Evelyn who said, "You and Kera, you were ahead of your time, but NASA's catching up. I'll send everything I know about the conference. Keep me informed." (183)

As Jillian recalls the rest of this critical evening, she does not minimize Jack's contributions to family time. He participates in the preparation of dinner, he is focused on the conversation with the children, and he takes charge of the kitchen cleanup. While Jillian "listened to Peia's songs and helped Manny with Algebraic equations," Jack gets the children into their showers and their pajamas and bed.

Their quarrel is key to understanding how tension-filled family life has become for both of them. She says to him, "No one ever looks at you and makes you feel small, do they, for having kids." (185) And he asks, "What the hell happened today?" Then she confesses, "I still want all of it...But every time I try to talk about it, the only thing you seem to be able to do is help me accept less." (185) And when his response is to look "sorry," Lesert makes clear that he is as tired of looking sorry as she is of being denied her work as a scientist. The reader knows that this is part of an old and repetitive script. The children know, for Jillian remembers that Manny puts his hands over Peia's ears so that she might not hear the rising voices. They continue to quarrel; though Jack is eager to stop, Jillian cannot.

The day has been too much for her, and the only way she can deal with the impasse is, first, to search for the box of her old studies and masks, and then to escape from the bedroom and the family by taking the box with her and climbing through the bedroom window out onto the dormer roof. On that relatively mild January evening, she begins the planning of her ten days in the wilderness.

Lesert has portrayed Jack with sympathy, as a man who believes— or wants to believe—that Jillian is as happy as he with their children and their life together. But either he cannot or will not recognize that, in significant ways, she also feels "diminished" because she is not doing her work as an astronomer. Indeed, there is no way she can do it in Ann Arbor, Michigan. She is not a whiner, and she is not a wife who blames only her husband for her own failings. She is wise enough to know that she has made choices that bind her. She doesn't want to abandon her life now, but she does want to renegotiate some of her choices.

Is the ten day hiatus a kind of warning to her husband and children? Perhaps. Her husband and children use her absence to plan for at least minimal reforms of their lives together. Clearly, that is one piece of wisdom that feminism has offered all of us: Changing women's lives won't work unless their partner's lives change as well.

Women and Astronomy

The chapter that follows the memory of an open quarrel between Jillian and Jack—set more than twelve years before, in 1987—opens with the sentence, "Walking through the entry doors their first time at the observatory, it was love at first sight. As Kera's voice whispered, it was 'Rapture.'" (193) The adored is not a lover, but a giant telescope and a hall filled with the Pleiades and photographs of women astronomers both from the past and the present.

While physics continues to be regarded as a masculine field, astrophysics is quite distinctively somewhat more gender-neutral. Historically, astronomy has included more women, some of whom have made major discoveries in the discipline. Maria Mitchell, for example, discovered a new comet in 1847; and even before her, Caroline Herschel discovered three new nebulae in 1783 and eight comets between 1786 and 1797. The tradition continues: Annie Jump Cannon simplified and perfected the spectroscopic analysis of stars in the early twentieth century, applying her methodology to a comprehensive survey of the heavens. Today, ten of the eighty-seven astronomers in the US National Academy of Sciences are women. Forty-seven percent of the bachelor's degrees and 17 percent of the doctorates in astronomy go to women, while comparative figures for physics are 22 percent at the bachelor's level and eight percent at the doctorate. Today, a list of famous astronomers would include Jocelyn Bell Burnell, who found the first pulsar when she was a graduate student, and Vera Rubin, who discovered dark matter. In particular, Vera Rubin serves as an especially powerful role model for Jillian.

After graduating from Vassar College, Rubin accompanied her husband to Cornell, where she completed an MS degree with a thesis that suggested that galaxies might be rotating around an unknown center, rather than expanding out as predicted by the big bang theory. Rubin's PhD dissertation, completed at Georgetown University where she took night courses while her parents cared for her two children and her husband waited for her in the family car, demonstrated that galaxies weren't evenly distributed in the universe, thus once again contradicting the big bang theory. But her work was not immediately praised. Fifteen years later, she obtained evidence for dark matter through another discovery—of the curves of galaxy rotation—which forced the scientific community to accept her earlier work and which further stimulated significant research on the identification and description of dark matter.

In *Base Ten*, historically significant woman physicist Mileva Maric, Einstein's first wife, haunts Jillian whenever she fears that she will never receive credit for her discovery and her work. Maric may have contributed significantly to the first four papers Einstein published in 1905, which provided the framework for twentieth-century physics, in the most well-regarded European physics journal, *Annalen der Physik*, with only his name on them. Several scientists believe that Maric may have contributed to some or all of these papers. Soviet scientist Abram Joffe claims to have seen her name as well as Einstein's on two of the papers, which prove the special theory of relativity and demonstrate the equivalence of mass and energy. When Einstein won the Nobel Prize, he gave Mileva Maric the award money, though they were already divorced. But the editors of *The Collected Papers of Albert Einstein* and a group from AAAS who debated her possible contributions failed to settle the question, concluding, "We simply do not know" (www.pbs.org/opb/einsteinswife/science/1905htm).

Although astronomy may be more open to women than some other sciences, it requires long hours in the field or away from home at one of the several unique telescopes in the nation. In other words, one cannot be an astronomer just anywhere: cities even as small as Ann Arbor may make viewing stars difficult, and in major cities such work is impossible. Sandra Faber, who appears briefly in the novel to welcome Jillian and Kera to Lick Observatory, is a professor of astronomy and astrophysics at the University of California, Santa Cruz, and a leading authority on telescopes and instrumentation. Her research focuses on the evolution of structure in the universe and the evolution and formation of galaxies. She headed a team known as the Seven Samurai that discovered a mass concentration called "The Great Attractor."

The Novel's Unique Elements

Few novels portray a close-up of motherhood and marriage in a family in which both husband and wife see their working lives as important to themselves and as contributing to society. Further, the portrait is not of a family made dysfunctional through some excessive use of alcohol, drugs, or some strain of morbid behavior. Lesert attempts to depict a normal academic family in which, even after ten years of marriage, the husband and wife still love each other. The children, lovingly and creatively drawn, seem healthy, even happy, and the twelve-year-old boy appears especially sensitive to his mother's moods. Jillian recognizes her mood swings as harmful to herself and her relations with her husband and her children, even to her children's healthy maturing.

The novel also contains unique elements particular to the wilderness Jillian chooses for her path to a healthy recovery: the physical challenges of the Manistee National Forest, the solitude of the Manitou Islands, their steep dunes, icy waters, and animal population. Jillian uses physical exhaustion as a means of clearing her brain and honing her energies for changing her life. After ten years of family life, Jillian needed to go alone into the wilderness. She says, near the close of the novel, "She'd found strength in solitude."

Further, Jillian is attracted to legends and subject to dreams, particularly of a great mother bear, Mishe-Mokwa, and her two cubs for whom the Manitou Islands are named, two cubs who allegedly drowned when they could not swim the distance to another shore. In a dream, the bear urges Jillian to "keep swimming," and clearly that is the advice she takes when, at the novel's close, she learns from phone calls to Kera and Jack that she has a job offer. At the end, instead of going directly home to her children, her husband encourages her to drive further north to see the man who will be running the project she is going to join. She will return to her family, but this time she will also be able to keep swimming. (298)

Most unusual for fiction—there is no other novel like this one—is Maryann Lesert's deliberate decision to make her central female characters astrophysicists, to show them at work on a giant telescope, and to fill her pages with authentically-checked scientific information about stars in a manner that is both educational and entertaining. She has been taught by scientists who vetted sections of the manuscript for accuracy, including four non-narrative chapters that describe, in accessible terms, the lives of different kinds of stars. In short, writers and literary critics, as well as scientists may well wonder why, even in 2009, writers do not choose to focus on characters who are scientists more often. Since the 1950s science has been key to American desire for world dominance; nearly sixty years later, it has become key also to the continued existence of the planet.

Jillian's Future

At the end of the novel, Jillian fuses her vision of astronomy with a vision of relationships. She is working out a solution to her struggle that would allow her to be a scientist as well as a mother and wife. She recognizes that she must take the initiative and no longer simply depend on other women astronomers who have kept her connected while her children have been growing up. She uses the Pleiades as a model for the Seven Sisters, who will amaze the astronomical world and compete successfully against "the boys at Princeton playing around with the same ideas." (297) Some of these sisters are "real," and some are characters in the novel: Kera, Sandy Faber, Evelyn Young, her mission partner Patty Hall, Vera Rubin, and a younger researcher she doesn't yet know, Sravani. Jillian herself would become visible, like Merope, one of the Pleiades:

> Since the time of the Greeks, it had always been agreed that there were seven sisters, but only six were readily observable with the naked eye. The seventh, Merope, had earned the name "the lost one" because she was visible only to those with the keenest of sight. Whether she'd been wooed by Orion (unlikely) or had married a mortal, Merope had lost her place—supposedly. The Greeks might have lost track of her, but her sisters never had. (295)

Jillian recognizes that it's time, if not beyond time, for her to lead: "First we must imagine. Then, of course, we model. And if there was one thing Jillian knew, she knew how to make a damned good model." (298)

Thus, Jillian provides the potential suggested by Evelyn Fox Keller for seeing science in a different way and for new approaches that women can bring to science. Their creativity and the new approaches women may bring to science represent a significant reason for attracting more women to science. Women scientists, of course, enrich their own lives with the work they do, but ultimately, they enrich the field of science itself.

As important, *Base Ten* attempts to make palpable the living story of a woman—and one expects also, her husband—learning to balance their careers and their family lives. We think the portrait is accessible, not overly-idealized. These people are made of flesh and blood. We would agree with the scientist asked in 2008 whether her children had hindered her professionally. "The most important thing," she tells younger scientists, "is to pick a partner who will *really* share the work of raising a family." (Gornick, 139)

Author Maryann Lesert

Given the scenic structure of *Base Ten,* it will come as no surprise that Maryann Lesert is a successful dramatist. Her full-length productions include *Superwoman* (1998), a tragicomedy about being human in a world driven by technology; *The Music in the Mess* (2001), and *Natural Causes* (2003), a finalist for the Princess Grace Foundation's National Playwright's Fellowship to New Dramatists. In 2003, she published two short plays: "Bump" and "If, When, and Only." She is writing a second novel, an excerpt of which was published in 2007. In the mid-1980s, Lesert studied biomedical science in equal measure with art and writing, and in 2003, she earned a Master of Fine Arts in Writing from Spalding University in Louisville. She teaches creative writing at Grand Rapids Community College.

Base Ten is her first novel, written, she says, because "I felt betrayed by my own body and by love when I found that my ability to maintain a career and my own passions was severely limited when I had children. It was as if I had made some silent pact with my family and society at large that I would put myself on hold, indefinitely, because my children needed their own good beginnings." Like the husband she created in *Base Ten,* hers, she writes, is "one of the 'good guys.'" Still, "he did not feel the same pressure," for "the social structure

When asked why she chose to make Jillian and Kera scientists, she offered her own interest in such learning, but as important, she "wanted to buck the system that tells us that only special women have what it takes to achieve in science. I've witnessed many women simply giving up. What to sacrifice when husbands do not seem able or willing to truly share the responsibilities of home and family." She added: "First we must imagine; then we model. *Base Ten* is my attempt to model a 'someday' without obstacles."

Florence Howe and Sue V. Rosser

Works Cited

Gornick, Vivian. *Women in Science: Then and Now.* New York: The Feminist Press at CUNY, 2008.

Keller, Evelyn F. *A Feeling for the Organism: The Life and Work of Barbara McClintock.* New York: W.H. Freeman, 1983.

_____. *Reflections on Gender and Science.* New Haven, CT: Yale University Press, 1985.

Marasco, C.A. "Women Faculty Gain Little Ground," *Chemical and Engineering News 84.* 2006: 58-59.

National Science Foundation. *Women & Science: Celebrating Achievements, Charting Challenges,* Conference Report, March 1997. http://www.nsf.gov/pubs/1997/nsf9775/start.htm

_____. *Women, Minorities, and Persons with Disabilities in Science and Engineering,* February 2007.

Ogilvie, Marilyn Bailey. *Women in Science: Antiquity through the Nineteenth Century. A Biographical Dictionary with Annotated Bibliography.* Cambridge, MA: MIT Press, 1986.

Pbs.org/opb/einsteinswife/science/1905htm. Retrieved 8/29/06.

Rosser, Sue V. *Women, Science, and Society: The Crucial Union.* New York: Teachers College Press, 2000.

_____. *The Science Glass Ceiling: Academic Women Scientists and the Struggle to Succeed.* New York: Routledge, 2004.